Y 542

GW00371894

LONDON BOROUGH OF ENFIELD
LIBRARY SERVICES

This book to be RETURNED on or before the latest date stamped
unless a renewal has been obtained by personal call or post,
quoting the above number and the date due for return.

A CENTURY OF SERVICE TO MANKIND

A History of the St John Ambulance Brigade

A CENTURY OF SERVICE TO MANKIND

A History of the St John Ambulance Brigade

Ronnie Cole-Mackintosh

Century Benham

Copyright © The Order of St John, 1986

All rights reserved

First published in 1986 by Century Benham Ltd
An imprint of Century Hutchinson Ltd
Brookmount House, 62–65 Chandos Place, Covent Garden
London WC2N 4NW

Century Hutchinson Australia Pty Ltd
PO Box 496, 16–22 Church Street, Hawthorn, Melbourne, Victoria 3122 Australia

Century Hutchinson New Zealand Ltd
PO Box 40–086, Glenfield, Auckland 10, New Zealand

Century Hutchinson South Africa (Pty) Ltd
PO Box 337, Bergvlei 2012, South Africa

Set by Rowland Phototypesetting Ltd,
Bury St Edmunds, Suffolk
Printed and bound in Great Britain by
R. J. Acford Ltd, Chichester

Designed by Roger Walker

ISBN 0-09-167500-6

FOREWORD

I am always glad that I live in a community with a fundamentally Christian tradition, where the concept of helping a total stranger is not in conflict to one's loyalty to family and friends. The St John Ambulance Brigade provides a system whereby that concept and that tradition can be provided with the training and the equipment to maximize the effectiveness of that help. By anticipating the need for that help at any large public gathering, the St John Ambulance Brigade has brought great relief to many thousands of people suffering from accidents and disasters, and through their practice of First Aid saved many lives and reduced the seriousness of injuries. All this has been provided entirely voluntarily.

This history, which marks a century of service to the highest of ideals, describes its beginnings and its development, especially through two World Wars, and how it has matured with the use of modern technology yet never losing its humanity and sense of caring for others. I am proud to be associated with this most worthy charitable institution and I hope this history will be both of interest and an example of the best community spirit to those who read it.

Richard.

HRH The Duke of Gloucester, GCVO
Grand Prior, The Order of St John

CONTENTS

APPENDICES

INTRODUCTION

It was a privilege to be asked to write the story of the St John Ambulance Brigade for its centenary year. This is a story rather than a history, which does not claim to be a definitive work, although there is room for such a project. My aim is to present the development of the St John Ambulance Brigade in Britain, so that the devoted service of its volunteer members can be fully appreciated both within and outside the St John fraternity. It is a story which includes many instances of loyal routine service, corporate duty and individual acts of selflessness or bravery undertaken in the service of mankind. The story of the Order of St John in Britain is briefly outlined and there is also a chapter dealing with the expansion of the Brigade overseas, for the Cross of St John has served mankind in most Commonwealth countries.

In June 1877 the Order of St John of Jerusalem in Britain founded the St John Ambulance Association to teach first aid and distribute ambulance material in areas where the risks of accidents were high, and within a few years trained members of this Association were forming themselves into teams prepared to help their fellow citizens. In June 1887 the Order created the St John Ambulance Brigade, acknowledging the need for a formal structure within which trained men (and later women) could carry out medically approved first aid and assist in the transport of the sick and injured. The Brigade was formed to meet the needs of a Britain experiencing the effects of the industrial revolution. Since then, however, the world has been changed by social, economic and political upheavals as well as by the more normal and peaceful evolution of a gradually changing society. The Brigade has continued its service throughout these long years – in times of peace and war, on the sidelines of pageantry and amid the turmoil of crisis, earning an honoured and respected place in modern Britain. The path which it has had to follow has not always been easy but, once launched, it soon gained credibility and earned the support of the public and the encouragement of the Crown. Members of the Royal family have always held important posts in the Brigade as well as in the Order of St John, and their contribution to the motivation and morale of a volunteer organization in these changing times has been of the greatest importance. Among the general public, many people understand and accept the presence of the Brigade at sports or ceremonial functions, but do not know of the numerous other regular duties and 'unofficial' work which is done. Part of my task, therefore, is to illustrate the wide scope of the Brigade's work.

I have attempted to put into words what others have put into deeds and if, in foreshortening the tale to meet the tight limitations of time and space, facts have been omitted which others find important, I can only ask their pardon. Never having served in the Brigade, I have no personal experience to draw upon and this has posed its own problems. I have consulted a large number of published works, both official and private, and also some unpublished material. A list of these sources is contained in an Appendix, together with acknowledgement for the photographs which we have used. Many men and women who are or were members of the Brigade have corresponded with me or given me the benefit of their experience in conversation. There are too many for me to name them all and it would be invidious to attempt any selection, but I am most grateful for the assistance they have given. I must, however, formally and sincerely acknowledge my debt to the staffs at National Headquarters and of the Library and Museum at St John's Gate, who have answered my many questions and amended my drafts; they have all been very patient and cooperative. May I also express my grateful thanks to HRH The Duke of Gloucester, Grand Prior of the Order of St John, who has very kindly consented to write the Foreword.

As the modern Brigade which is part of the new St John Ambulance steps forward into its second century, I hope that its past achievements will have been reflected in such a way that its members can be proud of a job well done and prepared to continue their voluntary efforts to serve their fellow men. There can be no doubt that such service will still be required, even if not on the same scale or in the same way as in previous times. Equally, there can be no doubt that the men and women of St John can and will respond.

24 June 1986

1
ORIGINS – THE HOSPITALLERS

The game is not yet over, but already violence on the terraces has claimed its customary victims. To the small knot of people in black uniforms and white belts, it matters not who is winning; they are dealing with three casualties, one of whom is in a serious condition. They have stemmed the bleeding and carried him from the ground to the ambulance point. Their driver has already contacted the local general hospital by radio and now, before the three patients can be put on board, the most seriously injured of them has become unconscious; another life is at stake . . .

Meanwhile, 200 miles away an air traffic controller is in touch with an aircraft bringing a matched kidney from the Continent in a life-saving mission to a national hospital for major transplant surgery. The pilot is a volunteer in the St John Air Wing, prepared to answer urgent calls at any time of day or night. Waiting to receive the organ and transport it to the hospital is a vehicle provided by the local St John Ambulance Division and a police escort to clear the route. Far away in Jerusalem, the staff of the St John Ophthalmic Hospital are beginning an operation, one of some four thousand performed annually – this time on an Arab mother to prevent blindness caused by trachoma.

As they work, quietly and skilfully, these members of St John may not consciously acknowledge the thread of hospital tradition – woven first into the fabric of chivalry and then into the daily life of modern Britain – which has brought them to this vital form of service to mankind. There is too much at stake for any lapse in concentration. Deep down, however, they are aware that for centuries the Order of St John has played its part in providing skilled medical aid to the sick poor as well as to those wounded on campaigns. Only when their patients are in professional medical care can they relax and then perhaps recall at leisure the long and noble path taken by the White Cross of St John of Jerusalem.

When the Crusaders entered the Holy City in 1099 they found a flourishing hospital, founded and directed by the Blessed Gerard, and it was here that many of the Christians were nursed back to health. It is not surprising, therefore, that the hospital earned the respect and gratitude of European chivalry. At about this time a brotherhood of Hospitallers, working in this hospital, was founded by Gerard and St John Baptist was adopted as its patron saint.

In 1113 the Pope recognized the work and growing influence of the brotherhood and its hospital by taking them under his protection and granting them the right to elect their own Superior, thus effectively creating a religious Order of Hospitallers. Their founder Gerard was referred to as the Venerable Provost of the Order and in this we see the origins of the present description of the Order in Britain.

The knights and wealthy merchants of Europe had always felt a strong desire to visit the Holy Land and some years later, under Gerard's successor Raymond du Puys, the Hospitallers found themselves allied to the Templars in defending Christian pilgrims from attack. They naturally took part in the battles between Muslims and Christians and, like the Templars, were feared and respected as military opponents. Thus the military branch of the Order flourished until the Order of St John had grown larger than had originally been intended, was directly under Papal control and, of greater importance, its military arm had become too powerful for some western rulers. However, one aspect of the Order's work remained unchanged: the hospital and its concept of service to 'our masters the sick poor'. The hospital at Jerusalem had been allowed to carry on its work even during the most violent struggles, but slowly European rulers were becoming weary of supporting the Crusaders in the Middle East. They had more pressing and more local causes in which to invest their revenues. This loss of support coincided with increased military pressure on the Church, on the holy places and on the military fortifications in the Levant. Slowly the grip of the Christians on the Middle East was loosened and as their castles were taken and their towns destroyed, the Hospitallers fell back on their most famous castle, Krak des Chevaliers; when that had been captured, the Christian foothold was confined to Acre. In May 1291 Acre fell in a savage engagement which cost many lives including that of the Prior of England; the weakened Christian Orders, weary and lacking support and encouragement from Europe, could not hold out and were driven from the Holy Land.

The years passed and as the number of recruits increased the Order assumed an international nature; the members of each individual nation tended to work and live together, forming national groups called Tongues or *Langues*. The headquarters of the Hospitallers in England was established at Clerkenwell in 1144, following a gift of five acres of land by Jordan of Briset.

The Hospitallers had owned property in Cyprus, and for a short while the Order established its headquarters and its hospital on the island, but eventually the King of Cyprus expelled them, fearing their local power and the international effect of direct allegiance to the Pope. By now the Order had evolved into a sea power with the aim of defeating Turkish Corsairs in the Mediterranean, thereby protecting the sea route for the pilgrims. In order to maintain their aim of re-establishing themselves in the Holy Land, they decided to go to Rhodes and from there continue their attacks on the Muslim fleets. Once again their first task was to build the hospital and this was followed by the 'inns' or 'auberges' for the national *Langues*. The Order of St John became a sovereign power and ruled Rhodes for nearly 200 years, its hospital attracting world-wide praise and its seaborne expeditions striking hard at the Turks. It was in Rhodes that a more formal structure of the Order was instituted, with specific responsibilities being given to the senior member or 'pillar' of each Tongue. The Pillar of England was the Commander of the Turcopoles – mounted archers in the Holy Land and in Rhodes – who was responsible for the important task of coastal defence. He was known as the Turcopolier.

In 1480 the Turks, having made numerous raids on the islands throughout the fifteenth century, decided to dislodge the Hospitallers from Rhodes, but despite being heavily outnumbered the Order stood firm and the Turks retreated. In 1522 they tried again and once more the defence was stubborn, but Grand Master Philippe de L'Isle Adam was forced to surrender rather than subject the ravaged city to further death and destruction. The Hospitallers were accorded the honour of leaving Rhodes with dignity, but they had nowhere to go and the Grand Master spent the years from 1523 to 1530 seeking support for a new home. Meanwhile, inevitably, the morale of the Knights and brethren had been sapped and their personal standards declined.

In 1530 they were offered Malta by Charles V of Spain, for the double purpose of carrying out their peacetime vows and also maintaining an armed force to prevent Muslim aggression. The Emperor required only nominal rent – one falcon to be presented to him annually. Late in 1530, therefore, the Order's ships sailed for the first time into what we now know as the Grand Harbour; its flagship, the *Santa Anna*, was commanded by Sir William Weston, Grand Prior of England. As usual, one of the first tasks was the establishment of the hospital, but now there was also an urgent necessity to improve the defences against an expected Turkish invasion.

While these great events were taking place, the English priory had flourished as the Order became more influential and more young men were recruited as Knights. In Jerusalem, sisters of the Order had lived in their own convent but helped with the hospital work. In 1180 the English sisters were given a nunnery and lands at Buckland in Somerset. The Order gradually acquired further properties including former Templar estates following the final dissolution of the Templars in 1312.

For a while during these turbulent years it seemed as if the Grand Prior of England, Thomas Docwra, might be elected to the Grand Mastership of the Order. However, de L'Isle Adam Grand Prior of France, obtained the honour and with it the responsibility of defending Rhodes. Thomas Docwra was instrumental in rebuilding much of the English Priory Headquarters at Clerkenwell and in particular the Gatehouse, which dates from 1504 and is today the headquarters of the modern British Order of St John.

As relationships between King Henry VIII and the Pope became more strained, the King came to doubt the loyalty of the Knights of St John because of their allegiance to Rome.

When Henry was excommunicated, the Catholic religious orders were a natural target for his vengeance and in 1540 he dissolved the Hospitallers in England, confiscating all their property. Of the few Knights remaining in Britain, some left the country but others were imprisoned or executed. After only a brief revival in 1557 under Mary Tudor, the Order again suffered sequestration of its property under Elizabeth I, but although she took their estates and plate the Queen did not remove their title, so that technically and legally a Priory of the Order of St John could still exist in England.

Returning to the Mediterranean sphere, in 1564 the Turks massed an enormous fleet of troopships in the Bosphorus and began the loading of an invasion force including large siege guns and supplies for a long campaign. Over 40,000 Turkish troops were being concentrated in Constantinople. The Grand Master, de la Vallette, was not unaware of these preparations and he summoned Knights and Brothers from the European nations, at the same time pressing ahead with continuing the construction of fortifications. When the Turkish fleet was sighted on 18 May 1565, the Order could muster about 8,000 men for the defence of Malta. Within a week the Turks began the bombardment of Fort St Elmo, but despite many assaults and sea bombardments the little fort held out until 23 June; on the eve of St John's Day, not a man was left unwounded, over a thousand men had been killed and garrison supplies were exhausted. The Turkish janissaries thus took the fort but at a cost of over 8,000 troops, considerable supplies of ammunition and the loss of a vital month. The Turks now turned their attention to the Order's other defences at the Birgu and Senglea and moved equipment overland; their siege guns and even some ships were dragged around the western shore of the Grand Harbour in order to encircle the Hospitallers. La Vallette's 'little army' – for we must use this term after all they had experienced – still held firm, inflicting casualties on the Turks, despite their own losses and the physical and mental fatigue which affects a besieged force. This long phase of the siege, during July 1565, was a particularly savage and bloody affair with no quarter asked nor given. By the end of August the Turkish leaders were desperate; they had launched many massive assaults against the southern defences, but had been thrown back in confusion at every attempt. Now the autumn weather would make their task much harder and they were not able to keep their ships at sea. They had already lost over 20,000 men and those who remained no longer had the will to continue the siege. During the night of 7/8 September the Turks accepted that they had no further hope of success, embarked their troops and departed. The siege of Malta had lasted slightly less than four months and the Order of St John had withstood the fiercest Turkish attacks, but at heavy cost: 7,250 casualties and considerable destruction. Two of the senior English Knights known to have been in Malta throughout the siege were Peter de la Nuça, the Bailiff of Egle, and Oliver Starkey, Commander of Quenington, who was the Grand Master's Latin secretary. To Oliver Starkey belongs the unique distinction of being the only person not a Grand Master to be commemorated in the Crypt of the Grand Masters in St John's Co-Cathedral in Malta.

If the cost was high, the gains to the defence of Western Christendom were very considerable in that Turkish capability to continue the assault on Europe had been very seriously reduced. For the Order itself the defence of Malta was a glorious victory, hailed as such by the ringing of Church bells even in Protestant England. Once again the White Cross had retained an honoured place in Europe. Now, with the many gifts showered upon the Knights and the Grand Master, they set about rebuilding Malta – with pride of place given to Valletta, de la Vallette's 'humble city'. Sadly, however, the great Grand Master died in 1568 before the work was finished.

The years following the defence of Malta saw the gradual demise of the English Tongue of the Order. Although several attempts were made to recover property and revive the Priory, they all failed. For a short while the English Tongue was allied with that of Bavaria, but eventually the Bavarian branch was suppressed and the few English members of the Order had no official base.

Meanwhile the Order lost its home in Malta when Grand Master von Hompesch tamely handed over the island to Napoleon in 1798. This was a severe blow, causing most Knights and members to disperse to their countries of origin. Now the Order in Western Europe had no home and no role, while its most treasured religious relics were in the personal keeping of the Russian Emperor. The Pope could see no reason for supporting the Order in this disorganized form and so no Grand Masters were appointed. It was a time for taking stock and adjusting to a new international situation in which the military aims of the Order no longer applied and there could be no claim to sovereignty so far as Malta was concerned. Some French Knights from the former Tongues of Auvergne, Provence and France formed themselves into a Capitular Commission with the aim of reviving the claims to Rhodes or seeking compensation for the loss of Malta. One of the constituent parts of their policy involved the raising of a large loan in England and to give this a better chance of success they recommended the revival of the English Tongue. They believed that the difficulty of Britain's Protestant religion could be overcome; there was a precedent in the case of Brandenburg.

In 1831 an English clergyman, the Reverend Robert Peat, accepted nomination as Prior of England and it was hoped to rebuild the Order by admitting new English brethren, but in 1837 the Lieutenant Grand Master ruled that a special dispensation would be required for each English candidate. The reaction to this in Britain was the preparation in 1841 of the St John's Day Declaration, a series of resolutions which were designed to allow for a more precise understanding of the

philosophy surrounding the English revival. They set out the requirements for a specific British and Protestant branch of the Order reviving
the Hospitaller cause, owing allegiance to its own monarch and having
equal standing with other *Langues*. Negotiations were continuing
when, in 1848, the French monarchy was again overthrown and with it
all the members of the Capitular Commission. There was no support
for the English revival and indeed the whole subject was surrounded
by bitter controversy, with Rome insisting that candidates must be
Catholic. In 1858 the Lieutenant Master in Rome declared that the
whole concept had been unconstitutional from the beginning. However, the interested parties (members) in England decided to continue
and to find and develop outlets for their charitable aims in the Hospitaller tradition. On St John's Day 1858, therefore, following
Rome's disavowal, 'The Order of St John of Jerusalem, Anglia' was
proclaimed with a Master at its head, a Capitular Commission and a
Chapter to give effect to its policies.

In 1867 they first suggested the creation of some form of ambulance
service for the poor, but although a carefully prepared scheme was
presented, prevailing medical opinion at the time indicated that the
difficulties would be almost insurmountable. However, the members
persevered and during a busy, productive and successful period of
some twenty years the Order's work became organized throughout Britain – it established the Ambulance Department and made
application for land in Jerusalem on which a hospital could be built
(though the grant was not confirmed until 1882). In 1877 the St John
Ambulance Association was founded and then ten years later – based
on the phenomenal success of the teaching which the Association
provided – the Brigade was formed.

The development of the St John Ambulance Brigade is the central
theme of this story, but the detailed study of this is left for subsequent
chapters. It will be helpful now to complete the account of the history
of the Order in Britain and look briefly at its Headquarters, Church and
Hospital.

The success of the Order, the dedication of its members and the
devoted work of the Ambulance Department, Association and Hospital attracted widespread public support as well as the encouragement
of members of the Royal family, and in 1887 the Prince of Wales
presented a petition to Queen Victoria requesting a charter for the
Order. On 14 May 1888 the first Royal Charter was granted to 'the
Grand Priory of the Order of the Hospital of St John of Jerusalem in

England'. The Queen was to be Patron and Sovereign Head of the Order, while the Prince of Wales would be the Grand Prior with effect from the next St John's Day (24 June). One of the main objects of the Charter was to enable the Order 'the more effectually to carry on and conduct the hospitaller and other charitable works of the said Fraternity'. The Order's aims, as shown in a schedule to the Charter, remained those which had been followed for centuries: 'works of humanity and charity in the relief of sickness, distress, suffering and danger without distinction of nationality or creed, and the extension of the great principle of the Order, *Pro Utilitate Hominum*. Other objects can be summarized as aid to the sick poor, aid to the sick and wounded in war, the maintenance of the St John Ambulance Association and through it the provision of first-aid instruction and equipment. The Charter also provided for 'the organization of ambulance corps, invalid transport corps and nursing corps; the formation of provincial associations to further the general objects of the Order' and finally but of great importance, the maintenance of the British Ophthalmic Hospital in Jerusalem.

In 1907 King Edward VII granted a supplementary Charter which empowered the Order to create Priories and Commanderies as subordinate establishments. In 1926, King George V authorized a further Charter, which confirmed the earlier documents and recognized the antiquity of the Order's Hospitaller traditions by granting the prefix 'Venerable' to the title. In addition, the spread of St John work throughout what was then the British Empire resulted in an expansion of the title using the phrase 'the British Realm' instead of simply 'England'. In 1955 Her Majesty the Queen approved the term 'Most Venerable' for use in the Order's title and in a further supplementary Charter in 1974 the words 'in the British Realm' were removed so that the correct title today is 'The Grand Priory of the Most Venerable Order of the Hospital of St John of Jerusalem'. The official short title, 'The Order of St John', is most often used and the term 'The Venerable Order' is employed to distinguish the British Order from the Sovereign Military Order in Rome, which is the direct descendant of the medieval Knights of St John.

The status of the Order of St John in Britain is unique. It is an official Order of Chivalry, but differs from other such Orders in that most of those who are admitted actually work *Pro Utilitate Hominum*, following the Hospitaller tradition of old. The Order carries no post-nominal letters but is acknowledged by the Sovereign. As Patron and Sovereign

Head of the Order, Her Majesty the Queen approves all admissions and promotions. There are five grades – similar to the junior Orders of Chivalry – and their insignia are worn as official decorations, with specific rules applying to precedence when other decorations are worn.

When in 1939 Prince Henry, Duke of Gloucester, succeeded the Duke of Connaught as Grand Prior of the Order of St John – becoming the fourth Royal Grand Prior since 1888 – his first great challenge was at the outbreak of war. Most of the Order's work during the war was undertaken under the Joint War Organization and The Duke of Gloucester's Appeal, which raised more than £50,000,000, was one of its most outstanding successes. After the war the Grand Prior went as Governor-General to Australia, where his interest in autonomous Priories developed and it is significant that the years between 1943 and 1952 saw the establishment of all the present Priories as well as the Commandery of Ards. In 1958 he opened the Garden of Remembrance when the restored Priory Church was reconsecrated, and two years later he visited the Hospital at Jerusalem. He was an advocate of closer relationships between the Alliance of the Orders of St John in Europe and with the Sovereign Military Order of Malta, and these aims were given effect in 1961 and 1963 respectively. To the Duke of Gloucester, the Order owes the Grand Prior's Advisory Council and the Grand Prior's Trophy, the award for the premier first-aid competition for statutory services in Britain. In all his work for the Order, the Duke was supported by his wife, Princess Alice, who became the Deputy Commandant-in-Chief of Nursing Corps and Divisions.

Prince William, the Duke of Gloucester's elder son, had obtained a first-aid certificate at school and had joined the local division as an ambulance member. In 1968 he became Commandant-in-Chief of Ambulance Corps and Divisions shortly before going to Tokyo. On his return to Britain in 1970, he renewed his involvement in the Order and Brigade, becoming particularly interested in their history and traditions. His tragic death in 1972 deprived the St John movement of an effective leader with an active mind and an original outlook. For two more years after his son's death the Duke of Gloucester held the office of Grand Prior, completing a total of thirty-five years at the head of the Venerable Order before his own death in 1974. Prince Richard succeeded him as Duke of Gloucester and became Grand Prior of The Order in February 1975, to continue his family's service at a critical time in the Order's history. He delegates the management of the daily work of the Order and its foundations to the Lord Prior and his executive officers who work from St John's Gate, Clerkenwell. The Duchess of Gloucester is now Commandant-in-Chief of Nursing Divisions in Wales.

'The Gate' is the affectionate term given to the Order's headquarters; it is all that remains of the ancient Priory, originally built in about 1148, and has witnessed some of Britain's more turbulent history. During the peasants' revolt in 1381 the Priory was partly destroyed by fire; in 1504 Prior Thomas Docwra rebuilt the Gatehouse and refurbished the Priory, but in 1540 the Priory was taken into Crown hands by Henry VIII, who reserved the timber and lead for his own use. During the short re-establishment under Mary Tudor, the Priory reverted to the then Lord Prior, but only one year later Queen Elizabeth I granted its freehold to private owners. It later became the property of the Master of the Revels, then of Lord Burleigh. Later the Gatehouse belonged to a printer and publisher and finally in the eighteenth century it became an inn – The Old Jerusalem Tavern. We know that a restoration committee successfully fought against the demolition of the building in about 1845, and that in 1874 the Order was able to take possession of the Gatehouse through the generosity of Sir Edmund Lechmere; he purchased the freehold and made it over to the Order through the St John's Gate (Clerkenwell) Company Ltd., which had been formed in 1866 by members of the Order with the specific aim of acquiring the Gate and the advowson of the Church.

The Order's church in St John's Square was built in about 1144 with a round nave, and was enlarged and reconsecrated in 1185. It was damaged by Wat Tyler's fire in 1381. There followed a chequered history as the fortunes of the Order waned in England, and it became a source of stone for Protector Lord Somerset, whose palace in the Strand owed much to the masonry of St John's Church, and particularly to its bell tower. In the early eighteenth century the building was purchased by the Church Commissioners and it became another parish church for Clerkenwell. The Order was given the advowson early this century and later granted ownership of the church as Clerkenwell no longer needed two parish churches. The long history of the Church very nearly ended on the night of 10/11 May 1941 when it was virtually destroyed in a German air raid; showers of incendiary bombs fell on the roof, gutting the building, though miraculously the twelfth-century crypt, all that remained of the first Priory building, survived. After the war it was necessary to raise large sums of money for restoration and the Order, Association and Brigade at home and overseas gave generously. On 17 October 1958 the Duke of Gloucester presided at the reconsecration of the church by the Archbishop of Canterbury and dedicated memorial gardens as witness to the sacrifices of two World Wars.

The Ophthalmic Hospital in Jerusalem is the second great foundation of the Order of St John. Since the 1858 revival there had always been an interest in returning to Jerusalem in some way and by 1873 it became clear that Britain was the only European nation not to be represented by some form of charitable work in the Holy City. In 1876 the Secretary-General of the Order applied for land on which to build the hospital and after delays and the personal intervention of the Prince of Wales, a site near the Jaffa Gate was granted in 1882.

The Order wished to make ophthalmic medicine its prime contribution and an eye hospital was opened on this site in 1882. Its staff quickly overcame the fear and mistrust which would naturally be the first local reaction; during the first three and a half years over 58,000 people had been treated and the hospital progressed, gaining friends and doing good until the First World War. The Turks entered the war on the side of Germany and the St John staff had to leave Jerusalem, whereupon the Turks took over the hospital buildings and later used them as an ammunition store which was blown up just before being retaken by the British Army. Between the two World Wars the hospital staff earned the gratitude of the local Jews and Arabs for their impartiality and by 1935 the number of persons treated had reached an all-time high. Moreover, a training school had been set up for Arab girls who were interested in the medical or nursing professions.

Palestine after the Second World War was a violent area; the British Mandate had ended in 1948 and the hospital, damaged yet again, was placed within Israeli jurisdiction, inaccessible to the Arabs who had formed the majority of patients; and so the old building had to be sold. Despite a deteriorating Arab–Israeli situation the Order continued its research into eye diseases and maintained its support for the hospital, one of the general aims of its Royal Charter. In 1960 a new hospital was opened, but this too was slightly damaged during the war of 1967. In 1981 the hospital began its 'Outreach Programme' which was designed to carry facilities and expertise to poor people who could not travel to Jerusalem. This new development flourished and during 1984 the number of mobile clinics held was 150; throughout the West Bank and Gaza over 23,500 people were examined, 5,000 of whom were in need of treatment. These cases are additional to the 42,500 patients seen at the hospital itself, so that in one year some 66,000 people benefited from the presence of St John in Jerusalem.

The work of this important hospital has caught the imagination of men and women from many nations. Surgeons and nurses have come from Australia, Canada and the United States. King Hussein of Jordan remains a generous benefactor and his wife, Queen Noor, is Patron of the Friends of the Hospital. In 1983 the Saudi Royal family made extensive gifts to further the hospital's work, whilst in London the Ladies' Guild has collected money to endow a bed. Of the hospital's 80 beds, five have been endowed at a cost of £70,000 each, the Friends of the Hospital and the St John Cadets being among the donors. The American Society has provided generous donations from its members and has declared its support for the eye bank and the children's ward. All this activity is vitally necessary if the hospital is to obtain sufficient money to continue its work. But money does not go very far in an area of 100% inflation; nor is money all that matters. The staff of the hospital, now led by Sir Stephen Miller as Hospitaller, continue to show the same dedication as their predecessors, whilst their professionalism and technical skill have made the most remarkable progress. One of the key members of the staff is the Matron and when Mrs Ruth Parks retired in October 1984 after nine busy and successful years, the Priory of Canada paid her the unusual compliment of establishing a division in her name. Her successor, Pauline O'Donnell, was recruited through the Priory of Scotland.

Today St John's Gate is the headquarters of the Order of St John housing the Chancery of The Order, and its museum, as well as the St John Ambulance Museum. Nearby, the Church bears the scars of war quietly but proudly, restored in unaffected simplicity, the historic crypt surviving to remain a focus for worship and tradition. Together they retain their places at the administrative head and religious heart of a working British Order of Chivalry. In the Holy City the Ophthalmic Hospital plays a role of world importance and reaches back to the very origins of the Hospitallers. In the United Kingdom and overseas, Priories and Commanderies have been established to support the work of the Order. The Priory of Scotland still uses the ancient Commandery title of Torphichen and, more relevant to the modern age, provides invaluable support for ski and mountain rescue and its own Cadet unit. The Priory for Wales has for long supported a wide variety of welfare projects and still provides help for mountain and marine rescue units. In the Priory of South Africa, decisions about the future work of St John were taken in 1982 and 1983 and must now go forward in a deeply troubled nation. New Zealand's Priory is currently reviewing its structure. The Priory of Canada has welcomed the first Lady Prior. The Priory in Australia has recently published a major first-aid manual, whilst in the Commandery of Western Australia over 19,000 students have qualified in first aid. The Commandery of Ards – official name for the Order in Northern Ireland – continues to provide a service to all its citizens under the most taxing conditions. Elsewhere in the world, in forty-three different nations of the Commonwealth, St John flourishes, not perhaps as Priory or Commandery, but as teams of men and women working to serve mankind and earning respect for themselves and for the cause which they serve. The Order of St John is unique as a Christian Order of Chivalry in that its working foundations embrace all religions.

2
G̲R̲E̲A̲T̲ ̲E̲N̲T̲E̲R̲P̲R̲I̲S̲E̲S̲

During the second half of the nineteenth century two separate developments were unfolding, both of which were to affect the Order. In Britain industrialization had brought greater risk of accidents and more awareness of the need for first aid. In Europe the minor but bloody wars of the 1860s and 1870s highlighted the plight of war victims. After the battle of Solferino (1859) Jean Henri Dunant called for international recognition of the need to alleviate the suffering of sick and wounded soldiers. This led to the first Geneva Convention of 1864, which introduced the revolutionary idea of neutrality on the battlefield for medical personnel and gave rise to various national aid societies and, later, the International Red Cross movement. The detailed development of the British Red Cross organization is not part of this story, but the role played by members of the Order of St John in its creation is very important and must be recorded not only in the context of the Order's early work but also because it provided a strong base for the work of the Order's foundations.

By 1867 the Red Cross movement in Europe was growing fast, but Britain was not taking part. During 1868 the Order had been in touch with the War Office and Admiralty, inviting them to recognize the potential value of a national society for Britain. At a Chapter meeting on 6 April 1869, seven members of the Order formed themselves into a Provisional Committee* to establish how this could be done. Thomas Longmore, professor of surgery at the Army's hospital at Netley and a firm supporter of the new movement, made himself available as an advisor and the Committee was given the support of the Army Medical Department. This link between the ambulance work of the Order and the Army's medical authorities was of great importance as the

* Chapter-General Report 1870.

Ambulance Department of the Order evolved and as preparedness in peace became an accepted aim of voluntary societies.

At the third Red Cross conference in 1869 John Furley, representing the Order of St John, pledged Britain's commitment to provide help for the sick and wounded, and in July 1870 this pledge was made good. Immediately on the outbreak of war between France and Prussia on 15 July 1870, Charles Burgess – Secretary of the Order's Provisional Committee – wrote to *The Times* and a public meeting was held in Willis's Rooms on 4 August under the chairmanship of the Prior of St John, the Duke of Manchester*. The Committee put forward the idea of creating a national society, recommending that Colonel Lloyd Lindsay, VC, veteran of the Crimean War, should become Chairman. Lloyd Lindsay accepted the challenge and within a week he too wrote to *The Times* seeking national support. Twenty members of the Order immediately joined the new Committee with Burgess as Secretary and within twenty-four hours Furley set off for France with Dr William MacCormac. Lloyd Lindsay's call for help was successful and the new society played an important role during the Franco-Prussian War. The need for a peacetime organization was recognized in the following lines from the Chapter-General Report for 1871:

> It is earnestly to be hoped that this Society may be continued as a permanent national institution, retaining such organisation in time of peace as may ensure its efficiency in case of war.

The British National Society for Aid to Sick and Wounded (BNAS), with its component members of the Order, also took an active part in war relief measures during the Turco-Serbian War in 1876. Again the Order took the lead by creating a relief fund and establishing a register of qualified volunteers prepared to serve in the war zones. A medical team was sent out and this, together with the fund, was later controlled by the BNAS. However, the role of the British Order of St John in these formative years was important and of lasting influence because its initiatives drew public attention to the need for assistance and were crucial to the creation of the National Aid Society, from which the Red Cross Society of Great Britain would be formed. The Order's pride in this achievement must not be dimmed by the passage of time, nor damaged by subsequent differences of opinion or changes of direction; it deserves its honoured place in the records of humanitarian work.

* Chapter-General Report 1871.

The peacetime work of the Order had now gained impetus and in 1869 the Chapter decided that it was time to publicize more widely the charitable objects of the Order of St John in England. At first they had proceeded 'as quietly and unostentatiously as possible' but now extension of the work would only be possible with increased public sympathy and support. By 1870 the work of the Order in a number of hospitals and in the provision of free meals for the sick and poor was earning praise from patients and doctors alike – but again, more work meant greater need for finance.

In 1872 the Order had suggested that some form of ambulance organization would be required in industrial areas and the first ambulances – Neuss litters – were purchased for use in Burslem and then Wolverhampton, where local ambulance committees were formed with a member of the Order as chairman. In this lay the seeds of what was to become the Ambulance Department of the Order, for in 1874 at the first Chapter-General to assemble at St John's Gate since the dissolution, reference was made to 'the general superintendence of an Ambulance Department'. At the same meeting three other matters of long-term importance were discussed: the possibility of purchasing the freehold of St John's Gate; the provision of Neuss litters for industrial areas; and Sir Edmund Lechmere's suggestion of a medal to be awarded for bravery in saving life on land. It was during this period that Francis Duncan began his association with the Order and its ambulance work and in 1876 he took over the Ambulance Department, absorbing himself in the work of the Order with phenomenal energy. In 1873 the Order had first raised the question of schools to train nurses for work in districts where the sick poor needed help. The Order also expressed its concern at the growing risks on the railways; in three months there were 75 collisions, 315 deaths and almost 2,000 casualties of all kinds. Something needed to be done, some organization was required – and quickly. At Edmund Lechmere's suggestion, Thomas Longmore presented a paper dealing with the care and attention required for accidents in mines and industrial establishments. This was a most effective scene-setting paper, drawing attention to the fact that there was no civil organization despite evidence that accidents were increasing. The Order had again taken an initiative by bringing this situation to the attention of the public and the stage was set for the formation of the St John Ambulance Association.

The creation in 1877 of the St John Ambulance Association, the first great Foundation of the Order, was one of the most far-reaching and wide-ranging steps taken by the Order at any time in its long history. The men and women who created the Association and Brigade and guided their destinies in the early years were people of independent spirit and often of independent means. They were determined, dedicated, sometimes eccentric but always sincere in their work for humanity. Their spirit of adventure – no less than their sense of purpose and devoted labour – generated the energy and gave rise to the most important long-term decisions of the modern Order. They were pioneers of first aid in peace and also of aid to the wounded in war. Today we might describe Furley as the 'action man' of the early years, Duncan as the articulate orator and Lechmere as the philanthropist and quiet authority. These, with such friends and supporters as James Cantlie, Thomas Longmore and Major Peter Shepherd, combined to form one of the most influential groups of men in modern social history. There were others who at this time did not occupy central positions: Ella, Lady Strangford; Vincent Kennett-Barrington; Charles Burgess; Major George Hutton, and William Church Brasier of Margate; but their work and their loyalty was of lasting importance for the development of the Order. Lady Strangford and Vincent Kennett-Barrington had been tireless workers for the relief of suffering, operating sometimes independently, sometimes for the International Red Cross and also for the St John Ambulance Association. Kennett-Barrington was Deputy Chairman of the Association from 1882 until his death in 1903, very ably supported by his wife Alicia who did much of his Association work during his frequent absences. Also in 1882, at the request of the Order, Lady Strangford established the Victoria Hospital in Cairo, where many sick and wounded British soldiers were nursed back to health. Individually each achievement was in itself remarkable, but taken together the combined effort was of considerable international significance.

We have already spoken of Sir John Furley, albeit briefly. Born in Ashford, Kent in 1836, he had always wanted a military career and became an energetic officer of the local unit of Volunteers. In 1864, during the Prusso-Danish war, he visited the Danish HQ and saw for himself the plight of the wounded. It was the very year of the first Geneva Convention and Furley's experience here was the spark which ignited his subsequent long-term interest in the victims of war. In the same year he became a member of the Order of St John and it was as the representative of the Order in 1869 that he pledged the creation of a British national aid society. From this point onwards Furley's name is inextricably linked with national aid, first aid, Red Cross and naturally, St John. As the first Director of Stores of the Order's Ambulance Department, his inventiveness and his ability to turn his experience to practical use were invaluable. The Ashford litter, an ambulance hamper, horse-ambulance carriages, an electric light device for searching the battlefield – all were invented or modified by him. The first Princess Christian hospital train in 1900 and the second in 1915 also owed something to his energy. In 1883, at a time when there were no municipal ambulance services, Furley formed – with William Church Brasier – the Invalid Transport Corps, forerunner of the modern ambulance services. He was a man of vision, energy, organizing capacity and inventive genius whose gifts were brought not only to the Order of St John but also the International Red Cross at a vital time in the development of both. He was to play a most important role in the provision of Red Cross aid during the Boer War and at the age of 78 his advice was sought in the First World War. When he died on 26 September 1919 he had been awarded honours by many nations and was acknowledged as one of the greatest pioneers of the ambulance movement.

Sir Edmund Lechmere was born in 1826, descendant of a famous family which reached back to the Norman conquest. A successful and enlightened businessman and landowner, he was admitted to the Order of St John in 1860 and quickly became involved in its policy and administration. He believed that the Order should do more to live up to its ancient Hospitaller traditions and used his influence to encourage this. In 1868 he became Secretary-General of the Order, a post which he held until 1890. This vitally important post at the administrative centre of the Order was in many ways shaped for the future by Lechmere, who brought all his considerable business and organizational gifts to the task. But he was more than just an administrator; in 1869 and 1870 he was one of the group which influenced the formation of the National Aid Society. Described as amiable, courteous and hospitable (his home was often the venue for important if informal discussions), he was also a man of immense energy who worked very hard to further the aims of St John. He loved tradition and had a strong sense of history; it is not surprising, therefore, that he should want to recover and restore the Gatehouse at Clerkenwell and in 1873 he purchased the freehold of the building which was later transferred to the Order, although in the meantime the Order leased two rooms in the tower which now houses the library. To Lechmere must go the credit for the purchase of land in Jerusalem on which the first Ophthalmic Hospital stood and also for the institution in 1875 of the life-saving medal of the Order of St John, which he hoped would be the equivalent on land of the Royal Humane Society's medal for bravery in saving life at sea. He died in 1894 shortly after purchasing a sixteenth-century Processional Cross for the Order. For thirty-four years Sir Edmund Lechmere had served the cause of St John; his influence on the development of the Order was outstanding and his contribution to its traditional base remains unique.

Francis Duncan, an Aberdonian brought up in the strict faith of the Kirk, was an officer of the Royal Artillery and the author of its early history. He was a natural leader and an excellent lecturer who combined these gifts with an inquisitive approach and the courage to question authority, but above all he had an extremely high sense of duty and possessed phenomenal energy. He was a gifted orator and when later he became a Member of Parliament his maiden speech was greeted with acclaim by Members and the Press. He directed the Ambulance Department of the Order during the critical period when the Association was formed and supervised the development of the new Foundation. As his parliamentary duties increased he became much in demand as a speaker, and eventually gave up his positions in the Ambulance movement although still working for the Order whenever he could. However, the strain of constant work took its toll, his health deteriorated and on 15 November 1888 he died; however he had lived to see the Order's work recognized, due in no small measure to his own gifts. His position as the persuasive orator during the formative years of the Order's work remains unchallenged.

Surgeon-Major Peter Shepherd was involved with the ambulance work of the Order almost from the outset; in 1872 he was instrumental in starting the ambulance service in the Potteries. He supported the formation of the Association and became the first instructor at the Woolwich Centre. He is the author of the Association's first training manual, published in 1878 under the title *Aids for Cases of Injuries and Sudden Illness*, and he acknowledged the help of James (later Sir James) Cantlie and Mitchell Bruce in writing this first and all-important textbook. Regrettably this busy but gentle man was killed during the Zulu War on 22 January 1879, while attempting to save the life of a soldier at Isandhlwana. Despite many revisions the book was known for many years as 'Shepherd's manual' as a mark of respect for the man and the manner of his death. There was no intention to attempt any pretence at medical skill; the preface makes this clear:

> This brief manual is simply intended for non-professional readers. There is no attempt made to popularize medicine or surgery; the object is to furnish a few plain rules which may enable anyone to act in cases of injury or sudden illness, pending the arrival of professional help.
>
> 30th October 1878

There was an air of expectation when, on St John's Day 1877, John Furley read a paper at the Order's invitation with the title, 'The proper sphere of volunteers for the relief of the sick and wounded soldiers in war'* and he was quick to remind his audience that he spoke as a senior Council member of both BNAS and the Order of St John. He advocated the need for establishing some organized system of training in peace if war victims were to be helped. This would provide a base of help for the victims of civilian accidents who were no less deserving of immediate aid. Britain was still only partially prepared and this was unfortunate, because untrained medical help could be more dangerous than no help at all. Furley claimed that support for the Red Cross, the Geneva Convention, was right in principle and he hoped that the BNAS and St John would be able to work together; 'Whatever we both do will be in harmony with our support of what is popularly called Red Cross work.' The Red Cross is the badge of a modern crusade, he said, ready to support without displacing the established medical authorities in the field. Furley pointed out that the need for a permanent organization and training had been suggested to the BNAS, but they declined to accept the responsibility; it was 'too great an enterprise'†. The way was open to the Order of St John to take up the vacant ground. In future the desire to volunteer would be insufficient; there would be many volunteers but only those who had been trained would provide effective assistance, whether in peace or war. Furley predicted that if professional medical men could work together with men and women who had received basic first-aid training, St John would soon possess an organization which would be of value in civil life and could also provide reserves for the Army hospitals.

Lechmere formally supported Furley's paper, getting to the heart of the matter by claiming that such an organization was within the spirit

---

* Chapter-General Report 1877.
† Corbet Fletcher, 1929.

Above: The Priory of
Clerkenwell, after Hollar, 1656
Right: The Great Ward of the
Hospital in Malta. 17th century
Statutes of the Order

Sir John Furley

Francis Duncan

Sir Edmund Lechmere

William Church Brasier

Brigade Nurses in the Order's crypt at Clerkenwell c.1890

FACING PAGE:
Above: The first Officers of the Brigade
Below: Tibshelf Colliery Ambulance Corps c.1887

Above: The first uniformed duty –
Queen Victoria's Jubilee 1887

Left: Denaby Main Colliery
Division's cycle ambulance

FACING PAGE:
Brigade members mobilized for th
Boer War. Clerkenwell April 190
Top: The St John V.A.D. Hospita
Rochdale

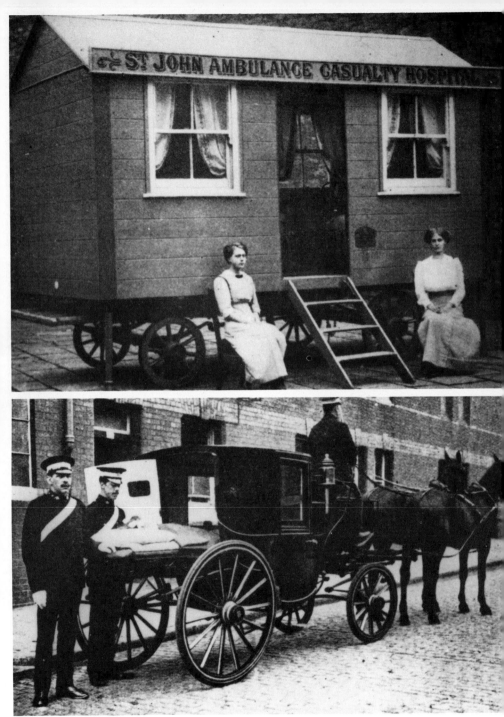

Top: First Mobile Unit – 1912
Above: Bristol City Corps' Ambulance – 1912 *(N.L. Display Services).*

of both the Red Cross conference of 1869 and the earlier initiatives of the Order of St John. There was no organization which trained and maintained its skills in peace – supporting a civilian need – which could then support the sick and wounded in war. The Order should fill the gap and provide such an organization. Francis Duncan spoke with his characteristic oratory and honesty, calling for support for the new association: money, men, women and the exertion of influence so that there could be some first-aid facility in each factory or mine.

There was no time to lose if this new venture was to gain support and recruits and so at Woolwich on 6 February 1878 a public meeting was held, designed to make the Association widely known and to publicize its aims. The Articles of Constitution listed five objects.*

a. Instruction in first aid, for accident and sudden illness and transport of sick and injured.
b. Instruction in elementary nursing.
c. Manufacture and distribution of material and the formation of ambulance depots in centres of industry and traffic.
d. The organization of Ambulance Corps, Invalid Transport Corps and Nursing Corps.
e. Promotion of instruction and work to alleviate suffering of sick and injured in peace and in war, independently of class, nationality or denomination.

Essentially the new organization would teach first aid and distribute ambulance material, the two great streams of activity which have been recognized by St John people for a century. It is, however, worth looking at the five objects to see the breadth of other activities envisaged, for in these we observe the origin of the Brigade, Medical Comforts Depots and the development of Nursing Divisions. We also see clearly the desire of the Order to serve without distinction of colour, class or creed.

Inevitably Lechmere, Duncan and Furley spoke at the meeting. Lechmere, the chairman, referred to the Order's search for Hospitaller work and his hope that the sick and injured in peace would be catered for as well as the victims of war. He wove the central thread of the concept – that people should be encouraged to devote something of their time or their means for the help of the suffering and the sick. Duncan referred to the changing circumstances of the world they lived in, suggesting that the new organization could achieve local results but

---

* Public meeting 6 Feb 1878, Woolwich.

with centrally controlled policy and records, so doing more to relieve pain and suffering than any other organization of modern times. When Furley's turn came to speak, he suggested that the new Association would form an indispensable part of voluntary assistance and the Army would look upon it as a valuable reserve; the word 'ambulance' had taken on a military flavour, but he defended the term as being of civilian application too. Finally he claimed that this would be no spasmodic effort, to be adopted for a moment and then forgotten. General Brackenbury, who had left the BNAS, felt it was the duty of the Society to organize in peace a system which could come into effect in the event of war. He, Longmore and others had tried to persuade the Society, but Lloyd Lindsay had said that the BNAS could not take 'so considerable an affair upon itself', though he wished the Order's new venture well.*

So the first centre of the Association was formed at Woolwich and others quickly followed in Kent: Ashford, Sevenoaks, Maidstone; then Chelsea and Lavender Hill in London; later in Worcester and Southampton. The Metropolitan Police asked for their own centre and other police forces followed; railways, potteries, mining areas and other industrial areas soon provided their own centres. The idea caught on rapidly and although some people considered it to be an 'ephemeral female fashion' there were many from all walks of life who saw the real value to the community and gave their support. Wherever possible a centre was formed; if that was not possible, detached classes were arranged for interested pupils. Within six months 1,000 people had been trained and so rapid was the progress that by 1880 over 70 centres had been formed and 40 detached classes were in progress; by 1881, over 30,000 people had been trained. Duncan could boast that despite the high number trained there had been not one complaint that any had exceeded the proper bounds of first aid, that classes were being held for working people and that the supporters and instructors 'did not do this to get rich'.

The main object of the Association was instruction and the 1879 syllabus for training consisted of a set course of six lectures, two of which were designed as separate subjects: one for men – stretcher drill and lifting – the other a nursing lecture for women. A year later a second course was set up for home nursing and hygiene, available for those women who had already passed the first course. At the same time

* Public meeting 6 Feb 1878, Woolwich.

the concept of annual requalification was adopted and with it the award of the Medallion, that much prized symbol of continuous training. By a resolution of 25 July 1879, anyone who successfully sat a second examination could purchase a Medallion in bronze, silver or gold. It is of interest that the cross depicted on the first pieces is the plain White Cross worn on the surcoats of the Crusader knights – the Arms of the Order. In 1883 a bronze Medallion was provided free to those who requalified, and in 1884 the eight-pointed cross was used on the Medallion.

The second great aim of the Association was the design and provision of ambulance material when and where it should be needed, and in the latter part of the nineteenth century this was a particularly important requirement. The embryo stores department began with one triangular bandage and a wheeled litter, but before long the inventive genius of Furley and the willing help of his assistants had been rewarded with improved designs and manufacture on a scale which could meet most local needs. An ambulance hamper was designed and modifications were made to the Beaufort litter. Indeed, in 1879 the Order was able to offer a limited amount of stores for use in the Zulu campaign.

The governing body of the Association was to be the Central Executive Committee with a Chairman, Deputy Chairman (who was also the Director of the Ambulance Department of the Order of St John), Director of Stores and Chief Secretary. A separate medical committee was formed, on to which members of London hospitals were coopted. Local centres were headed by a President and local committees were formed, each with its own secretary and treasurer. It was accepted that a substantial number of working-class people should benefit from the training, but would not be able to make any financial contribution. As early as 1878 the Ambulance Department recognized the need for emphasis to be placed on the practical side of the training, and at the same time began to maintain a roll of personnel who were prepared to volunteer for service in hospitals. In fact the hospitals welcomed the Association and were pleased to provide instructors and examiners for the various centres, as well as practical work in the hospitals for members taking the second certificate.

The St John Ambulance Association was created to fill a need which was recognized as equally valid in peace and war. There was no doubt that it was an important and relevant new development, undertaken for pure humanitarian reasons and able to meet the real needs of the time. There was no stopping this great new enterprise; ambulance centres and classes sprang up all over England and Wales. The public was only too willing to support an organization which so clearly demonstrated its desire to serve all people. The ten years between 1877 and 1887 were years of expansion followed by consolidation; acceptance, then active support. Working men and their representatives were naturally interested in the Association – the Chairman of the Mineworkers' Union was keen to see more first-aiders amongst mining staff and the same was true on the railways. At sea the Merchant Navy had suffered over 3,000 deaths from accidents on board ship and was quick to see the value of obtaining first-aid instruction for deck officers. Francis Duncan could justifiably claim that 'the Association has become a national work and the nation is realising the fact'. The progress of the Association attracted the attention of members of the Royal family; in 1879 HRH The Duke of Edinburgh accepted the Presidency of the Ashford centre, whilst Prince Leopold became President of the centre at Oxford. Four years later the Duke of Connaught became President of the centre formed at the Royal Military College, Sandhurst. Princess Beatrice gave her support to the Shetland Islands and Princess Christian, already well-known for her charitable works, decided to support the general ambulance work of the Order.

For the men of St John, 1879 was a busy and very productive year. First the Metropolitan Police Commissioner issued an order dated 27 June, to the effect that any assistance offered by a certified pupil of the St John Ambulance Association would be accepted. This, coming only two years after its birth, was real recognition. Secondly, it became necessary to publish a supplementary report in February to take account of the phenomenal progress of the new movement. The first report had been divided into two sections: 'Aid to the Injured in Peace' and 'Aid to the Sick and Wounded in War', thus identifying the concept of a working, practical organization in peace which could provide a civilian reserve for the medical services in war and which demanded high standards. The term 'First Aid to the Injured' was now placed at the top of the papers describing the syllabus. Finally William Church Brasier, a bookseller, formed an ambulance 'Corps' at Margate and this – the first organized unit of trained first-aiders – worked with the lifeboat as well as in the town. It was a success, earning the respect of the townspeople and, of importance for the development of the Brigade, bringing Church Brasier to the notice of the leaders of the St John Ambulance movement; Furley in particular was impressed by the Margate experiment and in 1883 he invited Church Brasier to work with him on the development of an 'Invalid Transport Corps aimed at transporting the sick poor without charge', bringing the carriage of the sick 'within the means of all classes'. This venture began with a single horse-drawn carriage, two litters and four staff, and was the fore-runner of the Metropolitan Corps. Already, however, new corps had been formed at Leicester and in the north of England.

At a time when there was no radio or TV and the newspapers were certainly not read by everyone, the best methods of attracting support and publicity for the Order's work were by personal visits and public meetings. The Ambulance movement was very fortunate in having Major George Hutton as one of its working supporters. He began a series of visits known as Ambulance Crusades to areas where first aid would be most needed and described the work of the Association on land as the equivalent of the lifeboat at sea. A tireless worker, a persuasive speaker and totally committed to the general aims of St John, Hutton's contribution to the expansion of ambulance work – particularly in the north of England – was considerable.

In 1884 the Order sanctioned the use of its eight-pointed Cross surrounded by a garter as a badge for certified members of the Association, and in the following year Lechmere obtained approval for his idea of awarding a Life Saving Medal for bravery on land in the same way as the Royal Humane Society's Medal was granted for life saving at sea. It was also in 1884 that the importance of coordination was brought to the public notice when a bridge collapsed at Coppal Station between Wigan and Preston, injuring a number of people. *The Times* was able to describe the 'excellent system' of the Association when they tackled the accident. In 1885 the Order's Stores Department sent out ambulance material for the troops in the Sudan and for the builders of the Sudan railway, and John Furley was asked to modify a horse-ambulance for use by the Army in the Sudan. Furley was seeking a degree of uniformity and interchangeability, so that patients would suffer the minimum of disturbance; his designs were awarded gold medals at the International Health Exhibition, repeating his Brussels success of 1877 and bringing further international recognition to the Association.

The movement had caught the imagination of a public only too aware that first aid was necessary – in 1885 there were 8,500 reported accidents in factories and of these over 400 were fatal; on the railways over 1,000 people had been killed in a single year. People from all walks of life came forward and by 1887 over 100,000 had been trained by the

Association and 270 centres had been officially formed. Thus by the middle of the 1880s the Association had established itself at home and in addition it was influencing first-aid work overseas. In Germany, Professor Esmarch established the *Samaritaner Verein* based on the British Association and very soon similar organizations were developed in other European nations and in the United States. Further afield, in what was then the British Empire, centres of the Association were formed; the first of these was in Victoria, but within a year other cities in Australia had followed and during the same period centres were started in Singapore, Rangoon and in China.

By 1887, therefore, the Order of St John could be proud of its achievements:

a. The crucial role in the formation of the National Aid Society
b. Diets for convalescent and sick patients
c. The formation of 'cottage hospitals'
d. Training for local nurses to help the sick poor and the foundation of a nursing training society
e. Establishment of ambulance litters and material in mining and industrial areas
f. The Eastern War Sick and Wounded Relief Fund
g. Institution of Medals for Life Saving on land
h. The creation of the St John Ambulance Association, the first great Foundation of the Order in Britain
i. The foundation of the St John Ophthalmic Hospital in Jerusalem
j. Promotion of greater awareness of the needs of the sick, poor and wounded
k. Distribution of ambulance material generally
l. Improved standards of practical first aid.

Through the Association the great concept which the Order had sought since its revival was now being put into effect and as the numbers trained by the Association increased, they had grouped themselves into 'corps', training and working together. These corps did not, however, have the benefit of a national organization and co-ordinated fund raising, indeed some local organizations were very basic.

On 31 March 1887 officers of the Ambulance Department met twenty-four of the more eminent physicians with the aim of establishing a 'proper system of transport of invalids in London'. As a result of this meeting the Central Executive Committee of the Ambulance Department decided that the various corps should be brought into one centrally controlled national organization and 'banded together as a brigade' for civilian needs and as an Army reserve. On 19 July 1888 a special memorandum was issued announcing the decision and instructing the corps that henceforth one generic name would be used, 'The St John Ambulance Brigade', to be followed by the name of the corps on a separate line. The new organization was a genuine extension of the Order's work as approved by the Charter. It was to be a voluntary civilian organization for providing assistance in civilian emergencies and also a form of medical reserve for the Army and Navy. All members were to be certified personnel who had been trained by the Association and no corps could exist independently of the Brigade. The corps which had been founded before 1 June 1887 retained their identities; the most prominent at that time being Margate (1879), Ashford (1879), Brighouse (1882), Leicester (1882), Northampton (1886), Wigan and Tibshelf Colliery, whilst the Nursing Corps were represented by Oldham (1885), Leicester and Hull. The Ashford unit, formed on 4 April 1879, now has the privilege of being the most senior division in the Brigade because Margate – formed a little earlier – seceded from the Association following a difference of opinion.

At first the Brigade was organized into two regions, Metropolitan and Provincial, and the units were renamed 'divisions', but the spread of interest in the Ambulance movement continued and in 1894 it was found necessary to reorganize on a regional basis. There were, however, teething troubles to be put right; some divisions appeared to model themselves on the Army's volunteer units and adopted military ranks and unauthorized uniform. This had to be brought under control, but tactfully, since it would be all too easy to destroy the local potential of the Brigade units by a heavy-handed response from London. There was also the question of overcoming the prejudices of those who called St John men 'body-snatchers' or who believed this was no more than 'an ephemeral female fashion'. It says much for the leadership of the time that a degree of order and discipline was soon established with no loss of goodwill in the Brigade and the gradual retreat of the sceptics.

We must make a special mention of the first official 'Public Duties'. In 1886 the Invalid Transport Corps offered its services to the Commissioner of the Metropolitan Police to establish ambulance stations at the Lord Mayor's Show. The offer was accepted and this first public duty was a resounding success. Immediately there were requests for other duties, including the establishment of first-aid stations at the Military Tournament. In 1887 the Commissioner of the Metropolitan

Police asked Sir John Furley to provide medical and trained first-aid assistance for Queen Victoria's Jubilee on 21 June and Furley, Dr Sam Osborn – one of the Metropolitan surgeons – together with fifty Brigade men took up their posts at Buckingham Palace, Westminster Abbey and Spring Gardens. Each detachment had its own horse-ambulance and first-aid kit. They were considered part of the police contingent, for these men were awarded the Metropolitan Police version of the Jubilee Medal; Furley was described as 'Director of Ambulance'. On the following day, for the Hyde Park celebrations nursing members took their turn at public duty, while during the weeks that followed Brigade personnel were on duty at the many official functions which formed part of the Jubilee celebrations.

One of the great advantages of a centrally controlled Brigade was the ability to achieve and maintain consistently high standards and uniformity of both practical first aid and administration. In 1889 the first issue of Brigade Regulations was made, outlining the objects of the Brigade, the personnel for each corps and such detail as the wearing of uniform. Each corps was to have a minimum strength of eleven, which was to include a surgeon, a superintendent and an inspector of stores. Uniform was to be optional and, if worn, would consist of black serge trousers and jacket with the Association's badge on the arm and a black peaked cap with the Brigade badge. One important regulation included in this first issue was the requirement for annual re-examination by a surgeon in order to maintain membership. Some sort of central registration and control was clearly necessary, because by 1889 there were 10 Divisions in the Metropolitan area and 35 Corps or Divisions in the regions. As one might expect, the greatest strength was to be found in the industrial and mining areas of the Midlands, Derbyshire, Yorkshire, Lancashire and Kent. It was in Middlesbrough in January 1889 that the Prince of Wales inspected over 1,000 members, following a successful 'crusade' in Yorkshire by the indefatigable George Hutton.

The following year saw the first Brigade competition which was held at Birkenhead, the object being to maintain high standards – as was the concept of the annual training camps which were begun in the same year. The first of these was at Muswell Hill and included physical fitness, fire drill, demonstrations and practical first aid. It was not long before local camps and competitions were arranged, so that efficient, coordinated training and teamwork spread throughout Britain. Two years later, the railway companies granted a reduction in the fares for St John personnel travelling on duty.

Apart from the local training there was a great deal of work done at St John's Gate, mainly administrative and organizational. Annual inspections of Corps and Divisions were authorized, officer appointments were formally granted by a warrant, uniform was standardized and made compulsory for public duty. But perhaps the most important decision of this period was the appointment of a single officer as Commissioner to control the Brigade, the first being Colonel E. T. Thackeray, VC, CB. Until this time the Brigade had been administered by the Directors of the Ambulance Department, John Furley being known as 'Hon. Director of the St John Ambulance Brigade' during his tenure of office from 1887 to 1890. The first Brigade Chief Superintendent, HQ assistant to the Commissioner, was also appointed – William Church Brasier, whose conscientious approach was to bring great credit to the Brigade and influence the lives of many members, young and old. It was to Church Brasier's guard of honour that the Prince of Wales turned on 24 June 1893 when he unveiled the memorial to the late Duke of Clarence and said to the representatives of the Press: 'Gentlemen, this is a good uniform. I believe much good will come of it.'

By September 1894 the Brigade had been divided into five separate districts: No. I, Metropolitan; No. II, South and West; No. III, Central and East; No. IV, North West; No. V, North East. Its total strength, including surgeons and nursing members, stood at 4,706. The districts were divided into Corps and Divisions and these local organizations needed their own headquarters for training and the safe custody of their stores; Wellingborough (Northampton) became the first corps to obtain its own Ambulance Hall in 1894. A few years later Accrington and Colne followed suit, while the Association's 29 London ambulance stations were now staffed day and night by St John men and women. These halls and stations provided a link with the population, who now realized that the service provided by the Brigade was of real and lasting benefit. More people came forward to join, so that in 1895 the Brigade strength had reached 150 surgeons, 6,603 ambulance personnel and 778 nursing members. The organization of these personnel into Divisions and Districts had gone smoothly and Deputy Commissioners were now appointed to supervise each District. A Brigade conference was convened at Northampton and the 185 delegates who attended approved the Metropolitan District uniform for general use throughout the Brigade. The next year saw a joint demonstration of fire drills and first aid under realistic conditions laid on by Church Brasier, who was a voluntary fire officer as well as well as a Brigade member. In 1897 the Brigade prepared for the celebration of Queen Victoria's Diamond Jubilee, its largest public commitment. Colonel C. W. Bowdler, the Deputy Commissioner of the London District, organized 95 ambulance stations along the main processional route and in the City and these were manned by 803 men – of whom 349 came from the provincial corps – and 103 women. Throughout the celebrations the Brigade treated over 1,700 cases, including the Duke of Albany and Coburg, and for the first time members were posted with the police in front of the crowd.

It was in this same year that the first inter-railway competition was held and the Brigade competition became formalized with the presentation of the Dewar Shield. 1898 saw the official approval of the design for the Service Medal of the Order of St John which had first been authorized in 1895. The bust of Queen Victoria, which still features on present-day medals, was executed by Princess Louise. For a short period, this award had been given for meritorious service, but is now given for fifteen years of efficient Brigade service and a bar is added for each further period of five years.

The Brigade had progressed overseas as well as in Britain. In 1887 Victoria, Australia, had set up the first overseas centre of the Association; the first overseas corps of the Brigade was formed in Dunedin, New Zealand, in 1892 and the following year units were formed in Cape Town and Auckland. Nursing units were established in Cape Town in 1894 and in Dunedin in 1895. The overseas development of the Brigade is dealt with in a later chapter, but here it is important to recognize how early in the general development of the Brigade the overseas expansion began.

So, as the nineteenth century drew to its close, St John Ambulance work had become an established and respected part of the British scene. In a little over ten years the Brigade had built upon the solid foundation laid by the Association and was now recognized in its own right, its organization stabilized and its uniform well-known at many public occasions. Of the great trio, Lechmere and Duncan had died but Furley remained to serve both the Red Cross and St John. By 1899 the strength of the Brigade was nearly 9,000, of whom just over 1,000 were women, and recruits were still coming forward. All seemed set fair for expansion, but there were troubled times ahead and the Brigade would soon prove itself to be just as dependable in war as it had been in time of peace.

3

A NEW CENTURY

By the end of 1897 Britain was at the peak of her power as leader of an empire. Queen Victoria, now nearly eighty, had emerged from her self-imposed wilderness of widowhood and was once more a popular figure. The most prominent national characteristic was the deep sense of patriotism which overrode some of the social injustice of the times. The spirit of volunteer service flourished throughout Britain, and within the St John fraternity there was a justifiable feeling of pride in the great progress which had been made. It was becoming generally accepted that the Order of St John provided policy and direction through its Ambulance Department, the Association being responsible for training and teachers whilst the Brigade supplied a trained, uniformed body of men and women volunteers to carry out first-aid duties. Life in Britain was proceeding much as normal for the period; in London there were still many horse-drawn buses, while many more people were emigrating from the country areas to find work in the major cities. A housewife would pay two old pence (1p) for a pound of sugar or a loaf of bread, and for the same money her husband could buy his pint of beer. Social improvements were on the way, but slowly, and Britain saw no cause for great alarm.

This was not the case in South Africa, where a much more volatile atmosphere had been created by the grave differences in approach between Britain and the Boer leaders who were seeking their own independent republics. British dominance in the area and her insistence upon specific concessions for British-born settlers had already caused great resentment, which would soon explode with the Boer invasion of Natal on 11 October 1899.

The spread of voluntary service had already given rise to the need for some form of control over the various strands which would work together in peace and war. On 8 July 1898, the Secretary of State for

31

War convened a conference with the aim of coordinating voluntary medical aid and in November that year, the Central British Red Cross Committee was formed, consisting of representatives from the National Aid Society, the War Office, the Army Nursing Reserve and the St John Ambulance Association. In January 1899 this committee was officially recognized as Britain's national Red Cross organization. Meanwhile Colonel Bowdler, Commissioner for the Brigade, had written to the War Office seeking guidance as to whether the trained men of the Brigade should be mobilized to assist the medical department. By October, having had no reply, he wrote again and by now there was a real need for urgency. Agreement was given to enlist Brigade personnel and formal documents were to be prepared. However, Bowdler did not wait for these; instead he issued a special memorandum to the Brigade on the 27 October calling for a return of volunteers and outlining the general terms of service. It was accepted that the Central Red Cross Committee would coordinate the general support for the British Army, the Association would help with the provision of comforts and parcels for the troops, but the Brigade would be the sole channel for the provision of men as auxiliary orderlies. When the first call came for these men, the Brigade was ready; Bowdler's initiative paid dividends. They came from many walks of life, some giving up good salaries, to enlist under two general categories: those who served under the War Office and were paid by the Army and those who joined under the aegis of the Brigade as part of the national Red Cross effort.

The country in which they were to serve needs some description, for its character and climate were as much responsible for casualties as were the Boers. It was a vast place in which the main area of operations was over 3,000 ft above sea level. Day temperatures in summer were very high, but the nights were bitterly cold. The dry air in the high veldt would aid recovery from wounds, except where it became dust-laden due to the passage of troops and horses. Then the dust carried the germs which caused gangrene. The rivers became polluted as the war dragged on and thus sources of typhoid and enteric fever; and in some parts of the theatre of war the shortage of water presented serious hazards.

On 14 November, Brigade Order No. 16 (BO 16, as it was called) was issued, setting out detailed items of service and rates of pay. Volunteers were paid according to their rank and qualifications; the officers received 38s 6d (£1.85p) per week, while privates were paid 23s 4d or 21 shillings per week according to grade. Most of the work for the Brigade involved hospital duty including, to quote from BO 16, 'removing, nursing and tending the sick and wounded, cleaning their eating utensils, bedpans and so forth and keeping the wards clean. Men on board ship will be amenable to ship's discipline and must be prepared to sleep in hammocks.' Officers of the Brigade who volunteered would rank with RAMC Sergeants, to be employed as Wardmasters if they held the Association's Nursing Certificate as well as that for first aid. Privates in the Brigade were classified as Ward Orderlies First or Second Class according to their qualification, but there were some men who became stretcher-bearers, moving forward with field hospitals.

The uniform consisted of a shirt, a khaki drill tunic and trousers, boots and puttees, topped by a pith helmet or field cap and with an overcoat for inclement weather. The men wore the black St John buttons and a St John badge on their sleeve. They carried a holdall with toilet items, a first field-dressing and their knife, fork and spoon, and were also issued with a clasp knife and the Red Cross brassard. They were expected to bring some of their own basic uniform, but the bulk was provided by the Order and the Red Cross Committee at a cost of about £2.10s.

Bowdler's system for mobilizing the Brigade involved the allocation of quotas to each of the districts, dependent on their numerical strength, and the selection of personnel to fill these quotas was delegated to the Deputy Commissioners. This speeded up the Brigade reaction and allowed for accurate selection of those best qualified. Headquarters tried to give a week's notice of the date when men were required to report, and a further week was necessary for preparation before the drafts could be sent to their ports of departure. The early drafts naturally found themselves the centre of interest for both local press and public as they boarded their trains bound for London. Their destination was St John's Gate, which had been turned into a Brigade mobilization and training centre. On arrival in London, the new recruits were met by a 'heavily moustachio'd soldierly officer' who welcomed them, allocated their accommodation and saw that they were settled in. This was William John Church Brasier, one of the pioneers of the Ambulance movement and of the Brigade in particular. He was Brigade Chief Superintendent at the time of the Boer War, one of the work-horses of the period, serving alongside William Morgan who acted as the main quartermaster. The two men dealt with all the administration and training requirements for the draft, and for the first six months of the war they only rarely left the Gate. Training was coordinated by Dr Sam Osborn, Chief Surgeon of the Metropolitan Corps, and Stores Superintendent A. J. Trimmer who gave up all his spare time to assist the mobilization programme. After a week of revision training the men were fit to join a draft, but in the early stages demands for orderlies followed in quick succession and the men were sent off after only four or five days.

The first call for men came from the War Office on 13 November and telegrams were immediately sent from the Gate to the districts. Within forty-eight hours men were reporting for training, and on 23 November the first St John Ambulance orderlies left the Gate to join the hospital ship *Princess of Wales*. There were three officers and twenty orderlies in this first draft, and each was presented with a special brassard bearing the monogram of the Princess, later Her Majesty Queen Alexandra. The second draft, totalling fifty-five men, joined the transport ship *Simla* bound for Cape Town. These were the first Brigade members to set foot in the war zone. By June 1900, 1,500 men had been mobilized and the final total was 2,046. We must stop a moment to consider what these figures mean – that one man in five was accepted and went to South Africa and in No. 4 (Lancashire) District – commanded by Colonel Charles Trimble – the figure was as high as one in three. In fact a quarter of the medical orderlies serving in South Africa were St John men.

Those who sent the British Army to the Boer War in 1899 believed that their task would soon be over – if not by Christmas, then soon after. In the event, their first Christmas was made memorable by a personal gift from the Queen in the form of a tin of chocolate for each man. This gesture of the Sovereign was eagerly awaited and the gift was highly valued by the servicemen in South Africa, including the men of the Brigade.

Apart from the official military hospitals, there were a number of private hospitals working in South Africa. These ranged from the large Imperial Yeomanry hospitals to small sections provided by individual benefactors – the Langman and Portland hospitals, for example. These were provided through Central Red Cross Committee, but some of the staff came from the Brigade. The Army field hospitals were closest to the scene of action, where wounded were brought from the battlefield for immediate treatment. Stationary hospitals, mostly tented, provided for longer treatment and rest for about a hundred men before they could be moved back to the base general hospitals of 500 beds where long-term treatment was available in either tented or hutted accommodation.

Some men served in the field hospitals and bearer companies and assisted in the removal of the wounded from the battlefields to the first casualty clearing units. The cold night temperatures made it necessary for this to be done quickly, and Edward Halstead from Hebden Bridge describes this in his diary for 20 and 21 April 1900:

> . . . went out with a party of 10 to search for wounded, we being provided with canteens. Returned to camp after losing our ambulance waggons with five men, one seriously wounded . . . Boers started shelling and we had to remove all sick and wounded out of range.

The bulk of the Brigade worked in the stationary and general hospitals, and work they certainly did. Several diaries written by Brigade men – in particular the letters of W. S. Inder of Kendal – show a daily routine which began at 5 a.m., breakfast at 6, treatment and bathing of patients until 9.30 when the medical officer did his rounds. The midday meal was at 12.30 and during the afternoon the orderlies helped the sick and wounded by doing shopping or writing letters. Evening duty ended when patients had been washed, utensils had been cleaned and the tent walls had been fastened down. There were, however, frequent extensions of duty as, for example, when new batches of wounded came in from the front or when the orderlies had to mount guard. But the biggest single cause of an increased workload was enteric fever; Orderly Beardsmore from Wellingborough records in his diary that he and his friends had only four hours off duty in a period of forty-eight hours during the 1900 epidemic. That these men earned the respect and gratitude of the wounded is indicated by the friendly use of a nickname, not lightly given by the British soldier, and in the case of Brigade orderlies the natural choice was 'Johnnies'.

Apart from the hospital, the Johnnies served in ambulance trains and in hospital ships. The Princess Christian was the best-known of the ambulance trains; prepared in England to specifications worked out by Longmore and Furley, the train was completed in ten weeks, then inspected by the Princess herself before being dismantled, sent to South Africa and reassembled there. Furley was on board when this train became the first ambulance train to enter Ladysmith after the siege. There were seven coaches, of which four were hospital cars containing cots and stretchers for a total of just under eighty patients, one acting as a surgery with Roentgen-ray equipment and the other two providing staff accommodation and a galley. Brigade men also served on No. 4 Train, known as the 'White Train' because this was the first British hospital train to be painted all white with its Red Cross on each coach.

Many hospital ships were employed to bring the sick and wounded from South Africa to Britain. We have already seen how twenty-three men served on the *Princess of Wales*, but Johnnies also served on other ships. The *Maine* was presented to the Central British Red Cross Committee by a group of American ladies and fourteen St John Orderlies served on her. When, later in the war, the *Maine* was sent to serve in the China campaign, these same men all sailed with her and thus became the only St John personnel to qualify for the China 1900 campaign medal. St John men also served on other hospital ships as the campaign evolved, and personnel were transferred between hospitals to meet changing priorities.

Although the provision of trained men was the principal task of the Brigade, the Order as a whole contributed in a different way by the collection, sorting, storage and despatch of parcels of clothing, medical effects and comforts for the hospitals and for the troops. This was a most important service, conducted under the aegis of the Central British Red Cross Committee and one which attracted the sympathy and support of the whole population. It was a service in which the nursing members of the Brigade and other women connected with the work of St John played a notable part. They wished to volunteer as nurses in South Africa, but as the authorities would not permit this they turned their energies to the vital task of providing assistance to the troops in hospital. Depots were set up at Norwood and in St John's Gate and 150 stretchers were built and despatched from Ashford, home of the Ashford litter. A total of some 500 tons of goods was prepared in this way and sent to South Africa in specially built cases. It is perhaps worth noting that for the first time we see the Red Cross and the White Cross of St John side by side on official stationery.

War demanded its sacrifice from the Johnnies, just as it did from the troops at the front. It was inevitable that men who were so closely involved with nursing the victims of typhoid, dysentery and enteric fever would themselves become sick. There were over 74,000 reported enteric and dysentery cases amongst the troops, and of these 8,000 died; in fact, far more men became incapacitated due to sickness than through enemy action. Of the 2,046 Brigade men who went to South Africa, 65 died, 61 of them while on Brigade duty. At the end of the war in May 1902 the Order provided a memorial to these 61 casualties in the church at Clerkenwell, but a later war was to witness its destruction – with that of the church – in an air-raid.

That the men of St John proved their worth during the Boer War is undisputed. They served alongside the Army Medical Corps, shared their discomforts and dangers and earned their share of recognition. Two men, C. W. Baker and E. H. G. Wynyard, were awarded the Distinguished Conduct Medal, the first gallantry awards for active service gained by the Brigade, while a further eight men were Mentioned in Despatches. Cecil Baker, who was also known as Cecil Graeme, was later invalided home, partially paralysed as the result of an accident. A successful benefit testimonial and concert was arranged for him in London. Mr Murray Guthrie, MP, who visited South Africa, included in the term 'Trained Orderlies' 'the men of the St John Ambulance Corps . . . perhaps the branch of the Red Cross Society that was the most useful of any of the organizations of that admirable institution . . .'*

The overall achievement of the Brigade during the Boer War was remarkable not only for the number of men who volunteered for this first duty in direct support of the Army, but also for the efficiency of its mobilization and the quality of the men who went to the war zone. We must remember that this was the first time in Britain's history when an entirely civilian voluntary medical organization had been invited to select and mobilize its own personnel. The need for Brigade personnel continued even after reserve units had been called up – proof enough of their value. The whole concept was an unqualified success and was recognized as such by patients and policy-makers alike; these men had already volunteered to help their fellows in a civilian capacity and now they stepped forward to volunteer for war. The women of the Brigade would have gone willingly to serve in the hospitals if the authorities had allowed it, but this disappointment did not prevent them from working in comforts depots. The Brigade had been able to play its important role because it was relevant, motivated and trained – it was ready.

During and after the Boer War, the Brigade prospered in Britain and was firmly accepted by the public. The numbers of divisions had increased and many more recruits – men and women – were coming forward, so that when the men came back from South Africa the total strength was just over 12,000. At the same time, new ideas were being discussed; the first juvenile unit of the Brigade was formed at

* *First Aid*: October 1900, p. 27.

Nottingham as early as 1903, but this pioneer effort was not to last, though ultimately it would lead to the cadets. The first proposals were made for overseas units of the 'Brigade in British Dominions Beyond the Seas' and this is not surprising when one considers the number of people who had by now received some form of training. Within five years well over 2,000 members would have enrolled. Competitions became popular as methods of retaining skills and greater realism was injected into the actual tests. The police forces and railway companies formed their own units, continuing to use the Association's handbook for training. In Rotherham a group of steelworkers who were keen to start their own St John unit had to hold their first meetings in 'the back-yard of a house', but this brave little unit prospered and became very successful. Thus the Brigade expanded and with it the work of the Order; indeed this expansion created a need for more office space in St John's Gate, resulting in an extension which was opened by the Prince of Wales in 1903.

The first service medals of the Order – originally proposed in 1895 and approved in 1898 – were presented on 6 January 1900 at Marlborough House. The obverse of the medal shows a bust of Queen Victoria designed by her daughter, Princess Louise; this same design has been used through all the succeeding reigns and is still used today, unique among the medals approved by the sovereign. The medal was awarded for fifteen years' efficient service in the Brigade, and also in certain other appointments. In May 1911 the award of a bar for a further five years' service was approved. Initially the bar displayed the words '5 Years Service', but in 1924 the design was changed to a St John Cross flanked by St John's wort.

In 1909 the No. 1 (London) District of the Brigade was granted the honour of being designated 'the Prince of Wales's Corps'. This not only recognized the work of the Brigade in London at its many public duties, but also reflected 'the valuable services rendered by the Brigade gener-ally'. We know that many provincial units had assisted at public duty in London (and to this day they still do so). It is then possible to take the view that the King was granting honour to the whole Brigade through the medium of the unit most closely connected with the capital city and the Royal family.

A further extension of the Brigade's work into a form of welfare took place in 1910 when a division at Brighouse (No. 5 District) organized a 'camp' for crippled children. The authorities at the time believed that the St John Ambulance Brigade could help with the evacuation of civilians, especially the sick, during a national emergency and this camp was held by way of a rehearsal. Regrettably the experiment, though successful, did not lead to further such camps and the Brigade's entry into specific welfare work would wait several years.

On 21 January 1901 the whole nation was saddened by the news that Queen Victoria had died, having served her people for sixty-four years. She had witnessed the development of the Order and its foundations from the beginning, and as late as 11 January had sent a telegram expressing her admiration for the work of the Brigade in South Africa. At her funeral on 2 February there were 851 Brigade men and women on duty in London and Windsor, all wearing the black crêpe armband of formal mourning. The Queen was succeeded by her son King Edward VII; his support for the objects of the Order was well-known and it now seemed natural that Brigade personnel should take their place on public duty at his Coronation on 9 August 1902. Nine hundred personnel, mainly from London, reported to the various stations along a route which had been shortened because of the King's recent illness.

There were many lessons to be learned from the Boer War, for there had been adverse comment about both official and voluntary medical arrangements. Indeed it would have been surprising if there had not been some criticism. Although a Central British Red Cross Committee had been formed for the duration of the war, it was now proposed to create a permanent National Red Cross Society by merging the National Aid Society with the Central Red Cross Council. The preparatory negotiations for this step had caused some differences in approach between the Society and the Order and for a while relations were strained. There was criticism that although the Order had sent its representatives to every International Red Cross conference, the Society had not done so; however, the fact remained that international Red Cross work required the creation of national Red Cross organizations such as those formed in France, Japan and Germany. The British Order of St John could not expect to be accorded this status, despite its initiatives in 1870. Matters were resolved on 17 July 1905 when a conference was convened at Buckingham Palace at which the British Red Cross Society was officially created with Her Majesty Queen Alexandra as president. Its objects, so far as they affected the Brigade, can be summarized as the coordination of all offers of voluntary assistance during peacetime emergencies and in war. The War Office and Admiralty expressed some reservations, the former claiming that it would coordinate all its own requirements, whilst their Lordships decided to opt for the maximum flexibility and confirm their agreement with the Order of St John for the provision of trained personnel. Time and goodwill healed the rifts and in less than a decade the Brigade would be supporting the Red Cross in another war.

The naval and military authorities had begun to consider the creation of medical reserves as early as 1900. The Navy needed a unit of trained sick-berth attendants, while the Army required trained stretcher-bearers and orderlies for duties mainly at home. The success of the Brigade in South Africa made it an automatic selection for these tasks, and in 1900 five bearer companies were formed at Bolton, Bristol, Preston, Sheffield and Oldham; a sixth was formed at Shipley in 1904. Meanwhile the Navy began to recruit its reserves, so that by 1905 there were some 900 men enrolled from a total Brigade strength of about 14,000. Within a few years Brigade personnel were able to serve in four separate organizations which acted as reserves for the Army and Navy. These were all placed under the control of a Commissioner for Special Services, Colonel C. W. Bowdler. The bearer companies were increased to eight and recruiting began under Brigade Order No. 28. In fact this concept was overtaken by other organizations, but for some years it was the first military medical reserve.

In 1907 the Army Council asked the Order whether the Brigade could provide complete hospital staffs numbering 2,000 to undertake duties at the military hospitals at home. In Brigade Order No. 132 of May 1907, the Chief Commissioner Belgrave Ninnis asked for a nationwide response for the Military Home Hospitals Reserve. The original request is interesting, first because of the Army's faith in the Brigade's capability and second because of the Brigade's faith in its members. The order read: '. . . in enrolling himself the Brigade volunteer pledges his word . . . A man would therefore be untrue to himself, disloyal to the Brigade and wanting in patriotism if he volunteered for this duty without conscientiously believing that he would be able to serve.' Those who joined received no pay or capitation grant in peace, but were paid according to their RAMC rank on mobilization.

The Voluntary Aid Detachments were formed to support the newly reorganized Territorial Forces who would be called out in time of invasion. The RAMC would be responsible for the field and general hospitals, while the VADs would have the task of transporting and caring for the sick and wounded between the hospitals and during convalescence. The War Office believed that in the event of war they would be able to depend on sufficient voluntary assistance from the public, hence the title. The men and women who joined were formed into detachments with a minimum strength of 66 men and 22 women; members would be given special training by the Association and would be permitted to retain their membership of the Brigade.

The Admiralty's agreement with the Order of St John concerned the Royal Naval Auxiliary Sick Berth Reserve (RNASBR). The work done by the orderlies aboard the hospital ships had impressed the naval authorities with the need for a standing reserve trained to that standard. Approval for its formation – with an establishment of 1,200 – was given in November 1902 and the first personnel, all from within the Brigade, began training with the Royal Navy, operating under Brigade Order No. 77 dated 20 February 1903. This Reserve was to remain available to the Navy until 1949, when it was disbanded after two World Wars and half a century of service.

Three famous figures who had been giants in the International Red Cross movement were lost to the world in 1910: Florence Nightingale died, richly honoured for her great service in the Crimea and in the years that followed. In contrast Henri Dunant – whose experience of Solferino had sparked off the whole concept, but whose gentle, unassuming nature had kept him out of the limelight – died virtually unrecognized. The third great figure to die during 1910 was Gustav Moynier, the man whose efficient, businesslike attitude turned Dunant's dream into a world movement and who became the first president of the International Red Cross Committee. We are not concerned here with the details of their work, simply to pay tribute to the memory of three people whose efforts on behalf of the sick had already resulted in St John men and women serving alongside other societies to support the objects of general International Red Cross policy.

In Britain, the year 1910 brought further sadness to the nation with the death of King Edward VII on 7 May. The King had always been a staunch friend of the Order and Brigade and was greatly liked by the population as a whole and by St John men in particular. His funeral on 20 May saw 1,700 Brigade members on duty, caring for the vast crowds who turned out in London and Windsor to pay their respects. It was perhaps fitting that at the funeral of the man who had expressed his faith in 'a good uniform', those who wore that uniform were placed with the police line and given full control of ambulance arrangements.

They did not fail him then and they have not failed his successors. The new King, George V, immediately appointed the Duke of Connaught as Grand Prior of the Order, thus beginning an association which was to last many years and be of enormous benefit to the Brigade. When the King's Coronation took place on 22 June 1911, again the Brigade was on duty; this time 1,756 men and women reported on the 22nd and 2,600 for the celebrations on the 23rd June. In addition, many members of No. 2 District did public duty for the Review of the Fleet at Spithead. In July the Prince of Wales was formally invested at Caernarvon Castle and again the Brigade provided men and women for duty. One group of men from the Barclay Perkins Division of London District typified members' dedication and dependability when they travelled 500 miles by train, walked 16 miles to Caernarvon and carried out 12 hours of public duty, all within the space of 30 hours! Add to this fact that each man paid his own fare and provided his own haversack ration, and we begin to get some idea of the voluntary spirit which motivated the Brigade at this time.

Another death occurred in 1911, this time one which touched the hearts of all Brigade members when at the age of 55, William Church Brasier died after a long illness. His Margate initiative has already been mentioned, so too his part in the mobilization of the Brigade in 1899 and 1900. If what he did was remarkable, then what he was as a man is even more so. His kindness, understanding and sympathy were natural traits of a character which also included enthusiasm, energy and a love of hard work. He was a dedicated first-aider and served St John (and the fire brigade) with distinction until retiring through ill-health in 1905. He was the first and only Brigade Chief Superintendent and was affectionately known to all ranks as 'the Chief'. Many tributes were paid to him during his life and a further mark of his claim on the affection of St John men and women was seen in the attendance at his funeral. Many men had been given more honours, but very few had earned greater affection. His place in the history of the Brigade is assured as the man who, more than any other, guided its work in the formative years.

The 'good old Chief' would have been proud of the Brigade as it formed up in Windsor Great Park on 22 June 1912; 13,000 men and 2,000 women from all parts of Britain and also from overseas territories gathered in uniform to be inspected by the King and Queen and then took part in displays of rescue work and first aid. The parade accounted for almost half of the total Brigade strength and this in itself is remarkable. Even more noteworthy is the fact that some fifty members from the Brigade overseas were on parade. It was a most effective and efficiently organized review which attracted praise from the public and encouraged more men and women to volunteer. The King himself was pleased with the review, which was then counted as the official Annual Inspection for the whole Brigade.

By 1913 the Brigade had expanded to such an extent that reorganization was necessary. The original five regions were now insufficient for effective control and efficient administration and so the country had been divided into eleven Districts during the later part of 1911. Nursing divisions were being given greater responsibility and specific hospital training. Lady Perrott convened a conference of nursing officers in the Chapter Hall at St John's Gate; this was the first nursing conference in the Brigade and among the subjects discussed were two which were seen to have particular relevance – the work of a voluntary hospital in war and the organization and functions of Voluntary Aid Detachments.

In the twenty-five years of its existence, the Brigade could claim many successes. The first decade of the twentieth century witnessed the general acceptance of the White Cross and its White Cross belt into the fabric of society; there were over 23,000 Brigade members including nearly 5,000 women, all volunteers who gave their time, their energy and often their money freely and cheerfully to aid mankind. They had served not only on the sidelines of pageantry but also amid pain and poverty. Wherever there was a need – particularly in the growing industrial centres – the important if humdrum work of caring was continued. They were entitled to feel proud of their service and their success in an expanding nation, and the growing international dimension to their work was an equally valid source of pride. But now, as 1913 drew to its close, the European scene became more turbulent and once again the seeds of war were sown.

4
THE GREAT WAR 1914–1918

Events in Europe during the crucial period from 1909 to 1914 were dominated by the traditional enmity between France and Germany, the economic rivalry between Britain and Germany, the question of Belgian neutrality and the Balkan Wars of 1912 and 1913. On Sunday 28 June 1914 the Archduke Franz Ferdinand was murdered at Sarajevo; there were Serbian implications in the assassination and Europe was again in turmoil. Then on 2 and 3 August Germany invaded France and Belgium without warning. Despite pleas from the British government, the Kaiser would not withdraw and Britain honoured her 'scrap of paper' guaranteeing the safety of Belgium by declaring war on Germany on 4 August 1914.

During the latter part of July 1914, the British War Office had recalled reservists and cancelled the camps for the Territorial Army; on 3 August the Territorials were embodied into the Regular Army and one week later a British Expeditionary Force sailed across the channel. Soon after that the Western Front settled into the stagnant trench warfare which was to cause such misery. Meanwhile the Home Fleet had been called to preparatory war stations and in the industrial centres of Britain the civilian work force was being mobilized. The war which was now unfolding was to be the first involving the civil population to any great extent, the first in which poison gas was used and the first in which an air arm was deployed. The effect upon medical facilities was bound to be significant and the need for well coordinated, sophisticated voluntary support was already apparent.

Very soon after the declaration of war, the Joint War Committee of the Red Cross and Order of St John was formed and from 24 October 1914 the two organizations worked almost as one. It is impossible to separate many of the strands of this work, so closely were they coordinated, which is a compliment to those who managed the Joint

Committee and its detailed operations. There were, however, some activities which remained the province of each separate partner and this account will highlight some of them.

On Friday 1 August the Admiralty gave instructions for the mobilization of the RNASBR and within thirty-six hours over 850 men had reported to their barracks. In a few weeks some of them would be in action at sea. On 4 August the War Office ordered the hospital reservists to be called up as from 7 August and by the 10th all 2,000 men had turned up. At the same time the War Office made an additional unscheduled request for a further 500 men and the Brigade response was immediate and positive – before 30 August all these men had joined their units in an Army which earned that proud nickname 'the Old Contemptibles'.

Soon after the declaration of war trained nurses from the Brigade provided the complete staff of No. 5 Hospital at Wimereux – the nursing members were not being left out this time and in fact were to make a remarkably valuable contribution to the work of St John during the war, serving in all the main theatres of war as well as at home. Those who were sent to Serbia suffered extreme discomfort, working in severe cold under the most primitive conditions. During the retreat to Albania the dedication of Mrs J. C. Mullen, who had been the first Lady Superintendent at Newcastle-on-Tyne, was recognized by awards from three different nations. She was later to enlist – 'slightly over age' – to serve in the WAAF during the Second World War. Some of the St John Voluntary Aid Detachments who had volunteered for overseas service went to Belgium in 1914 and were taken prisoner by the Germans. At home the nursing members served in every capacity from cook to commandant in the large and small hospitals set up for long-term treatment. In the great St John Hospital at Étaples the women played another important role as field nurses under fire, and some would be decorated for their bravery and devotion. Over eighty nursing members were to die on active service.

The first unit under the auspices of the Red Cross to go to France was a detachment of St John men from Wales, who landed at St Nazaire in September 1914. Some of these worked with motor ambulance convoys, while others served on No. 11 Ambulance Train, earning the following praise from the CO:

> They were perfectly trained in all kinds of stretcher work and First Aid
> ... at their divisional HQ in England, the greatest credit is due to those

who brought these men to such a high standard of proficiency. It was
such a a pleasure to work with a personnel such as the above . . .

Calais, August 12 1915.

Other men from St David's District were at summer camp near
Aberystwyth during the last days of peace. Their Commissioner,
Herbert Lewis, was then given the task of raising a field ambulance of
240 men to serve with 38th Welsh Division. In a remarkable expression
of corporate loyalty the Brigade provided all these personnel: every
volunteer reported in little over two weeks and the War Office responded by giving the unit a special title: 130th (St John) Field
Ambulance. Herbert Lewis became the first commanding officer, but
soon after its formation Colonel John Davies took over and remained
in command throughout the war, being awarded the Distinguished
Service Order (DSO) for his work. Eleven of the men were awarded the
Military Medal for bravery either as drivers or as stretcher-bearers.
When the cry 'Stretcher Bearer!' or 'Orderly!' was heard, urgent above
the noise of battle, the men would run forward, crouching low as much
from urgency as from fear, and seek out the wounded. Some would be
easy to find, but others would only be found after a lengthy period
under fire in 'No Man's Land'. Some would not be found. It is difficult
for a man to remain calm, cheerful, efficient and sympathetic amid such
horror, especially when his own life is in great danger, and it says much
for the men, their leaders and their trainers that they achieved so much.
Because we lack space we must allow the achievements of these men to
represent the work of all St John men who served on the Western Front,
and let Colonel John Davies speak for all through his final Order of the
Day: 'You won a reputation you should ever be proud of.' The
Welshmen were indeed proud of it and for many years Corporal
Thomas, MM, played the 'Last Post' on the unit's silver bugle which
now has an honoured place in the Priory for Wales.

The men who had enrolled with the RNASBR or joined the medical
staffs of the Naval Divisions were soon under fire on land and at sea.
The Naval Division assisting in the defence of Antwerp in October
1914 particularly distinguished itself and it was here that Edmund
Walch of the Bolton Corps was awarded the Distinguished Service
Medal (DSM), the first to be awarded to a Brigade member. He was a
senior rank in the Naval Field Ambulance, with 25 orderlies and
stretcher-bearers, five of whom came from Bolton. The Gallipoli
campaign claimed the life of another member from Bolton, George

Stockham, who was sailing with the Plymouth battalion of the Naval Division. He too won the DSM on 9 May 1915, the citation simply stating that, 'in operations south of Achi Baba he worked splendidly under fire to recover wounded until he himself was severely wounded.' In fact his wounds were so severe that both his feet were amputated and he died shortly after the action. Conditions on board the hospital ships, where many casualties were brought, must have been particularly difficult and those St John members whose duties placed them here had no easy task, even if they were not under direct fire.

But the sea could claim its victims without the aid of the enemy, and so it was when the hospital ship *Rohilla* foundered near Whitby, taking the lives of five men of the Barnoldswick Division.

On the home front the Military Home Hospital Reserve was mobilized and men were sent off to various army hospitals around the country and to serve ambulance trains stationed at the ports. By October 1914 most of the reserve had been mobilized. At the same time voluntary hospitals were being established and it was one of these which had the unique distinction of being the first VAD hospital on British soil to come under enemy fire. This happened when German cruisers shelled the East Coast towns of Whitby, Scarborough and the Hartlepools on 16 December 1914. Sergeant Knaggs formed three stretcher-parties to recover wounded to the hospital, where over 400 cases were treated in just over 24 hours; it was during this period that Nursing Sister Birch was wounded by shrapnel. Later in the war the Germans returned to this same area on a Zeppelin raid and again the Brigade was in the forefront of rescue and first aid. When the Zeppelins raided the Thames Estuary and East Coast, the Southend, Felixstowe, Lowestoft and Brooke Divisions were particularly active.

The decision to create Voluntary Aid Detachments was now seen to have been correct, although when the expected invasion did not take place the War Office agreed in February 1915 that VADs could serve in hospitals at home and overseas. Although the R/D initial standards set by St John had been criticized as being too demanding, the effort put into training paid dividends. By 1913 two grades of VAD membership had been established: mobile members, willing to serve anywhere; and immobile members, who could serve only near their homes or work. As the war progressed so the VAD organization altered to meet changing priorities. A General Service Section was established, allowing more women to replace men and thus release them for military service, but the work remained much the same. The men became drivers and stretcher-bearers, whilst the women usually helped at first-aid dressing posts, railway or roadside rest stations or on administrative duties. Some worked for part of the time in the auxiliary hospitals as well as on VAD duty, while numbers of the mobile members volunteered for service in the overseas bases; indeed over 5,000 women VAD members were serving in military hospitals. By the end of the war there were 308 St John VAD units, with a total strength of over 9,000 members.

The establishment, organization and staffing of auxiliary hospitals at home was a major contribution made by both the BRCS and the Order of St John. The largest of those operated by St John – employing a number of VADs and nursing members of the Brigade – was at Southport, the largest voluntary hospital in Britain. In effect it combined two hospitals: 'The Grange' and 'Woodland', providing over 500 beds. The hospital operated under the direction of Dr W. C. Bentall until February 1919. Some idea of the pressure on this hospital can be seen in the figures for 1916; two thousand admissions, including over 700 seriously wounded, and 226 major operations. In 1918, 2,500 serious cases were admitted, with a consequent increase in all-round pressure on the voluntary staff.

The best known of the St John hospitals was the base hospital at Étaples, on the French coast. The Order of St John offered to staff and maintain a 520-bed hospital and this was accepted by the War Office. In a circular dated 8 December 1914, the Secretary-General informed the Order and its Foundations of the proposals and asked for support in terms of money and manpower. Each of the beds was estimated to cost £100 per year to maintain, so a great deal of money would be needed. The first Commandant was Colonel Sir James Clark, Chief Commissioner of the Brigade, then on 14 July 1916 he handed over to Colonel C. J. Trimble, who had done so well as Deputy Commissioner in Lancashire. The staff comprised 19 officers, 78 nurses and 141 orderlies, these last all Brigade volunteers. The formal title of the hospital was 'The St John Ambulance Brigade Hospital', a fine compliment to the men and women who served the Brigade the world over. The concept of a St John hospital aroused the sympathy of all members and supporters of the Order throughout the Empire and many beds – even entire wards – were adopted by divisions, districts or individuals. In addition to contributions from the Order, many industrial firms and business houses provided money and there were also donations from members of the public.

The design involved a prefabricated building set around a central square with covered interconnecting paths. There were 16 wards of 30 beds each and two of 25 beds, every bed in these wards being covered by a blanket with the Order's badge on a black circle. The hospital contained X-ray facilities and an electro-cardiograph instrument, possibly used for the first time in a military hospital. Its original size soon proved inadequate however, and a further 64 beds were needed for the casualties from the Somme. By the end of the war there were nearly 750 beds in use, and during April 1918 the number of admissions was 2,500, a remarkably high figure; on one day alone over 700 men were admitted. Throughout the war the efficiency of the unit attracted praise from all who had cause to visit it.

On 31 May 1918 the hospital came under very heavy air attack when the German Luftwaffe bombed and machine-gunned the complex. Considerable damage was caused, one ward being completely destroyed by a direct hit; sixteen people were killed and very many more were wounded. Six wards were uninhabitable and three more had been very severely damaged. The staff, led by the CO, displayed considerable bravery and devotion in rescuing and assisting the wounded and the Order awarded its Life-Saving Medal in gold to Colonel Trimble; two silver medals and thirteen bronze medals were also awarded. In June the Army medical authorities decided to move the hospital to the hills above Deauville and the prefabricated buildings were transferred and re-erected in time for patients to arrive in October 1918. During its life the St John Ambulance Brigade Hospital had dealt with 35,000 patients, nine members of its staff had been killed or died of wounds and a further twenty had been wounded. Colonel Trimble's last report contained these words: '. . . it built up a reputation and this reputation it sustained to the end'.

The declaration of war had not extinguished the Irish problem; it was perhaps inevitable that there would be further outbreaks of violence and in the spring of 1916 one such occurred. On 25 April an Army brigade arrived at Kingstown and proceeded to Dublin, where Sinn Fein rebels were in possession of some houses in the suburbs. A battalion of the Sherwood Foresters was advancing along Northumberland Road when it came under fire and suffered casualties. Almost immediately the crack of rifle fire gave way to the duller sound of explosions as grenades and bombs were thrown, causing further casualties. This was the situation when Corps Superintendent Holden Stodart, a Brigade man since 1904, went forward to the aid of a wounded soldier and was shot and killed. Elsewhere in the city the

Brigade joined with the medical profession to provide stretcher parties under the general direction of Dr Ella Wess, who organized a makeshift auxiliary hospital for the wounded of both sides – there was no discrimination in terms of help given.

At the Ophthalmic Hospital in Jerusalem, the situation had deteriorated to such an extent that for the first time since 1882 it was decided to close the hospital. The Turks took it over and used some of the buildings as an ammunition store, having looted much of the remainder. Then, in an attempt to deny ammunition to the advancing British, the Turks blew up their store and destroyed a great part of the hospital. A mammoth rebuilding task would be needed after the Armistice.

Throughout the Empire members of the Brigade and the Order offered their support to the Armed Forces, some enlisting with their national contingents while others did duty at home. From New South Wales came one officer who enlisted, went to Gallipoli and was wounded; after his release from hospital, he went back to the front and was killed in 1916. In Malta the local corps provided nursing staff for the service hospitals and some left the island to serve in Salonika. Many of the Anzacs wounded at Gallipoli received treatment at the Malta hospitals. From India came detachments designed to meet the stringent religious requirements of the Indian troops, facing totally new conditions on the Western Front. From Newfoundland, a small detachment was attached to their home regiment during that fateful first day of the Somme, 1 July 1916. Canada had provided VAD members to serve in France and Egypt and twelve Brigade members served at Étaples, whilst for all Canadian troops the St John first-aid syllabus was a compulsory subject. Halifax in Canada experienced one of the most dreadful tragedies of the war when two ships – one fully laden with ammunition – collided, the resultant explosion causing very extensive damage and loss of life. The nursing division of the city, under Mrs Clara McIntosh, dealt with the injured and cared for the homeless in a remarkably successful disaster relief operation. The Brigade in other countries was no longer 'beyond the seas'; it was well to the fore in serving Britain and her allies during the war.

The signing of the Armistice at 11 o'clock on 11 November 1918 ended the war in Europe, but the last St John men did not return home until early in 1920. Again there had been a price to pay; over a thousand men and women gave their lives and they are commemorated in a beautifully illuminated Roll of Honour kept at St John's Gate. So for the second time, the St John Ambulance Brigade had been asked to go to war and by the time compulsory conscription was introduced in 1916 over 25,000 people had been mobilized under Brigade systems, while a further 20,000 had joined their County or specialist units. As the men had gone to enlist, so younger men or those unfit for duty – and in some cases the women – took up the reins and looked after the home divisions. When the detailed response of the Order and Brigade during the first critical months of the war is assessed, it is difficult to find any other organization which would have been both willing and capable of producing 12,000 trained first-aiders and nurses for active service in just over six months.

There would be time for celebration and time to study the lessons of war, but for the present it was enough that it was all over and the nation was grateful for the services of the Brigade. The War Office wrote on 25 March 1919 to '. . . place on record its appreciation of the very valuable services which have been rendered', whilst the Admiralty recorded that the success of the RNASBR reflected the greatest credit on all concerned. But now the men and women who in 1911 had helped at the Coronation, viewing their future with hope, could look back over four years of war, four years of service to mankind in one form or another. They remembered their own friends amongst the one thousand St John members who had given their lives; but today was different and now they could look forward to a new peace.

5
INTO THE FABRIC OF THE
NATION 1919–1939

Britain came through the First World War to victory, but at a staggering cost in terms of human life. Throughout the country there was a considerable feeling of war weariness, men and women being only too grateful to have survived; the people were tired and reluctant to start work again. The conditions of trade were adverse for Britain and unemployment cast a black shadow over the major towns and cities. In such an environment it is not surprising that many men and women found it difficult to renew their first-aid voluntary service; indeed there were many St John men and women in the queues for work and amongst those displaced by the economic situation. Many of those who had swelled the wartime figure of Brigade personnel to over 100,000 did not retain their interest and there was an immediate drop in the total personnel. In some areas, however, particularly industrial centres with a Brigade background, the desire to continue St John work was very strong. In Bolton, for example, the Superintendent aimed to have a St John member in every street. In Hull over 4,400 cases were treated by Brigade members, although only £41 had been subscribed and the Division was inevitably spending much more than this in its desire to serve its city. This underlined the general situation in Britain; it was not possible to maintain an even level of financial support throughout the nation, and the major cities where the need was greatest were the very places where the people had been hit hardest. It says much for the determination of the Brigade in such cities that they continued to be effective, and also draws attention to the central position of working people in the St John Ambulance Brigade.

In 1919 district conferences were held again; first in Ireland, then in No. 4 District, closely followed by No. 6 District. The aim was clear: to re-establish the Brigade in its former position by maintaining the high standard of competence and the degree of commitment which had been

Right: St John in the Air c.1914

Below: Dowlais Division's
Ambulance – c.1890

Top: Canadian and Newfoundland Members of the Brigade Overseas 1912 Royal Review
Above: 130th (St John) Field Ambulance. Provided exclusively from Welsh members

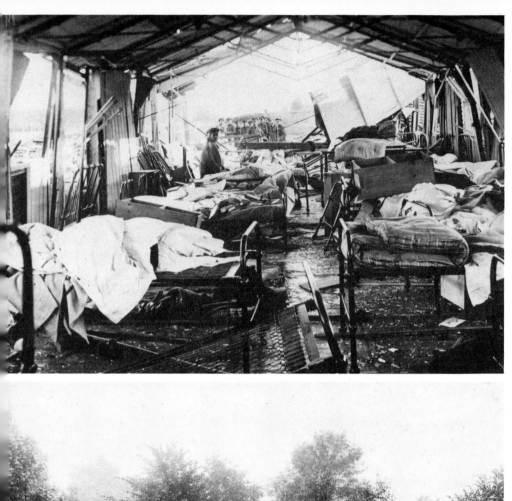

Top: The Etaples Hospital after the May 1918 air-raid

Above: Supplies and equipment leaving London for the Etaples Hospital

Colonel C.J. Trimble. Commissioner of No. 4 District. Commandant of the
Etaples Hospital. Holder of the Order's Life-Saving Medal in Gold

Edmund Walch. First Brigade member to be awarded the DSM, 1914

HRH The Duchess of York (HM Queen Elizabeth, the Queen Mother)
presents the Perrott Shield to Herne Bay Nursing Division, with Lord
Scarborough 1936

FACING PAGE:

Top: HRH The Duke of York (later H.M. King George VI) inspects nursing
members at Wembley, 1924. Lady Perrott is in the dark uniform

HRH The Duke of Connaught, Grand Prior, inspects a Cadet Unit at the
Royal review 1925. Sir Percival Wilkinson is on the left

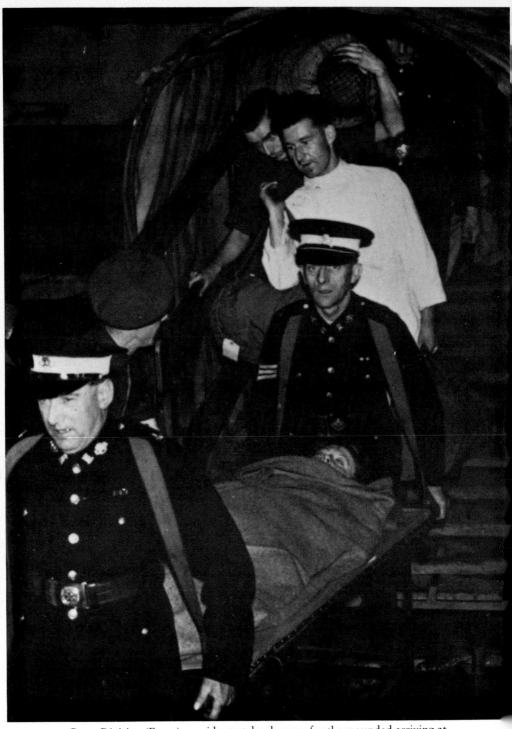

Grays Division (Essex) provide stretcher bearers for the wounded arriving at
Tilbury Docks during World War II

the central themes of the pre-war organization. It would not be easy to achieve this and it certainly would not be accomplished quickly. At Lancaster, Charles Trimble, Commissioner of No. 4 District, outlined his policy of disbanding ineffective divisions after a reasonable time had been allowed for them to resume peacetime work. There had been an inflated strength due to the war and it would be unreasonable to expect that all who had joined then would show the same motivation for duty in peacetime. Trimble's view was that the effective strength of the Brigade is the portion which works and feeble divisions who did not work should go; what remained would be the true active and efficient Brigade strength. That a strong and effective Brigade was still needed was shown by the remarkably high figure of 173,227 cases of injury or illness treated by members during 1921.

The joint work of the BRCS and St John during the war was continued in peace; in 1919 the continuation of this combined effort was effected by the creation of a Joint Council. An appeal to the nation by Sir Arthur Stanley stressed that money given for war work could now be used for war victims, so more money was required for the continuation of joint peacetime work by the two organizations. In Cheltenham a joint headquarters was opened on 25 September 1920 and throughout Britain welfare projects affecting ex-servicemen were undertaken by the Joint Committee. King George V personally expressed his pleasure that joint work was continuing at a time when demands for assistance were likely to increase. In his St John's Day address in 1921, the Grand Prior the Duke of Connaught wished the Association and Brigade to resume their former position as the leading ambulance organization, whilst working in accord with the Red Cross. One very important joint venture which had long-term effects was the creation of the Home Ambulance Service; instituted in 1919, within a year there were 264 vehicles operating on the roads of Britain. This activity reached a wider public and provided much-needed facilities, but it heralded a change in the status of St John. Before the war it had been virtually alone in first-aid and ambulance activity; now it would share the duty and therefore the influence. Whereas it had been possible for the British Red Cross Society to enter the field of first-aid as an independent organization, it was not possible for St John Ambulance to become involved independently in international welfare which was one traditional field of Red Cross activity. In some quarters, therefore, the BRCS was perceived as a competitor for public interest and therefore for financial support.

When, in November 1920, the Brigade wreath was laid at the foot of the newly dedicated Cenotaph, it was already clear that changes were needed within the St John Ambulance Brigade if it was to meet the altered circumstances in Britain and also be in a position to work alongside the BRCS. There was still a requirement and a firm commitment to provide trained personnel for the naval and military reserves and revised instructions for the Voluntary Aid Detachments were eagerly awaited. The structure of the Brigade was examined and it was decided to reorganize on a county basis so that the work of County Joint Committees of the Red Cross and St John could be reinforced. In 1921, Brigade Order No. 385 promulgated the new county organization. Each County would be headed by an Assistant Commissioner responsible to the District Commissioner and would have its own surgeon and other staff. Henceforth channels of communication between Corps and Divisions and District HQ would involve County HQ. Some large counties were sub-divided, but the principle remained valid. The system could not be applied to Ireland and London, nor to 'closed' divisions, including some railway companies – in particular the South Eastern and Chatham Railway which in 1919 had been authorized to raise Brigade units from its own personnel. By 1921 when the Company was merged to form the Southern Railway, there were 20 divisions with a total membership of 700 trained personnel. The involvement of railway companies with St John Ambulance began on 30 April 1878, when the Great Western Railway held its first ambulance class at Paddington. Classes were then held at other main stations and the separate railway companies later formed centres of the Association and issued their own badges and medallions for first-aid service. This situation existed until the railways were nationalized under the central title of British Railways, which then continued its association with St John. Some companies provided practical support by printing special SJAB free tickets for issue to personnel on duty.

In 1925 the Director of the Ambulance Department and Acting Chief Commissioner of the Brigade, Sir Percival Wilkinson, issued a memorandum dealing with the position of the Brigade in case of civil disturbance. Not for the first time, the motto of the Order provided the key: 'Help is to be given without discrimination of colour, race or creed . . . irrespective of any controversies and with a purely humanitarian object in view.' The memorandum recognized that certain people and 'closed' divisions (police divisions, for example) could not act in this way and that those who were unable to be non-partisan should not volunteer for a particular duty. This was an important instruction, since within a year Britain faced the General Strike and Brigade members knew then where they stood. During the strike from 1 to 15 May 1926, units of the Brigade undertook extra duties, the Ambulance Halls were used as first-aid and rest centres and municipal buildings were taken over by the Brigade for emergency centres. Arrangements in London were under the control of Commissioner Winny, who had to set up special detachments living in tents in Hyde Park and Regents Park. Elsewhere at the railway stations, in Divisional HQs and in local town halls, the Brigade stood to – prepared to help if the need arose. Although there were comparatively few casualties, the very presence of the Brigade in uniform allowed those on both sides of the dispute to recognize and respect the potential for speedy and effective relief.

The 1920s saw the deaths of two men who in different ways had made their mark upon the Ambulance movement. Sir Herbert Perrott had been appointed Assistant Secretary to the Order of St John and Chief Secretary of the Association from its inception, a post which he held for 38 years. Perrott's initiative and energy matched that of his other St John contemporaries and he can rightly be called one of the pioneers of the Association. His wife had been Commandant-in-Chief of the VADs and Lady Superintendent-in-Chief of the Brigade, shaping the work of the Nursing Divisions. It was therefore fitting that both these great workers should be remembered by the famous Perrott shield, presented to the Brigade by Lady Perrott in 1921 and first competed for in 1922. The other pioneer was Sir James Cantlie whose work for the ambulance movement took him beyond the confines of St John and into the field of general Red Cross work. He was one of the two doctors who assisted Shepherd in preparing the very first St John textbook. An enthusiastic and successful lecturer, he began a College of Ambulance which flourished for a while; his death in May 1926 represented to the Association the loss of yet another great pioneer.

During the 1920s it became clear that some of the poorer members of the population were finding it very difficult to obtain medical articles needed for sick-rooms and convalescent patients. To meet this requirement, a number of St John divisions established depots in which a huge selection of items could be stored and maintained for issue to those in need, either free or at a very nominal hiring charge. The depots were open daily, including Sundays, and staffed by members of the nursing divisions. The main articles stocked included Bath-chairs, air and water beds, hot-water-bottles, bedpans, bed-tables and pillow rests, waterproof sheets, thermometers, feeding cups, inhalers, crutches, some ointments and medicines, and packs for expectant mothers which they could take with them to hospital. All issues required the approval of a doctor or trained nurse. That the system fulfilled an important need was soon proved because the depots received many more requests for assistance and in some cases new premises were required. In Ipswich, the Cooperative Society worked with the Association and the Brigade, agreeing to construct a building for use as a St John Comforts Depot on a site provided by St John. In Bournemouth the Depot was co-located with the Brigade's Ambulance Hall and it too was much appreciated by local people. In Wales the Commissioner, Sir Herbert Lewis, declared that these depots played a most important role in the relief of distress, particularly in mining areas and those where poverty was greatest.

For many people there has always been a strong desire to spend some part of their holiday 'at the seaside' and inevitably the increased crowds mean greater risk of accident either on the sands or in the sea. The provision of a beach service was first provided by the Woolston Ambulance Division (Southampton) during the Whitsun holiday of 1912, the men carrying their tent to the beach every weekend between May and September until 1914. After the war the Division resumed this service until in 1933 the local authorities provided them with a mobile hut.

Bournemouth and Southbourne Nursing Divisions began to provide beach first-aid facilities in 1926 and 1928 and by 1934 most of the popular coastal resorts in Britain were served with a St John first-aid team. In 1926 the Brigade began its Road Service Scheme, designed to assist motorists at weekends and on public holidays. By 1935 over 200 staffed roadside huts and 950 first-aid posts had been established, and in the single year 1935 almost 25,000 accidents were treated. But the Association had experienced difficulty in keeping up with the constant drain on supplies and this, added to a marked reluctance on the part of motorists to offer thanks or contributions, made the roadside huts an expensive duty. At the same time the Association was providing first-aid kits in many police kiosks; 300 of these had been deployed by 1935.

By the end of 1929 the calls on the Brigade had increased considerably. Horsham Division's ambulance had travelled over 3,000 miles in a year, answering 149 calls for assistance. It is of interest that the police were authorized to drive the vehicle – and did so for some particular journeys – and the local council considered the Brigade's ambulance to be a most valuable asset. Northampton's ambulance had covered well over 50,000 miles in its sixteen years of service, carrying over 5,000 patients, and that excludes its convoy duties during the war. It was time to purchase a new ambulance at a cost then of about £400, but this money had to be collected by divisions, requiring extra organization for fund-raising and the willing support of the public.

In addition to the purchase of vehicles, the units of the Brigade needed funds to buy or renovate their local headquarters. Some were able to convert a barn or chapel, but others had to start from scratch. These were not easy times, however; the Depression exercised an unfortunate effect upon all voluntary organizations and St John was no exception, despite the public's increased appreciation. In Sheffield the Corps wished to provide a much needed first-aid post for motorists at a dangerous spot. They built it themselves, lodged the keys with the AA, the police and a local hotel, then staffed it regularly at weekends, being described as 'Samaritans of the wayside'. By now the number of road casualties was becoming alarming and the *St John Ambulance Gazette* for October 1929 called for legislation to force motorists to carry a first-aid kit in their vehicles. As always, St John was a little ahead of time!

There were the inevitable criticisms of the Brigade. In the early nineteen-twenties the frilled bonnets and voluminous cloaks worn by the nursing members came in for some well-meant and not altogether undeserved ridicule, but later complaints of 'meddlesome first aid' were less valid. The distinction between the work of the layman and that of the doctor was clear and followed most conscientiously throughout the Brigade. If mistakes were made, it was because the members were actually doing something and while those who act may sometimes err, they often save a life. The work of the Brigade was not, however, confined to on-the-spot first aid; the activities of its members during the General Strike of 1926 earned them the sympathy and support of both sides in the dispute. This was to be of value when, during the Depression of the early 1930s, the Brigade once again stepped in to provide medical comforts and trained manpower for the public as well as first-aid training for the unemployed; it also offered financial grants to help the cadet members from families in difficulty. In addition there was a great increase in voluntary duty at clinics, nursing homes and hospitals, whilst in one year over 470,000 patients had been carried in Brigade ambulances.

It would be possible to argue that there was too much interest in protocol, uniform and competitions and to some extent this is true, but pride in appearance and care in manner were necessary attributes of any good first-aider and it should also be remembered that in the twenties and thirties most other organizations were equally concerned with dress and discipline. There is another factor; pride in an organization reflects faith in its cause and this was particularly visible in the Brigade, demonstrated by the donation and consecration of banners or standards: first in Northern Ireland (1921), Lancashire (1924), London Central Area (1929) and Birmingham (1935). This pride in membership and achievement was given further impetus and recognition when, in February 1932, Army Order No. 26 authorized the wearing of special brooches by those who on or after 1 January 1931 had completed twelve years of active and efficient service in the VADs or Military Hospitals Reserve (MHR). These took the form of a bar bearing 'VAD' or 'MHR' surmounted by a crown; the same brooches were later worn with the Service Medal of the Order. Competitions were then – and are still – an extension of training, an opportunity to measure individual and team performances in a realistic situation and a focus for comradeship within the Brigade as a whole. They brought out the humour as well as the skills of the Brigade, as for example when a 'patient' at a regional finals was somewhat bandy-legged and a competitor called for barrel staves to use as splints!

Wembley during the first months of 1924 was a hive of activity because the British Empire Exhibition was to open in April, continue through the busy summer months until October and then be repeated in 1925. A Joint Committee of the Order and BRCS coordinated first-aid coverage, which was provided by St John and the Society during alternate months. For each day of the duty, 90 man-hours were required to cover the different locations from the opening until the gates were closed in the evening. Each monthly duty unit consisted of one hundred trained St John personnel; most of them naturally came from London, but almost every County was represented. This number increased on certain 'special days'. The Association provided medicines, equipment and a new up-to-date ambulance vehicle. The organization involved one main station which contained an HQ, two small wards and a garage with two ambulances. This was the casualty clearing station for the exhibition, controlling four ambulance stations which in turn controlled a number of first-aid posts deployed around the exhibition area, each in telephone contact with the main station.

Willesden General Hospital had earmarked thirty beds for use by the exhibition casualties and in fact nearly two hundred serious cases were admitted.

A further major international event which required the services of the Brigade took place on 7 September 1929, when the Schneider Trophy seaplane race was held in the Solent. The Chief Commissioner, Sir Percival Wilkinson, coordinated the duties at the request of the police and the Royal Aero Club. Units from London, the Home Counties and the Southern areas undertook the duty, which required nearly nine hundred members with fourteen ambulances. Apart from the first-aid posts at the event itself, all the approaches required some form of first-aid cover, and this was provided by Brigade road patrols with ambulances and motor-cycles.

If Wembley and the Solent were unusual public duties, the task given to Plymouth Division on 24 January 1932 must rank as one of the most unusual emergency duties. The headquarters of the Brigade in Plymouth was simply told to get together an ambulance and first-aid team and follow the Fire Brigade to an undisclosed destination. The police and City Council required absolute secrecy and so the men in the White Cross belts duly followed the lumbering fire-engine. Before long they found themselves on Dartmoor; not only that, they were approaching Princetown Prison. There had been a mutiny at the prison and help was urgently needed for a number of serious casualties. Additional St John men were sent out, while others were stationed in the city. Those who went to the incident were praised for the quality of their skill and their ability to assist the few medical officers available in tasks which were not simply a matter of first aid. The Chapter-General subsequently granted a vellum Vote of Thanks to the Division for this unusual but successful service.

In some cases their actions saved life, but in others they could not help. During one particularly severe winter in which gale-force winds and mountainous seas threatened our southern coasts, the Plymouth RNLI lifeboat was called out and the local Brigade immediately mobilized – manning the first-aid post and the ambulance. Three Brigade men of Plymouth were taken out to sea to board a fishing vessel which was lying crippled several miles out. Cole, Cornish and Rendle managed to clamber aboard and remained for nearly four hours attempting to dress the wounds of injured seamen, but although they were able to help some, one crewman was already dead. However, they had shown that the Brigade's work need not end at the shore. This type of emergency action occurred all round the coast and was part of an agreed procedure involving the RNLI and SJAB. The same was true inland – whenever the Fire Brigade was alerted, St John Ambulance men would muster at their own ambulance and accompany the fire-engine; thus the Brigade was on hand for immediate emergencies. There were, however, occasions when tragedy struck so quickly and with such violence that no help was possible. Such a case was the Wharncliffe Woodmoor Colliery explosion in 1936, when 55 men died from appalling burns and blast. The women of the local Nursing Division realized that nothing could be done for those involved, so they set up a makeshift mortuary where they cleaned and laid out the bodies, escorting the grieving relatives into the building for formal identification. What a harrowing task for those members and yet how important; they could not save life, but they gave dignity to the dead and some comfort to their relatives.

On 9 February 1929, King George V was taken by ambulance from Buckingham Palace to Bognor on the Sussex coast. He had requested that his team of stretcher-bearers should come from the Brigade. Superintendent T. G. Appleton, Sergeants J. W. Claridge and E. House and Corporal W. T. Puddifoot carried the King from the Palace and, on arrival at Bognor they conveyed him to his new quarters. His Majesty later gave each member a pair of silver cuff-links inscribed with the Royal monogram. But what was done for a King was also done for the commoner, as when members of Manchester and Preston Ambulance and Nursing Divisions were up very early in the morning to help and transport disabled pilgrims who wished to make the journey to Lourdes. The public was now beginning to expect a great deal from the Brigade and it was necessary to remind people that all this important work was entirely voluntary in nature, for the idea was circulating that men and women who gave so much of their time must in some way be paid officials.

The year 1931 saw the departure of three men who had served the Brigade very well during years of difficulty and subsequent consolidation. Sir Percival Wilkinson had been acting as Chief Commissioner since 1924, but his health had been failing for some time and in fact he was unable to take part in the Royal Review. Now his illness forced him to resign, to be succeeded by Sir John Duncan. The Brigade's Chief Surgeon, Sir William Bennett, also resigned on health grounds, being succeeded by a man who had joined the Brigade as a Divisional Surgeon, Clarence Isidore Ellis. Charles Trimble, who had done so much during the two wars and in peace was the driving force of Lancashire, also resigned due to age. He had been the Deputy Commissioner for No. 4 District since 1894, the longest serving senior officer in the Brigade at that time. His place was taken by G. W. Smith.

The progress of the Brigade during the late twenties and early thirties was marked by three important developments. The first of these was a much greater demand for the Brigade's services as the public became more aware of its real worth at a time of considerably increased risks in the factories, on the roads and on the railways. This brought with it increased financial support. The second, which flowed naturally from the first, was an increase in recruiting – in London alone, over a thousand new members were enrolled during 1929. Finally, with improved finance and numerical strength, it was possible to replace the overworked and outdated vehicles then in use and acquire new ambulances. By the latter part of 1934 many municipal authorities were entrusting their ambulance service to the Brigade, but this had serious disadvantages due to the voluntary position of the members who had their living to make at other jobs. Some councils became aware of this and provided an official service, with the Brigade as a reserve, but a few wished to carry on using the Brigade as long as it was possible to do so. New headquarters were bought or rented and the Brigade was able to staff the medical comforts depots which had been set up by the Association and provide a first-aid service at the roadside and on the beaches. None of this would have been possible had there not been a groundswell of support from the working population of Britain, matched by a determined approach to service within the Brigade.

In some respects the late 1920s and the 1930s were the years of greatest impact and resulted in the general acceptance of the Brigade into the working life of the nation.

In 1931 the Order celebrated a centenary based on the earliest attempts to revive the English Tongue in 1831. Over a thousand Brigade members – including 273 from overseas – attended a rededication service in Westminster Abbey on 24 June, when the Order's Cross and ceremonial banners were carried in procession. On 26 June an Empire Competition was held between teams from Britain and the overseas territories; Barnstaple (North Devon) railway team carried off the men's trophy, while a South African team won the nursing trophy with Liverpool coming second. On the following day, over 4,000 people assembled in Hyde Park to be reviewed by the Duke of Connaught, who in 1930 had granted to No. 8 District (Kent, Surrey

61

and Sussex) the privilege of using his name as an honorary title. At this time the strength of the Brigade was 62,000 at home and 11,000 overseas, and by 1933 the total strength had exceeded 100,000. The Chancellor of the Order, Sir Aylmer Hunter-Weston, looked forward to a time when first-aid instruction would be expanded worldwide, Medical Comforts Depots would flourish and the Brigade would have increased so that, 'Wherever men and women of the British race are congregated, there will be a unit of SJAB, well trained, well disciplined and carrying on the St John tradition.' He also hoped that in time to come the work of the Order would help to strengthen the intangible ties between Commonwealth nations.

The year 1935 marked the Silver Jubilee of King George V and once again the Brigade was on ceremonial public duty, providing over 3,000 men and nearly 1,000 nursing members to staff 71 first-aid stations. Within a year, however, this much-loved Sovereign had died and from every county in Britain, Brigade members took on the sombre task of providing staff at Sandringham, Windsor and of course in London as the King's coffin began its last journey from his home to the lying-in-state at Westminster Hall. They had served at his Coronation, carried him during illness and served at his Jubilee. Now they watched over the thousands who filed in sorrow past the catafalque, those inside the hall standing bareheaded as the four Princes took post for their own personal solemn vigil. In all, some 3,500 Brigade members undertook some form of duty for the King's funeral and over 8,000 cases were treated. That this was appreciated is evidenced by a letter from the Home Secretary which included the following:

> Their Majesties deeply appreciate the services which the members of the St John Ambulance Brigade rendered to the public during the funeral procession and they have no doubt that these services contributed largely to the comfort and well-being of the crowds lining the streets.

The year 1937 was an extremely important and very busy time for the Brigade; it was the year of the Coronation of King George VI and Queen Elizabeth and also a Jubilee year – the 50th Anniversary of the Brigade's formation. For the Coronation a great deal of preparatory work was necessary, including a number of full-dress rehearsals in the early hours of the morning. On 10 May at the Duke of Norfolk's rehearsal, those on duty were watching the procession of the peers – their pages carrying their coronets on red velvet cushions – when to their surprise and amusement one page appeared bearing his lordship's bowler hat on his cushion, but with no less dignity than his colleagues. On 12 May, Coronation day, 7,000 Brigade members including men and women from every division assembled. They were up at 4.30 a.m., reported for duty at 5.45 a.m. and remained on duty until after 6 p.m. A long day, a tiring day, but a truly memorable one for all involved. Over 9,000 cases were treated, including 162 people who were taken to hospital. The King sent a message of thanks, as did the Commissioner of the Metropolitan Police, and the work of the Brigade attracted the support and sympathy of the Press which reported the duty in some detail. The Brigade was delighted when Queen Elizabeth agreed to retain her position as Commandant-in-Chief of Nursing Divisions, which now numbered 897 with a total membership of 19,650.

The Brigade's Jubilee year began with a reception at St John's Gate, followed by a tea-party given by HRH The Grand Prior at St James's Palace which was attended by all representatives from overseas divisions who had come to Britain for the Coronation. On 22 May the Queen reviewed the Brigade in Hyde Park and was very pleased with all that took place, expressing her interest in the Brigade's achievements to Sir John Duncan, the Chief Commissioner, and Nigel Corbet Fletcher, the Chief Surgeon. The march past at this review was the first in which the surgeons – 111 men and 7 women – led the Brigade. Among the men who stood proudly on parade was District Officer S. A. Hill of Tibshelf Colliery Division who had been on parade in 1893 and was a stretcher-bearer at the 1912 Windsor review. Others, newcomers to St John, would remember that great review in later years when they themselves were given responsible posts within the Brigade. On Sunday 23 May, the Order and Brigade attended a commemorative service in St Paul's Cathedral in the presence of the Duke of Kent (where one young member was overjoyed at gaining admittance through the dubious expedient of helping the bass drummer to carry the drum). There followed an investiture at Buckingham Palace, a reception at the House of Commons and an Empire first-aid competition, but the final event was fittingly a working weekend involving home and overseas members. The Jubilee celebrations had been fun, but they had also reminded the public that this great voluntary movement which now spanned the Empire was worthy of their support; certainly in Britain the Brigade's work received widespread acclaim. The Queen recorded her appreciation of the Brigade's smartness and her admiration for their service, while Sir Arthur Stanley, Chairman of the BRCS, sent a letter of congratulation and fellowship: '. . . today when units of the

Order and of the Society are working side by side, we do not forget that the Brigade were the pioneers . . .'

The terrible legacy of illness resulting from the use of gas in the First World War and the rapid expansion of air forces led to two developments, at first independent but later fused. In 1923 a protocol of the Geneva Convention required adherence to the principle of prohibiting the use of poison gas and bacteriological virus as weapons of war. At successive International Red Cross conferences, the nations of the world were encouraged to ratify the protocol and so rid the world of this dreadful fear. Several nations did not ratify and the government believed that voluntary organizations dealing with first aid should undertake some form of training and thus be in a position to prepare the public should the need arise. The first anti-gas course was held as early as 1932 when No. 1 District organized training at Knightsbridge barracks. In 1935 the Home Office indicated the government's concern about the effects of air attack by publishing Air Raid Precautions handbooks and asked the Association and Brigade to organize ARP courses. From July until November 1935, special courses were run so that instructors could be trained. Some similar courses were held during the following years and then in 1938 the Home Office combined first-aid instruction and anti-gas instruction into a revised ARP syllabus. Two men prominent in arranging this training were P. G. Darvil Smith, the Brigade Secretary, and Dr W. C. Bentall who became ARP Staff Officer to the Chief Commissioner, following Herbert Blackmore who was the first holder of this post.

We might consider this to be the preparation of a trained civilian reserve for use in national emergency, and there is no doubt that only the Order of St John, the British Red Cross Society and St Andrew's Ambulance Association could undertake this work. Alone of these three, however, the Order had undertaken through the St John Ambulance Brigade to provide trained naval and military reserves in time of war. Therefore when the Munich crisis over Czechoslovakia cast its shadow over a complacent Europe, the British government instructed the Chief Commissioner of the Brigade to call out 755 men of the Royal Naval Auxiliary Sick Berth Reserve. The instruction came on 28 September 1938 and within 24 hours call-up notices had been sent out. At the same time plans were made for the speedy mobilization of the Military Hospitals Reserve and VADs. By 30 September the men of the Brigade had reported to their RN stations, but with the signing of the Munich agreement the preparations were suspended. By an intriguing coincidence one of the last overseas tasks of the Brigade in time of peace was the provision of escorts, an ambulance unit and nursing members to accompany the British Legion contingent to Czechoslovakia. There was a sense of relief at the outcome of the crisis, but Sir John Duncan wrote:

> In the future, as war will not only be waged against the armed forces as in the past but also against the civilian population, the Brigade should be available to render first aid to the civil population, should such a calamity ever arise . . . In any war which may be directed against this country, this service will be of far greater importance in the future than in the past.

That future was not far distant.

6

THE SECOND WORLD WAR
1939–1945

The international situation during 1938 and the early months of 1939 provided ample evidence that a European war had become a distinct possibility and an emergency committee was therefore formed of members of the BRCS and the Order of St John to prepare the way for joint activity.

Joint departments were organized and staffed, ready to operate at the outbreak of war. This high degree of preparedness differed greatly from the situation in August 1914, when the Joint Committee had only the experience of the Boer War on which to draw. In 1939 the experience of the Great War (as it was then called), the preparedness of the nation as a whole and – of vital importance – the continued joint activity of the BRCS and St John provided the basis for a smooth and efficient transition to a war footing. On 2 September 1939 the Joint War Organization was given formal and legal status with a central committee of 48 members, 24 each from BRCS and the Order. Once again, as in 1914, the White Cross would support the Red in war and the work would be a totally joint effort, but with the Red Cross having precedence because of the international recognition accorded to its name.

The role of the Joint War Organization was primarily one of coordinating the efforts of the two charities in order to supplement the work of the medical services and provide assistance to the sick, wounded and prisoners-of-war, as well as to civilians needing relief as a result of enemy action. Such coordination was designed to prevent the overlap of functions, with its consequent waste of energy and funds, and did not affect the internal structure or status of the two bodies. It is therefore impossible to separate the general work of St John from that of the BRCS during this period; the central direction of Red Cross effort involved both organizations, the two worked as one body for the duration of the war and must be treated as such. This short history cannot cover the enormous amount of work done under the aegis of the JWO, but instead must confine itself to a very brief note of the activities of its various departments. An excellent official history was published in 1949 and is listed among the references.

The Joint War Organization's immediate need for money was met by the Duke of Gloucester's Red Cross and St John Appeal, launched by the Duke on 9 September 1939. The Order and Brigade played their part in this, as in other aspects of war work, selling flags, making clothes and holding sales and raffles. The Order ceased the manufacture of medallions, pendants and its Service Medal, while divisions from the Commonwealth sent clothing to aid the victims of the Blitz. All these activities helped to conserve vital war material. By the end of the war the British public had subscribed over £50 million to this fund, which money would be used in accordance with two great principles of Red Cross work: first the relief was designed to aid the victims of war, not the everyday sick; and second, where there was an urgent need there would be an immediate response. The maintenance of the JWO cost on average £100,000 per week at 1940 values; for example, by the end of 1941 over £12 million had been collected, but expenditure was such that only £200,000 remained in reserve!

The general concept of Red Cross work in a theatre of war is the establishment of 'Commissions' whose task is the organization and provision of Red Cross aid required, within the terms of the Geneva Conventions. Commissioners are appointed with exclusive delegated authority to oversee the work and liaise with senior commanders of the Armed Forces. In December 1939 such a Commission was established in France, followed by a base depot and stores department to support the British Expeditionary Force. Sadly, because of the speed of the German advance and the evacuation from Dunkirk, this Commission had only a limited life. Other Commissions were established for North-West Europe, Southern Europe, the Mediterranean, South-East Asia and China; in addition, a special Commission was set up in Washington to coordinate joint effort with the American Red Cross. In North-West Europe, Red Cross and St John personnel were among the first voluntary units to enter the notorious Belsen camp, while the work of the Commission in South-East Asia was particularly harrowing with regard to the release of prisoners who had been in Japanese hands. In Thailand and Java, Burma, Singapore and Sumatra the determined leadership of one woman was to make a worldwide impact. That woman was Lady Louis Mountbatten, Superintendent-in-Chief of the Nursing Corps and Divisions of the Brigade. She visited isolated camps alone, cut through red tape and spoke sharply to ineffective officials and sympathetically to the victims of war. She seemed to be tireless, ubiquitous and always charming, caring and courageous. Virtually single-handed, she organized the evacuation and repatriation of many prisoners-of-war.

Towards the end of the war Lady Louis was touring hospitals and medical units in North-West Europe and visited Supreme Headquarters Allied Expeditionary Force (SHAEF), where Marjorie, Countess of Brecknock was serving. Lady Louis – accompanied by her staff officer Rosemary Eley, and Lady Brecknock – was due to visit forward hospitals in the Nijmegen area. They took off from Brussels, flying north-eastwards; after some time Lady Brecknock, who was studying a map, made an anxious enquiry and just then they encountered anti-aircraft fire. The plane was hit; one engine and the wing were damaged; pieces of metal and glass flew into the cabin where Rosemary Eley, who was sitting beside Lady Brecknock and immediately in front of Lady Louis, was slightly cut by flying glass. The aircraft returned to Brussels and the three intrepid ladies of St John were treated to a spontaneous champagne reception by the RAF, although they were hardly in a fit state to appreciate this, believing that they were drinking cider! Lady Brecknock's greatest worry was that she still had her SHAEF pass in her jacket pocket!

The main sections of the Joint War Organization were the Foreign Relations Department, which acted as a chief liaison agency for other national organizations; the Stores Department, which handled stores valued at £31 million during the war; the Prisoners-of-War Department, which dealt with correspondence and parcels for the POWs; the Wounded and Missing Department; and the Staff and VAD Department which recruited and deployed personnel. The JWO should be viewed not as a structural organization, but as a series of well-coordinated functional teams responding to shifting priorities and under constant pressure. At home the Joint War Organization formed 'flying columns' to work in areas which had been continuously and heavily bombed and where the local authorities found it difficult to staff rescue and first-aid teams because local people had been evacuated. The purpose of these columns was to provide special assistance to the sick, the elderly and children and to staff a mobile first-aid post. Each unit comprised a first-aid vehicle, one or two ambulances and a mobile canteen. The first-aid vehicle contained immediate welfare stores such as blankets, towels, baby napkins and feeding bottles, as well as a full range of normal medicines. With a total personnel of twelve, this was a very flexible mobile method of dealing with air raids and furthermore allowed for quick responses to changing priorities.

Although the Joint War Organization was the main channel for relief work, the Association and Brigade carried on with specific work of their own in addition to that done for the JWO. For the Association the pressing need for first-aid instruction continued and in 1940 a total of 298,343 certificates were issued to those who had successfully completed training courses. In addition they taught first aid and anti-gas measures to Air Raid Precaution teams in a combined operation with the BRCS.

As the war continued the Association became involved in continuous training for the War Reserve Constabulary, the Home Guard and other reserves, but as the danger passed the demand for training decreased and with it the number of certificates issued. The total number of people trained directly by the Association during the war exceeded one million. In addition the Association was able to send its famous textbook to prisoners-of-war in their camps. The Stores Department inevitably faced considerably greater demand for its textbooks, diagrams, first-aid kits and bandages.

The separate work of the Brigade followed the traditional patterns of the past: stretcher-bearers at the ports and railway stations and in the Home Guard; ambulance drivers, welfare officers and guides for evacuees. The Nursing Divisions played their part fully when the men went to war, as did the cadets. The Brigade in the United Kingdom reached a strength of 79,249 men, 47,911 women and 68,974 cadets – nearly 200,000 trained personnel at the call of the nation, in addition to those who had been mobilized for service with the Forces and the VAD. Overseas the situation was not so clear since several territories were occupied by the enemy, but whether occupied or free the Brigade members worked every bit as hard as their colleagues in Britain.

While all these activities were going on, the Admiralty and War Office mobilized their respective reserves within the Brigade. The Royal Naval Auxiliary Sick Berth Reserve (RNASBR) was called out on 25 August 1939 and 1,606 men reported to the Depots within 48 hours. The Military Hospitals Reserve was called out on 1 September and its Brigade personnel reported to a variety of army hospitals in the

UK. A week later the Director-General of Army Medical Services called for 700 men to join the BEF in France; there were more than enough volunteers from the Brigade, so a waiting list was drawn up. In December when a further 100 men were needed, these were taken from the waiting list, and by the end of the year nearly 2,500 men had been mobilized as army medical support. In addition the VADs had been activated and by the end of the year some two thousand men and women had reported for duty in service hospitals. These figures are eloquent in themselves, but the concept of providing military reserves within the Brigade and the commitment of the men and women who voluntarily formed those reserves is even more remarkable. First the Boer War, then the First World War and now the Second World War; in each of the three wars the men and women of the Brigade came forward to serve alongside the fighting men, to help them in times of stress caused by sickness or wounds. Some of the medical reserves – the RNASBR for example – were found only from the Brigade; no other organization matched this commitment. That all these people were prepared by training and experience to take up such additional tasks was a truly magnificent achievement of which any movement could justifiably be proud.

In January 1940 the Brigade had been warned to 'remain patient and ready to answer duty's call'. It was not long before the first calls came – for ambulance convoys and trained personnel to serve in France. The *St John Gazette* for February 1940 pointed out that volunteering would not absolve applicants from the national call-up and that the work would be unpleasant, arduous and dangerous. On Friday 15 March 1940, the first convoy with Red Cross and St John personnel formed up in the quadrangle of Buckingham Palace to be inspected by the King before leaving for France, its twenty ambulances manned entirely by unpaid volunteers. By August some of these ambulances had been captured and their crews had become casualties. At the same time emergency stretcher-bearers and orderlies for the civil hospital trains were required, and some men volunteered for these duties in addition to their normal work. Before 1940 had ended, Lady Louis Mountbatten was asking members of the Brigade to undertake yet another task – the provision of first-aid posts in the London tube stations which were being used as major air-raid shelters. As might be expected, the response was immediate and positive and in August 1941 Lady Louis was able to speak of the efforts made by provincial units to back up the work of the London District:

They responded magnificently, some came for permanent duty and are still here. Others came for relief work covering periods up to a month, paying their own fares and travelling expenses. They came from all parts of the country, even from Wales, Scotland, Ireland and the Isle of Man. Some had never been to London before . . . they never failed to report to their posts and gave invaluable help, inspiring confidence even in the worst ordeals. I have found their courage, coolness and competence deserving of the highest praise.

The first casualty lists of the war proved that Brigade personnel were sharing danger with the Armed Forces and that they were playing their part in the air raids. Staff Officer Rous of HQ No. 1 District was killed when a bomb exploded near his post. Two RNASBR men, Ernest Schofield of Crompton and Kenneth Parker of Bristol, were lost when the *Rawalpindi* was torpedoed and sunk on 25 November 1939; another, G. W. Hackett of Manchester, was killed serving in HMS *Courageous*. Gunner Lewis of Flint was captured in France and notified as a prisoner-of-war.

Life in a POW camp was more monotonous than we might conclude from the various stories of escape and the daring activities of the prisoners. There was certainly time to study and the JWO provided the necessary books and published a magazine with news of life in the camps. It was perhaps natural for prisoners to be interested in first aid and it was not long before those POWs who were Brigade members began to teach their colleagues, at first from memory but later from the textbooks provided by the Association. Medical Officers became temporary 'Divisional Surgeons', instructing according to the specific medical syllabus and conducting the examinations. In Stalag 383, located in the mountains of Bavaria, nearly three hundred prisoners-of-war successfully sat the basic first-aid examination and further classes were held in hygiene and home nursing, both important subjects for personnel living in such confinement. The instructors came from several different divisions of the Brigade: Sergeant Moffitt from Gateshead; Corporal Bramwell from Newport, Wales; Sergeant White from the Midlands; Private Lake from London's Special Constabulary and men from Exeter, Burton-on-Trent, Thornley Colliery and Liverpool. By the end of 1944 some 500 certificates had been awarded, 1,500 camp accidents had been successfully dealt with and the camp medical orderlies had increased their proficiency at dealing with common camp sicknesses. A high degree of improvisation was needed and this sometimes led to unexpected side-effects as when one man broke his wrist

71

and the first-aider used a bone from an animal as a splint; it was a source of great mirth that pieces of bone protruded from both wrist and elbow! One of the prisoners made a wooden shield depicting the Cross of St John from packing cases and when the camp was liberated it was recovered and later presented to 'The Gate', where it is now on display in the St John Ambulance Museum.

To assist with the expected increase in civilian casualties, the government created a Civil Nursing Reserve (CNR) under the control of the Ministry of Health. Members included the St John Ambulance Brigade and British Red Cross Society, who wore the uniforms of their parent organizations. Other members who were not already part of a voluntary organization wore a special CNR uniform, dependent upon their qualifications. Many St John members joined the CNR and worked in the hospitals which acted as casualty clearing stations for the victims of bombing raids. As the war continued and city after city faced the onslaught of the Luftwaffe, the ARP training which had been so skilfully and energetically undertaken by Dr W. C. Bentall before the war proved invaluable and members of the Brigade worked efficiently in a number of Civil Defence roles. At the height of the German bombing there were more than 50,000 St John personnel working in the Civil Defence systems. Experience – however bitter – and the sharing of common dangers and discomforts bred a new kind of teamwork and a different form of comradeship as the men and women of St John worked alongside the fire services, police and Armed Forces as well as with their colleagues in the BRCS. When the sirens wailed their air-raid warning the ARP and Civil Defence staff would quickly but calmly go to their posts. The St John Ambulance station would be manned with Brigade personnel, standing by with stretchers and first-aid kit ready to join the rescue parties. Those engaged in welfare would assist the elderly and the children to their shelters.

More often than not during the first two years of the war there was not long to wait before the dull thud of explosions and the crackle of incendiary bombs was heard, the glare of the fires they started painting a fierce lurid background to the work of the rescue teams. As they worked they were conscious of the creaking, crumbling masonry and timber which at any moment could fall on them and claim them as secondary victims of the raid. Eventually when the single-tone 'all clear' signal was given, the Brigade teams could count the cost, continue with rescue work and escort the survivors to their homes or a place of safety. They now faced dangers from burst gas and water mains, as well as from live cables which had fallen into the street. Many hours might pass before the work was finished and by then some members of the various teams would have changed into their day clothes and set off for work, while others would be doing their best to clear the streets and bring relief to the bereaved, the homeless, the injured and those for whom the shock of such savagery had proved too much. If they were lucky, they might finish just before the next night's raid began. The Brigade rose to this challenge as it had to others, and instances of bravery and devotion to duty under this ordeal were many. Some acts of heroism would receive recognition from the Sovereign, others would be acknowledged by the Order of St John and, as is the way of things, some would go unrecognized except by those most closely affected. Some men and women would give their own lives for the service of others during air raids. The sacrifice and service of all these members must be reflected in an account such as this, but space prohibits the inclusion of more than a few examples which we should accept as representing all who served in those dark and dangerous times.

Private Sidney George Wright of Luton Division was serving as an auxiliary fireman when, during an air raid, several serious fires were started in oil depots, wharves and factories. One fire was localized to two oil tanks which were blazing furiously; nearby were a number of full tanks, one of which had sprung a leak allowing a large quantity of oil to escape. The only way to check this rush of fire was to turn a drencher branchpipe into the blazing pool of oil. The officer in charge called for a branchpipe to be brought over and Wright immediately dashed forward and faced the burning oil. Although the fire was raging only two feet away from him he persisted in his efforts to get a branchpipe free from the branch holder and turn it over into the pool of oil, so driving the fire back. If he had not done this, five more tanks containing about 20,000 tons of oil would have caught fire. Mr Wright's name was among those listed in the *London Gazette* on 3 December 1940, when he was awarded the George Medal, the first St John person to be so honoured.

Just over a week later, on 12 December 1940, the *London Gazette* announced the award of the George Medal to Cadet Miss Betty Quinn, St John Ambulance Brigade, Holbrooks Division, Coventry. Miss Quinn thus became the first person described as of the SJAB, the first lady member and first cadet to be awarded the George Medal. She was rendering voluntary service at an ARP post when a shower of incendiary bombs fell in the district. Then, in the words of the citation:

> Without waiting for assistance she ran outside. At this time A.A. batteries were putting up a heavy barrage and shrapnel was falling all round. Bombs began to fall and a man was injured by one. Miss Quinn assisted him to a private shelter. A report came in of an Anderson shelter receiving a direct hit and although bombs were still falling, Miss Quinn ran there and commenced digging in the crater with a spade. She remained there and assisted to dig out seven persons who had been trapped and then attended to their injuries. She stayed until all had been removed by ambulance although shells were bursting overhead most of the time. She then returned to the Post and carried on with her duties assisting distressed people there.

Betty Quinn only stopped when the last person had been placed in the ambulance and she had handed over her patients to the professional medical authorities.

When the German Luftwaffe attacked Bristol, one member of the local Corps who had already given twenty-three years of service displayed such devotion to duty that he was awarded the British Empire Medal. William Thatcher was the Transport Sergeant of the Corps and on the night of the first blitz he should have gone off duty, but he remained until 3 a.m. the following morning having taken charge of the ambulance station. He had already taken one case to hospital when he was directed to another incident in which six people had been injured and he could only reach them by driving over debris-strewn roads. As his ambulance was being loaded, broken telegraph wires caused additional dangers. He continued to move patients to hospital and then found that his own home had been severely damaged although his family were safe. Called out yet again, this time he dealt with incendiary bombs which were falling near his ambulance, organizing the evacuation of the vehicle to a safe place. He then led a volunteer party to deal with more incendiaries. Throughout the intense period of the Bristol air raids he remained on duty through-out every raid, displaying high qualities of leadership and bravery.

In Lancaster, Sergeant F. Owens was awarded the BEM for a signal act of bravery when he climbed to the top of damaged gas-holders in order to carry out repairs which were necessary to ensure the safety of nearby houses. Owens worked at the top of the holder during an air raid when bombs were falling in the immediate vicinity. In Leicester,

Miss R. Lord of the Arthur Faire Nursing Division took charge of the St Philip's first-aid post and remained responsible for this duty through the worst of the air raids; she was later awarded the BEM for her consistently good service. On a beach in Wales, Mrs Clothier of Taibach and Port Talbot Nursing Division went into a minefield to help a soldier lying there severely wounded; she dressed his wounds and superintended his removal before leaving the area herself.

The Brigade Meritorious First Aid Certificate was not lightly awarded, yet the list of recipients includes every rank from Cadet to Commissioner. Cadet Leonard Skinner of Holbrooks Division remained on duty for over eleven hours during a heavy air raid on Coventry. During this period he prepared the ambulance for casualties and at one point he searched through the debris of a bombed house at great personal risk to rescue a woman and a baby. In Wales three cadets from Cardiff – L. Weeks, W. Rogers and R. Wilcox – were used as messengers during a raid in 1941. They maintained contact with rescue parties and Wilcox saved one team by his prompt action in pushing them out of the way of falling masonry. The boys later entered a burning garage, drove the vehicle to safety and then put out the fire.

Such heroism and devotion to duty was not without real sacrifice, as when Earnest Bealey of the Great Western Railway in Cornwall was severely injured in the left arm and leg while helping other victims to safety. He continued to provide help for people who were trapped in rubble until he was himself evacuated to hospital, where it was found necessary to amputate his left hand. During the intense air raids on Coventry, Corporal Harrison was on duty at the local hospital when it sustained a direct hit. Harrison was leading a party of patients and nurses to safety when another bomb fell and he was killed.

Under the impetus of war, many people who would not otherwise have done so joined the Brigade or took ambulance classes with the Association. By the beginning of 1942 the numerical strength of the Brigade had reached 147,000, of whom 3,000 were surgeons. A year later there were over 167,000 Brigade members serving at home, in addition to some 25,000 in the Armed Forces. Like others in the community, Brigade members were required to register for service and were called up with their age group. Those who were employed on vital ARP or Civil Defence work might be deferred until suitable replacements had been found for them. The call-up of the men inevitably placed greater strain on the nursing members of the Brigade who now accepted greater responsibility. At Beighton near Sheffield, for example, a new Nursing Division was soon in action when a serious railway accident occurred involving a troop train. There were many casualties and the nursing members were called to attend the injured, establish a first-aid post and accompany victims to the hospital. Some set up a local welfare station for those troops who had not been injured physically but who were suffering from shock.

The work of these women was described by the Army authorities as 'excellent', but it was not only at accidents that the nursing members proved their worth; in the everyday life of their divisions they put in phenomenal hours of duty. Nine members of the Littlehampton Division completed over 10,000 hours of voluntary duty in one year, a remarkable achievement. That the nursing members were able to bear their share of the tragedy of war is more than proven by the posting to Belsen of two St John members, Miss Brown of Cardiff and Miss Wilford of Leicestershire, who were with the earliest troops to arrive in that place of horror.

Life on the home front was bearable, but there were many restrictions which were accepted willingly and cheerfully: the blackout, controls on movement, rationing of food, petrol and clothes, the call for metals of all kinds to feed the munitions factories; all these affected the work and training of the Brigade. Coupons were needed for items of uniform and – as mentioned earlier – the manufacture of labels and pendants was discontinued. The Medical Comforts Depots continued to provide a valuable service at a particularly difficult time, especially since medical facilities were under ever-increasing strain. The members of the Association and Brigade played their part in raising money for the Duke of Gloucester's 'Penny a Week Fund' which was designed to assist in raising £1½ million per year for the Red Cross and St John Fund. There was always a need for more money to serve the needs of charitable relief, but this could not simply be provided by the government, for the aid would then assume the nature of a national effort by a belligerent country. Only by voluntary support could the privileges accorded to the International Red Cross be guaranteed and so provide help for prisoners-of-war and assist the tracing of wounded or missing personnel.

On 16 January 1942 the Order and its Foundations were saddened by the death of HRH The Duke of Connaught at the age of 92. He had succeeded King George V as Grand Prior in 1910 and held the appointment until 1939. His contribution to the development of the charitable work of St John in the twentieth century was outstanding and included changes to the Order's Royal Charter as well as taking a keen, lively interest in the work of the Association and Brigade. Not for nothing was he called 'our beloved Grand Prior'. In Wales there was particular sorrow at the loss of their own Prior, the Duke of Kent, whose death on active service deprived the Priory for Wales of a man whose interest and understanding of its work had already made its mark on the Welsh people. The loss of two such popular members of the Royal family at this particular time was bound to distress King George VI and Queen Elizabeth, but despite their grief they continued to provide support and encouragement to the St John members, as indeed they did for all voluntary organizations who were engaged in war work. On 25 February 1942 the King and Queen visited Coventry, paying a special visit to the hospital where 70 Brigade personnel were on duty; three of the people presented to the Royal visitors were Brigade members D. Bonham, Miss H. Finlay and M. Wellings, all of whom had been injured in the main blitz on the city. Personal touches such as this did much to warm the hearts and stiffen the resolve of the British people during the war. The younger members of the Brigade were also honoured when on Empire Sunday, 16 May 1943, Her Majesty Queen Elizabeth (now the Queen Mother) addressed over 2,000 members of the BRCS and St John Cadets. From the steps of Buckingham Palace, she spoke of the concept of service and the sacrifices which were being made both at home and overseas, calling for the youth of the nation to dedicate themselves anew to the service of others.

The men and women who joined the Armed Services, whether called up or as volunteers, did not all join the medical branches. A high proportion volunteered for combat duty at sea, on land or in the air, and many of them performed acts of bravery or gave such meritorious service that they were awarded decorations. However, *all* – whether decorated or not – upheld the great tradition of service which is the essence of the St John way of life. It would not be out of place to mention some of these members here, since they played their part in the most widespread war in all history and they are themselves of that history.

Dunkirk was the first major test of the British Armed Forces; the flotillas of little ships which made the hazardous journey to the beaches to take off the beleaguered troops caught the imagination of the nation as much as the dogged courage of the men themselves. HMS *Glendower* was one of the ships which made the crossing and one of the members of her sick-berth staff was William Griffin of Wigan. As *Glendower* arrived, another Navy vessel, HMS *Snaefell*, ran into the beach and went aground to pick up survivors. She immediately signalled for medical help and Griffin was sent over in a small boat to remain with *Snaefell* for the return journey to Harwich, treating a large number of serious casualties. *Snaefell* later returned to the beaches for another pick-up and Griffin worked tirelessly 'doing magnificent work' dealing with casualties under a hail of bombs and strafing by German planes. His commanding officer wrote:

> Griffin displayed courage and outstanding ability during a most difficult operation. The ship was continuously under enemy gunfire and air attack . . . I am proud to have him under my command.

William Wildey of Carlisle joined the Royal Air Force and became a wireless operator and air gunner with Bomber Command. His Stirling bomber was returning from a raid on 27 June 1942 when it was attacked by enemy fighters. The Stirling's gunnery accounted for three of the enemy before the remainder broke off the engagement and one more of our valuable aircraft was able to return to base. For his part in this action, Wildey was awarded the Distinguished Flying Medal (DFM). In the North African campaign, James Butler of Worthing was taking two wounded men to the rear when enemy aircraft began to machine-gun his ambulance. Butler was wounded, but despite this he jumped out and dragged the two casualties to safety just before the vehicle blew up. For this act of bravery he was awarded the Military Medal (MM). During the landing at Algiers, HMS *Ibis* was struck and began to sink. One of her sick-bay attendants was George W. Beeching of Wallasey, Cheshire, who had joined the Brigade as a cadet. He helped an injured man who had been badly burned to the deck, gave him his own lifebelt and then assisted him gently into the water. The surgeon of the ship wrote: 'The minutes that Beeching gave to save a shipmate cost him his life.' This heroic self-sacrifice was recognized by the posthumous award of the rare Albert Medal in gold, the only such award ever made to a Brigade member which the Brigade is privileged to display in the museum at St John's Gate.

Allied forces also recognized the devotion of St John personnel. Greece awarded its Red Cross Medal to Mary Maberley of Cardiff and perhaps it is no coincidence that her father had served with distinction in the Boer War and later became an Assistant Commissioner. William Nash of Haggerston and Gerald Jackson of Rugby received awards from the King of Norway for their service to his country. From France, Belgium, Holland, USA and Poland came awards to selected and deserving members of the Brigade.

The Victoria Cross occupies a unique and almost revered position in the eyes of servicemen, since it is awarded only for the most exceptional valour. Sergeant Henry Eric Harden of Northfleet Division, Kent, was serving as a Lance-Corporal of the RAMC during the battle of Arnhem when his personal bravery and determination gained him the Cross but cost him his life. The posthumous award was made in the *London Gazette* dated 8 March 1945 as follows:

No. 11006144 Lance-Corporal Henry HARDEN
R.A.M.C. (Northfleet, Kent)

In North-West Europe on 23rd January 1945, the leading section of a Royal Marine Commando troop was pinned to the ground by intense enemy machine-gun fire from well-concealed positions. As it was impossible to engage the enemy from the open owing to lack of cover, the section was ordered to make for some nearby houses. This move was accomplished, but one officer and three other ranks casualties were left lying in the open.

The whole troop position was under continuous heavy and accurate shell and mortar fire. Lance-Corporal Harden, the R.A.M.C. orderly attached to the troop, at once went forward, a distance of 120 yards, into the open under a hail of machine-gun and rifle fire directed from four positions, all within 300 yards, and with the greatest coolness and bravery remained in the open whilst he attended to the four casualties. After dressing the wounds of three of them, he carried one of them back to cover. Lance-Corporal Harden was then ordered not to go forward again and an attempt was made to bring in the other casualties with the aid of tanks, but this proved unsuccessful owing to the heavy and accurate barrage of anti-tank guns. A further attempt was then made to recover the casualties under a smoke-screen, but this only increased the enemy fire in the vicinity of the casualties.

Lance-Corporal Harden then insisted on going again with a stretcher party, and after starting on the return journey with the wounded officer, under very heavy enemy small-arms and mortar fire, he was killed.

Throughout this long period Lance-Corporal Harden displayed superb devotion to duty and personal courage of the very highest order, and there is no doubt that it had a most steadying effect upon the other troops in the area at a most critical time. His action was directly responsible for saving the lives of the wounded brought in. His complete contempt for all personal danger, and a magnificent example he set of cool courage and determination to continue with his work, whatever the odds, was an inspiration to his comrades, and will never be forgotten by those who saw it.

His Brigade colleagues in Kent have now built a Memorial Hall to honour this brave man whose sacrifice should inspire all who serve mankind.

When finally the war ended, the St John Ambulance Association and Brigade could claim to have played a positive part in supporting the Joint War Organization's work both at home and with its overseas Commissions. The Brigade had increased its membership and individual members had shown great loyalty, determination and courage in varied circumstances, upholding the magnificent traditions of the ancient Hospitallers. For some time before the end of hostilities the Headquarters of the Order had been considering the future development of the Brigade but for the men and women it was now time to be demobbed, to greet loved ones or to grieve for those who would not return. The Brigade and its people had once again served mankind when mankind needed it most.

7
THE BRIGADE OVERSEAS

Although this is primarily the story of the St John Ambulance Brigade in Britain, we cannot fail to recognize the growth of the St John work in the Commonwealth and in particular the development and achievements of the Brigade there. Each of the overseas territories could write its own fascinating story, justifiably proud of its own exploits, but here it is not possible to do more than outline the growth of the Brigade and illustrate some of the acts of service and sacrifice which have known no barriers of country, class or creed. In these few pages, therefore, the support of the overseas members and their incalculable contribution to the work of the Brigade worldwide is acknowledged.

The Brigade story began in Dunedin, New Zealand, on 21 December 1892, when the first overseas Ambulance unit of the Brigade was formed. In May the following year a Corps of two divisions was raised in South Africa and in December Auckland formed the third Ambulance Corps. In 1894 the first overseas Nursing Division was formed in Cape Town. The next year witnessed the birth of the second Nursing Division – in Dunedin. Then in 1903 Australia formed three Ambulance Divisions in quick succession, following a proposal made two years earlier suggesting overseas expansion. By September 1903 a separate organization had been created with the marvellous title of 'St John Ambulance Brigade in British Dominions Beyond-the-Seas'. Colonel Charles Bowdler, whose service as Chief Commissioner of the Brigade at home had spanned the Boer War, now became responsible for the Brigade overseas. Within a year the progress of the Association in India had given rise to the formation of the first nursing and ambulance divisions in Bombay. All these individual units were initially administered directly from London.

Meanwhile, the number of units of the Brigade had increased as people recognized the worth of trained and organized teams and it

81

became necessary to create Districts in each overseas territory, each District being responsible for its own national organization. By now New Zealand had 21 Divisions, Australia 15, South Africa 11 and India (Bombay) 3. Divisions were soon formed in Canada and Ceylon as well.

There is little point in producing a detailed catalogue of the formation of the various overseas units, for this would not recognize their actual service and the conditions under which the members worked. In almost every overseas territory the problems of climate, distances, water, availability of skilled resources and transport made the Brigade's service much more difficult than it could ever be in Britain where most of these things could be taken for granted. In Calcutta, for example, during a strike of sweepers and bearers, the members of the local Nursing Division worked on hospital duties including ward shifts and basic cleaning for over 48 hours, non-stop, in temperatures of over 110 degrees and amid the most primitive sanitary conditions. By the time of the Royal Review in 1912 the 'Brigade Overseas', as it was now called, had increased to a total of almost 3,500 and the Divisions were still growing. In India the nurses were soon at work on their very first public duty when a bomb was thrown during the Viceroy's official entry into Delhi. Lord Hardinge was himself amongst the many injured and was treated by the St John members.

During the First World War the overseas units played their part in many different ways. Canadian nursing members served in the Brigade Hospital at Étaples; Ambulance members from India, Australia and New Zealand served in their military or naval forces and Malta provided a hospital. After the War, the same weariness which gripped Britain also affected the Commonwealth and there was a slump in recruiting, accompanied by a period of inactivity. By 1928, however, the total strength of the overseas units had risen to just above 8,000. This was the beginning of the great period of expansion which coincided with the appointment of Colonel James Sleeman as Commissioner for the Brigade Overseas; between 1939 and 1940 the number of adult divisions increased five-fold to 1,546 and the cadet divisions rose from 32 to a staggering total of 414.

Expansion was not only in terms of members but also in achievements. It will be helpful to look at some examples of the work of the overseas divisions during this period to show the variety of tasks and the high level of dedication. In India the work of the Parsee Division during the Bombay riots of February 1929 when many people were killed and injured was described as 'grim determination and expert skill'. In Ceylon a police member saved the life of a woman who had been so viciously stabbed that parts of her intestines protruded. Doctors had given up hope but the policeman washed the intestines, replaced them, sealed the wound as best he could and carried her ten miles to a hospital. She lived only because of his dedication. In New Zealand during the Napier earthquake in 1931, Brigade members travelled over 500 miles to the scene and then worked for fifty hours without rest. Their quick reaction and efficient organization earned this praise: 'They know their work thoroughly and perform it most efficiently.' From Canada comes service of a different kind with the design and distribution of roadside first-aid boxes having an inner detachable box with carefully selected contents which could be taken to the scene of an accident. In Kenya, a Brigade member's first aid saved the life of an African who had been badly mauled by a lion – 400 miles from the nearest medical help. In Burma, Malaya and Singapore during the period before the Second World War, the St John Ambulance Brigade was the only ambulance service and naturally carried out all the duties of a public service. When the Government of the Straits Settlements required a blood transfusion service, the task was given to a St John Nursing Division. In India during the Quetta earthquake of 1935, a Nursing Division and an Ambulance Division from Lahore worked under the most trying and dangerous conditions, dealing with over 700 stretcher cases and supervising the evacuation of some 31,000 refugees. It was in Bombay that the first Muslim Nursing Corps was formed.

Hong Kong provides an example of corporate service which caught the imagination of the world. In 1932, during the Sino-Japanese War, a team of St John Ambulance Brigade from Hong Kong District was sent to organize an emergency hospital near Shanghai. There were two women doctors, 27 nursing members, 32 ambulance members and 10 drivers. This team faced a 'colossal workload', dealing almost immediately with 2,000 serious injuries. Their contribution was recognized by letters of thanks from the International Red Cross, while the citizens of Shanghai presented a trophy to the District and medals to the individual members. The Chapter-General also issued each member with a special badge.

The Second World War attracted overseas members, just as it had those of Britain. As men joined the services their places were taken by older men, new members or the women, more divisions being created to cope with increased requirements including air-raid and anti-gas training. Some of the greatest sacrifices were made in the Far East. Indian units worked ceaselessly during the evacuation of civilians from Burma and in the air raids on Calcutta, where the convalescent hostel for British troops was run entirely by St John nursing personnel. In Burma, members of the Nursing Divisions provided in two months 208,000 dressings and bandages, as well as doing duty as welfare officers or war staff at emergency hospitals. In Hong Kong 300 Brigade members were assisting the RAMC to evacuate wounded when they were captured by the Japanese and a number were summarily executed. In Singapore, too, the war took its toll; 91 Brigade members were killed, including the Nursing Superintendent Mrs Cherry.

In Malta, ravaged by German and Italian air raids day after day, Brigade personnel gave a very good account of themselves in first-aid posts, as drivers, welfare workers and in the civil and military hospitals. Despite the heavy raids and the many casualties, there was not one single case of a nurse leaving her post or failing to report for duty. It was during an air raid on 5 February 1942 that Mrs Caroline Yabsley – who had joined the Malta Brigade in 1910 and had also served in the Association as secretary – was killed by a direct hit on her home. She had already been bombed out of one home and her office had been destroyed. She combined her second home with an office and was working there when the bombs fell. The dedication of the Brigade in one of the Order's traditional homes led to a letter of thanks and praise which perhaps might apply to all overseas divisions: 'Their labours undoubtedly mitigated to a very great extent the suffering . . . a most valuable contribution to the war effort.'

With the end of the Second World War another period of stagnation set in and some of the divisions created during hostilities were now disbanded. But in India there was soon to be a fresh call for the services of St John during the rioting which followed partition and two members of the Parsee Division – one of whom had survived the war – were killed whilst attending the wounded. In a situation where Muslim and Hindu were intent upon killing each other, it says much for the Brigade's influence and the extent of real friendship among its members that men and women of one religion were prepared to go to the aid of the other sect, risking not only their lives but also the animosity of their own religious leaders. Partition brought with it a degree of disorganization within the Brigade which could not be overcome until the two nations had resolved the resultant conflict. Rioting in Durban, South

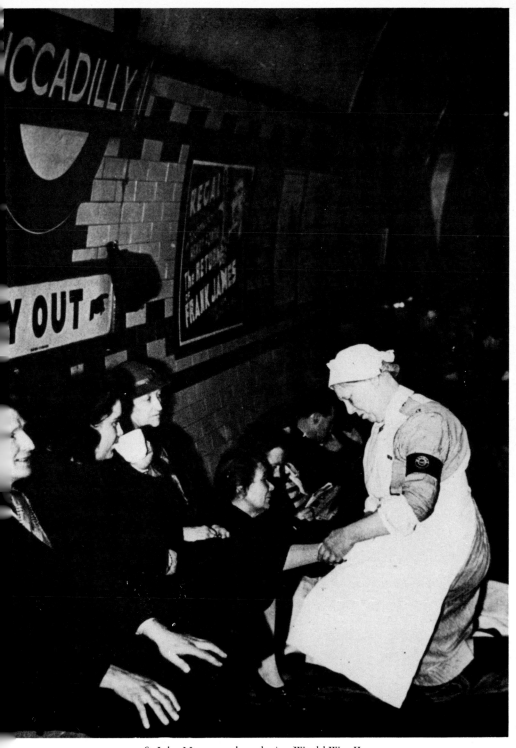

St John Nurse on duty during World War II

Sir Winston Churchill and two V.A.D. nurses on a flag-day

FACING PAGE:
Air raid precautions, World War II

Lady Dunbar Nasmith with the St John Air Unit at Woodley Aerodrome,
Reading 1947. (G.H. Metcalf)

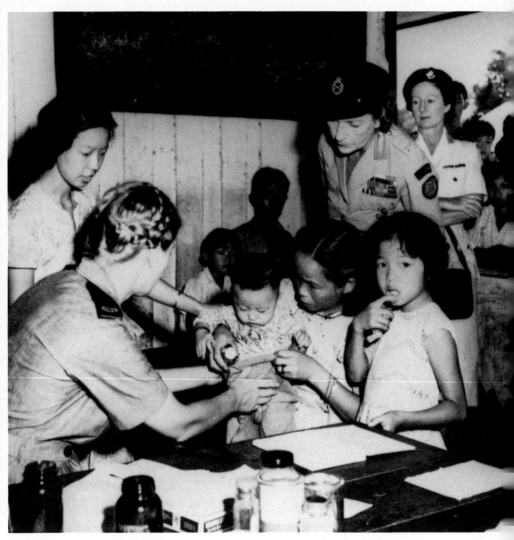

Lady Louis visits a St John Clinic on her Far East Tour 1954

Right: A public duty raises a smile

Above: Jamaica – A parade shows the Brigade's readiness for action *(Trinidad Guardian)*

Left: A training exercise in Western Australia, 1983

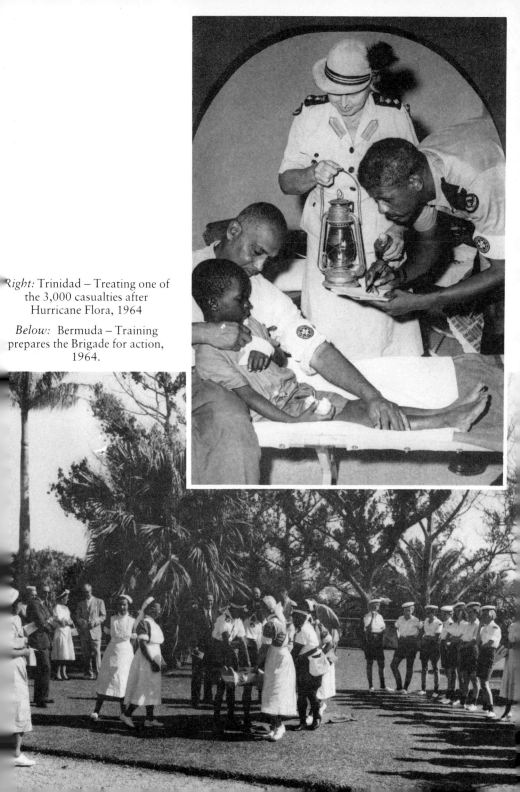

Right: Trinidad – Treating one of the 3,000 casualties after Hurricane Flora, 1964

Below: Bermuda – Training prepares the Brigade for action, 1964.

Public Duties – Beatlemania victim

Africa, resulted in many appalling injuries and the local Division worked solidly for four days in the streets and in the local hospitals. In Malaya, the resettlement policy required extra medical support and welfare teams. Twenty-five teams were formed by the Red Cross and St John, each having its own vehicle. It is interesting that nursing members from Britain went out to join their local colleagues for this task.

The war of 1939–1945 had transformed the world; apart from nuclear weapons, there were important changes in social and international relationships. However, there were still natural disasters to contend with, as for example the hurricane in Jamaica in August 1951 when the local Division dealt with over 2,000 cases and played a prominent part in arranging a programme of inoculations and in welfare work. When a hurricane hit St Lucia in August 1980 the Brigade contributed significantly to relief operations, several members of a Cadet Division being awarded Certificates of Commendation. From now on the Brigade in the Commonwealth would exercise a much greater degree of independence, though there would always be the link with 'The Gate'. By 1974, the Brigade Overseas was serving in forty-seven nations and had reached a membership of some 180,000. It will be useful to relate some recent achievements of these Brigade members, whose stories are not always fully appreciated in Britain.

Australia, which celebrated its centenary in 1983, has just cause to be proud of its 'Royal Flying Doctor Service', but the contribution of St John Ambulance to the aeromedical services of the Commonwealth may not be so well known. Derek Clark of the British St John Aeromedical Service visited South Australia in 1972 to study their systems, and discovered that in 1975 St John aircraft had flown 672 patients during a total of 1,545 flying hours. During one year the 3,685 St John members in South Australia gave a total of 400,000 hours of voluntary service. In New Zealand, when fumes escaped from chemical drums and many people were gassed, the members of St John Ambulance were quickly on the scene, carrying many victims to safety. Not too far away, Fiji is the first country of the Commonwealth to have created a mounted Division.

In Malaysia a rock-face at Ipoh crumbled and fell, crushing many homes in a village which had been built at the foot of the hill. Several St John men were killed or injured, but their colleagues struggled around the clock for four days searching for victims. Further south in Singapore, when building began in the industrial complex of the Jurong, the

St John Ambulance provided the first-aid posts for workers and residents. Jamaica honoured the unsung heroes of its ambulance movement when, to celebrate 21 years of independence, twenty-six St John members who had served for that period were given a special medal. From Bermuda comes an interesting comment from Mrs Dorothy Shirley, winner of the Westlake Cup for outstanding service in 1977. In a letter written to the *St John Review*, she compares the 'gives' and the 'gets' of St John service and suggests that the 'gets' would take up too much space and the 'gives' not much in comparison: 'help to a casualty, service to the Brigade, a small service to my country; a small act of thanks to God'.

In the Commonwealth countries of Africa and the Republic of South Africa members of St John continue their service. The Cape Flats is a depressing area outside Cape Town which is host to unemployment, alcoholism, glue-sniffing, violence and sheer despair. To some the only ray of hope they have seen has come from a community service project prepared and staffed by St John. Several centres have been organized where residents can obtain help, medical aid, child nursing, welfare and – most important – friendship. This service is carried out by a small number of paid St John workers backed up by many unpaid volunteers. The project, together with 'Care of the Aged' and 'Industrial Training', featured prominently in the Centenary Conference in 1983 when the decision was made to create a St John Ambulance division in Swaziland; this unit was inaugurated by the Chief Commander when he visited the Priory that year.

Further North in Kenya, the Brigade undertook one of its most sombre public duties. Jomo (Mzee) Kenyatta's death and lying-in-state in August 1978 brought tens of thousands of people to Nairobi. It was natural that the Brigade should honour the nation's President, but Mzee Kenyatta was also a Knight of Grace of the Order of St John, invested on behalf of the Grand Prior by the Countess of Brecknock during a visit. Members in Kenya did 2,000 hours of duty during one week and treated 5,000 people. In Uganda the only St John vehicle in the country was hijacked by an armed gang. Britain sent out a replacement and within three weeks this new ambulance had helped to save the life of a dangerously ill patient and had transferred two unconscious casualties to Kenya for treatment at the Kenyatta Hospital.

Canada has continued to demonstrate its flexible and innovative approach during the recent past. In 1975 Ski Patrol Divisions were created, five units with a total of 250 trained members. The same year saw survival cairns placed in the remote north, inside the Arctic Circle, containing food, first-aid kid, thermal blankets, location beacon and other equipment designed to aid survival for forty days. Two of the earliest cairns to be positioned were dedicated by Mr N. McClintock, Secretary-General of the Venerable Order, and a party of cadets, six of whom came from Canada and six from the UK. Their value was proved within a year when a man who had missed a meeting point for an aircraft walked for seventeen days and, near-starving, found the cairn – a life was saved. To Canada goes the honour of appointing the first woman to be Chief Commissioner of a Commonwealth St John Ambulance; Mrs Yvette Loiselle* was appointed on St John's Day 1978 to lead Canada's 12,500 members, who in one year provide 1½ million hours of voluntary duty.

The history of the modern Brigade Overseas, which now operates in forty-seven territories, is perhaps best left to the nations themselves to relate and an impressive history it is. For example, South Africa, Australia and Canada all celebrated their centenaries in 1983, followed by New Zealand in 1985. Finally, one other celebration should be recorded to end this chapter: the Diamond Jubilee of Malta District in 1969, which attracted members from almost every Commonwealth nation – proving, if proof were needed, that the bonds of friendship within the Brigade had remained strong enough to cross frontiers and overcome the stresses of emerging and changing societies.

* Now Prior of the Order in Canada

8

WALES, IRELAND AND THE ISLANDS

The highest forms of courage, service and sacrifice can often be found in the places of gravest danger and the areas where deprivation or despair exist. So it is with St John Ambulance in Britain; the mines and mining villages of Wales, the cliffs and mountains, the lakes and the coasts, and in particular the Channel Islands as well as the special problems of Northern Ireland, have all revealed aspects of St John work which warrant separate emphasis.

Wales has the distinction of pioneering the concept of Medical Comforts Depots to alleviate suffering and, because it has such a dense concentration of mining and industrial areas, the Brigade evolved a particularly valuable ambulance transport service. Both these initiatives display the essential characteristics of St John work within the Priory at that time – enthusiasm and relevance. Herbert Lewis was perhaps the man who, more than any other, helped to mould the St John organization and lead it to the point where at one time it was the most important and effective voluntary organization in Wales. Lewis spent a great deal of time encouraging or cajoling mine-owners to make arrangements for first aid at their pits; he personally organized the Welsh St John contingent for the Royal Review in 1912 and it required three special trains to get the men and women from Cardiff to London. He was also the first to go to France in 1914, was instrumental in raising 130th Field Hospital, and in 1918 was one of the men who campaigned for Wales to have Priory status. His contribution to the relief of suffering was recognized by his appointment to KBE in 1922 and he continued this work until his death in January 1931. Such a man deserves to be remembered with honour and the Welshmen erected a memorial tablet to him which the then Prince of Wales unveiled on 16 May 1933. Lewis's term of office as Commissioner of the Brigade here was one of constant progress, such that he could write in 1928 that the

Brigade was a power for good in Wales. In fact, during the period from 1920 to 1928 the numerical strength of the Brigade in Wales had almost doubled because there was so much to do. The demands on the St John Ambulance Brigade during 1928 and 1929 were enormous, not only because of the increased accident rate but also because the public knew that they could depend on this organization. Lewis was succeeded by the Hon. John Bruce, who was to see the Brigade through the thirties, the Second World War and the post-war period of nationalization. He saw the need for the voluntary organizations to accept even greater responsibility during the period of transition as the National Health Service settled down; they would still serve mankind, even if their own work would ultimately be reduced in a new social environment. The legacy from the Priory to the NHS was indeed valuable – a force of 30 ambulances, operating from 23 stations, using a staff of 60 men and women and covering 500,000 miles per year.

The Welsh St John leaders had not been content simply to approach the mine-owners regarding medical facilities; they also lobbied members of Parliament seeking legislation and eventually the colliery owners did provide first-aid facilities. The Brigade thus created specific Ambulance Divisions to serve every mine. It was then generally acknowledged that St John had done more than any other organization to establish a first-aid capability in the mines, and the men who joined the Brigade were themselves miners. Even today an accident in a coal-mine can have devastating consequences; in the 1920s and 1930s, the effect was even more shattering and in 1934 the serious explosion at the Gresford Colliery claimed the lives of all the men on one shift, including a Brigade man who was in the shaft. The police called the Wrexham Division and every man reported immediately. These men spent up to 28 hours on continuous duty amid the debris and with those who waited on the site, but there were no survivors. The pit then had to be sealed, and the St John personnel devoted further time to comforting the bereaved families – a different form of first aid and no easy task. There have been many tragedies in the mining villages of Wales, thankfully not all as catastrophic as Gresford but all with momentous consequences for the community. Few events, however, have called forth such spontaneous and widespread sympathy as the appalling disaster at Aberfan on 21 October 1966, when a mountainous moving mass of coal-dust engulfed the village school. The members of the Brigade from Merthyr Tydfil joined with the other organizations in a massive rescue and welfare effort. They may not have been heroes or

89

heroines, but they pulled their weight in a team of mercy in the highest traditions of service.

During the 1920s, the St John Motor Ambulance Transport provided a most welcome service in the villages as well as in the towns and cities at a time when accidents were becoming more frequent. Many industrialists became subscribers to a project which was designed to provide immediate removal from home or the scene of an accident to the nearest hospital. The mine- or mill-owners paid one shilling a year, while each individual paid one penny each week. Old-age pensioners and widows paid only a halfpenny per week. Even allowing for the purchasing power of the shilling of that time, this was by no means an expensive service and was generally regarded as being 'well worth it'. Another enterprise which was much valued and in constant demand was the chain of Medical Comforts Depots (MCDs they were called) which had been established throughout the Principality. In 1929 the Depots provided help for 5,400 needy cases and by 1947 there were no fewer than 157 of them which in one year issued over 16,000 items to deserving cases. The next year, however, was to see the nationalization of mines and the establishment of the National Health Service, so the subscribers' ambulance and the Comforts Depots would have only a limited future; indeed, by 1951 nearly a hundred Depots had been disbanded – a sad blow for Wales.

But work in Wales did not only concern the miners and the Comforts Depots. The Ambulance Divisions enjoyed the spirit of competition and for many years the inter-colliery contests attracted great interest. The National Eisteddfod also included first-aid competitions in its programme. Ambulance Halls, usually with adjoining social club, were popular and in 1949 when John Bruce opened the Abercarn Divisional HQ he was able to say that, whereas in 1931 there had been twelve Halls, he could now count well over a hundred. The members of the Nursing Divisions became directly involved in welfare during the Depression; Bargoed Nursing Division, for example, did remarkable work amid sickness and poverty, providing clothing, food and money to families who were experiencing real distress. The Cadet Branch in Wales flourished and gave good service, receiving a grant of £2,750 in 1933 following their smart appearance during the visit of the Prince of Wales. There was also a desire to get to know what was happening elsewhere and to exchange ideas. One excellent expression of this could be found in the 'health and mine' visits exchanged annually between the Rhondda and Harrow Divisions. Each division sent a group of members, including a competition team, to visit the other; playing host in alternate years. The competition prize was, appropriately, a miner's lamp!

The men of 130th (St John) Field Ambulance were not forgotten in peace. George Thomas, the unit's bugler, saw to that by maintaining a kind of benevolent society and organizing an annual reunion for the old comrades, dwindling in number as the years passed. In 1955, as he blew 'The Last Post' on the famous silver bugle, another Welshman – Lewis Evans of Clydach – was struggling desperately to remove heavy boulders which had trapped his workmate in mine workings. The victim was in fact trapped between tons of rubble, but Evans continued to try to save him until there was no more hope. On being brought to the surface, Lewis Evans said, 'As an ambulance man it was my duty to stay with him as long as he was alive'; that was an echo of the Welsh spirit of St John.

*

The development of St John work in the Channel Islands needs to be considered separately; first because the islands were the only part of Britain to be occupied during the war and St John personnel earned respect from both sides for their work; second because the islands have witnessed more tragedies and miraculous rescues than most other areas; third, so far as Guernsey is concerned St John provides a total rescue and ambulance service for the island; and finally, the only man ever to be awarded the Order's Gold Life Saving Medal *and* bar is a Channel Islander.

Guernsey's early invalid transport was organized by the poor law and hospital authorities. The island owes the establishment of its first full-time ambulance service to a serious road accident in October 1930, when R. H. Blanchford received serious injuries and nearly died for want of effective treatment and quick transport. In 1934 a Division of the St John Ambulance Brigade was formed on Guernsey and Blanchford – following recovery in a London hospital – came home and joined the new unit. The immediate aim was to acquire an ambulance and within two years sufficient money had been saved to purchase a second-hand Talbot. The St John Division spent the next year working extremely hard to prove that they could provide a reliable service rivalling the 'official' system. In 1938 they treated 60 accident cases, conveyed 625 patients to hospital and travelled nearly 38,000 miles – and Guernsey is not a large island! Meanwhile a Nursing Division had been formed in 1936 and Cadet Divisions in 1937 and 1939. The States then agreed that the Brigade could take on all ambulance work throughout the island, designating it the official Ambulance Service and providing an annual grant of £200. Barely a year later war broke out and on 20 June 1940 many islanders decided to leave their homes; for three days the St John personnel assisted the evacuation and then elected to remain on the island to continue their service. One week later, on 27 June 1940, the Germans bombed and machine-gunned the island; in the process they strafed the ambulance, wounding the driver, William Nicolle – whose leg had to be amputated – and killing the patient. Then on 30 June, the islands were occupied and the five long years of rationing and restrictions began. Despite the shortage of fuel, despite the curfews imposed by the Germans and despite a German attempt to commandeer the ambulances, the St John men and women were able to keep an ambulance service going by using horse-drawn vehicles and a charcoal gas engine obtained from France. The Germans were to be thankful that they had left the organization intact, because during occupation, their own men were rescued from cliffs and minefields or taken by ambulance for treatment. By the end of the war Reg Blanchford could claim that no person, friend or foe, had died for want of transport and no call for aid from either side had gone unanswered.

When peace returned the ambulance service was expanded and arrangements made to fly patients from the islands to Britain, an aspect of the work which is now a regular feature. At the same time the officers of the service organized their communications, providing two-way radio for the ambulances and the control room. The value of this initiative – the first unit in the UK to be so equipped – soon became apparent when in 1956 the St John organization was declared to be efficient and cost-effective and the States decided to increase their support. This requires some emphasis here, because the St John Division now consisted of some paid members of the local authority's service who also undertook the traditional volunteer work of the Brigade. To make the distinction clear, the official uniform of the Service was grey and the voluntary dress black. It is not simply a local ambulance service, although that is its main function; it operates the island's blood transfusion service, cliff rescue unit, sea rescue unit with its own high-speed launch, inshore craft and recompression centre – the first civilian unit in the British Isles – and finally a medical comforts store and escort service. The *Flying Christine* was introduced in 1952 and was immediately involved in sea rescues. She was the world's first marine ambulance launch, but in 1963 was so severely damaged that repair was impossible and in 1964 the *Flying Christine II* was launched. The following year this remarkable vessel was on show at the International Boat Show. In short, whatever is needed to save life and alleviate suffering, the Guernsey Service is trained to cope with it. There is not sufficient space here to list – much less explain – the complex equipment now managed by the Service, but it is comprehensive and extremely expensive. Without donations, legacies and assistance from the Hayward Foundation, such a venture could not continue to function and play its part in saving life. It is now called the St John Ambulance and Rescue Service and certainly lives up to its name, answering regular calls to the cliffs or the sea to rescue people in danger.

Reg Blanchford, the man whose injuries and subsequent dedication were to do so much for St John in Guernsey, has earned a unique place in history. He was the driving force behind the development of the Rescue Service, making it the professional force which it is today. He is also the only person to have been awarded the Life Saving Medal of the Order of St John in Gold, together with a bar for a second award, also the George Medal for bravery and the Order of the British Empire. He is listed in the *Guinness Book of Records* as the civilian with the greatest number of awards for bravery.

The voluntary St John Ambulance Brigade on Guernsey now consists of two Ambulance, two Nursing, two Ambulance Cadet and three Nursing Cadet Divisions. They carry out all the normal functions of the voluntary Brigade as elsewhere in the British Isles, but also provide the all-important back-up to the professional service. The Cadet Divisions have the support of a particularly active and effective Parents and Friends Association, which helps with fund-raising and maintains motivation.

Today, therefore, Guernsey possesses a professional and highly trained Ambulance and Rescue Service which owes its origin and early development to the St John Ambulance Brigade. It is not responsible to the Brigade, however; its funds – a grant from the States and public donations – come mainly from Guernsey and it is controlled by a civilian management committee answerable to the States. The voluntary St John Ambulance members on the island carry out the normal Brigade and Association tasks, but are not normally called out for emergency calls, this being the prerogative of the professionals. The two activities are distinct but not divorced, separate in function because some are paid and highly trained while others are volunteers. Both owe their existence to St John.

On Jersey as on Guernsey, the Germans imposed restrictions including a ban on the wearing of Brigade uniform, but Dr J. R. Hanna and Oscar Aubin pressed hard for permission to be given and finally the Germans relented. Thus on the Channel Islands we find a unique situation where the Brigade uniform was officially worn in the presence of an occupying power. Perhaps some of the men smiled as they remembered being in uniform at one of the last British Army parades on the islands before the war, when the White Cross belt marched past to the tune 'Oh Dear, What Can the Matter be?'

In September 1942 and January 1943 a total of 1,026 English-born residents, men, women and children, were deported from Jersey via St Malo to internment camps in southern Germany. On the direct order from Hitler, this was carried out as a retaliation against the British government because in 1941 Britain had asked that German citizens working in Iran against the Allied cause should be handed over. St John Ambulance members – both nursing and ambulance personnel – accompanied and cared for the deportees on the boat journeys from the islands to France. Well might the Constable of St Helier refer to the 'splendid service rendered' in a letter of thanks to Dr Hanna.

In December 1944, after 4½ years of enemy occupation, there was a serious shortage of food in Jersey. This situation was relieved by the arrival on 30 December of the Red Cross ship SS *Vega*, carrying Red Cross food parcels. Thus the imminent starvation of the civilian population was capable of being averted, but a further problem arose with regard to the collection, security and distribution of these parcels to the civilian people for whom they were intended. The task of handling the Red Cross supplies was entrusted to the St John Ambulance Brigade by the International Red Cross delegates who had travelled to the island in the *Vega*. There were to be three further visits of the ship and altogether there were six distributions of parcels to the civilian population in the ensuing five months. Over 236,000 food parcels and in addition supplies of flour, sugar, butter, footwear and so on were received and handled by the Brigade personnel, who also maintained an unbroken day and night guard over the supplies until the liberation of the island in May.

It is not surprising that at separate parades held on Guernsey and Jersey special certificates were presented on behalf of the Order, thanking the Channel Island Divisions for their tenacity and loyalty during five years of occupation. Although we have concentrated on only two islands, Alderney – the third of the Channel Islands – has its own Quadrilateral Division in which adults and cadets work and train together. There is no doubt that the presence of a strong, well-motivated St John organization in the islands did much to alleviate suffering on both sides and maintained the morale of the population during a most critical period. Britain's debt to the war services of the Brigade in the Channel Islands is enormous, and those who take their holidays on Jersey and Guernsey can be thankful that such well-trained and experienced men and women are prepared to give their time in the official Service and the voluntary Divisions for our safety. We have much to be thankful for.

*

The Isle of Man's contribution to St John Ambulance began in 1940 when Major J. W. Young started a Division there. In addition to the normal Brigade duties, this unit also operates the island's blood donor service in which the cadets play an important role. This was a particularly relevant function when, in 1974, the disastrous fire at the Summerland Amusement Park caused many casualties. The first ambulance on the scene came from the St John Division and while patients were being treated and conveyed to hospital, other members toured the streets to bring in blood donors from the public. Thus both aspects of the Brigade's work were brought together at a critical moment, providing a fast efficient service to the hospitals and making a significant contribution to the treatment of victims.

*

There had been a centre of the Association in Ireland since 1880 and in 1903 the first Division of the Brigade was formed with John Lumsden as one of the principal founders. Other units soon followed and their members served in the First World War, some with the British Forces and others at home in strife-torn Dublin. John Lumsden himself became Chairman of the Joint St John and Red Cross Committee and was the driving force behind the war hospitals and comforts depots, making his home available for Red Cross work. During the Easter riots in Dublin, his courage and leadership earned him the Order's Life Saving Medal in Silver, together with the Special Service Medal of the British Red Cross Society. When the District organization came into being, Ireland was allotted No. 12 with Lumsden as its Commissioner; at the end of the War he was appointed KBE for his services to the Joint Committee. Sir John Lumsden, as he now became, served through a troubled period of Ireland's modern history which led to partition in 1922. However, despite the inevitable effects upon training and morale, in 1921 one Division managed to gain the Symons Eccles Cup as runners-up in the Brigade finals. While competitions are good for morale, there is no substitute for proven success in real emergencies and there was no shortage of these during 1921. In Grafton Street, for example, Brigade member Albert Taylor was among a large group of shoppers when bombs were thrown; one bomb did not explode, however, whereupon Taylor immediately picked it up, made it safe and gave it to a policeman! He then set about helping the many injured. During the major street battles near the Four Courts, 180 Brigade members were on duty over a ten-day period, going to the aid of stricken men from both sides and with their calm efficiency gaining the confidence and respect of everyone. Barricades were lifted so that the ambulances could remove from the scene a wounded man and a woman who had just had a premature baby.

Sir John Lumsden was naturally proud of the impartial dedication of his men and women, but he expressed grave doubts about the long-term future. Then in 1922 came partition and the establishment of a totally new political system. Lumsden would continue to serve the ideals of St John until his death in September 1944, but from now on the Irish Brigade would be divided and the Ulster units became a sub-district of 4 Lancashire District, serving with another great Commissioner, Charles Trimble. The first Brigade units in Ulster were formed in 1932 and quickly assumed responsibility for first aid at major sporting occasions such as racing at Dundrod circuit and horse shows, as well as at smaller local events. They also agreed to provide cover for the various marches which are part of Ulster's life and it was during one of these demonstrations in 1935 that very ugly scenes erupted. Missiles were thrown at the procession and a full-scale street battle ensued. Brigade personnel were on duty all night and saved the life of a man who was being savagely beaten to unconsciousness. They then assisted the public and the police.

Following the Second World War, the Association and Brigade in Ulster were reorganized and in 1947 new regulations specific to Northern Ireland were published. The following year saw the whole Brigade in the province assembling for the St John's Day service in

Belfast Cathedral and in 1949 there was a great parade at the Balmoral Show ground. The pace of Brigade activity in Ulster quickened and in 1950 Lord Dunleath presented a cup for the most outstanding voluntary individual public duty, won that first year by a Belfast man named William Longridge who gave up all his spare time to look after a war veteran who had lost both his legs. Over a period of some six months, Longridge played a major part in teaching the patient to use his artificial limbs. This was not a matter of first aid, but an immensely valuable contribution to make. In 1951 a historic event took place when the Order purchased a new Bangor HQ – the first acquisition of land since the confiscation of the Ards Commandery – and the next year witnessed the reconstitution of the Commandery of Ards by the Duke of Gloucester, accompanied by members of the Chapter General. At a different level the men and women of the Ulster Divisions were buying their own HQs, often spending their own time and money to rebuild or modify an old property and raising money by street collections throughout Ulster. Despite the social deprivation which was affecting the Province following the war, the people were most generous – indicating perhaps the trust which the St John personnel had earned. But these same social conditions generated much more work for the Brigade and in 1954 the ambulances carried 3,000 patients, travelling a total of 32,000 miles; no duty was refused, no call for help ignored.

The Province of Ulster was to witness violence in the shape of terrorist activity in 1956, and this lasted until 1961. The years between 1962 and 1968 were comparatively peaceful so far as the Brigade was concerned, though with the now inevitable outbreaks of local violence. Then in 1968 and 1969 the situation deteriorated, giving way to the long years of violence which have not yet subsided and which affect the whole fabric of the Province. Naturally the Brigade was on call, the heaviest pressure being in Belfast and Derry. The first Brigade casualty was Divisional Officer Petticrew from Belfast, who received a serious head injury as he drove an ambulance on duty. He was one of five members of his family to be serving in St John at the time.

Since then the terms 'public duty' and 'first aid' in Ulster have acquired a new meaning. No longer was the Brigade dealing with sprains and cuts, but with multiple casualties with complicated, serious injuries; no longer with straightforward shock but outright horror, and always amid personal danger. There is insufficient space to catalogue all the incidents which have involved the Brigade members, but mention of several should ensure that their service can be properly appreciated and also indicate the degree to which this service was recognized at the time. The first story concerns a member of the Ryan family and his ambulance team – Ellen Dickinson and Driver Piggott – who in ambulance No. 15 began a period of duty which took them into the Shankhill Road to recover two policemen and one soldier who had been shot. When they arrived, they were confronted by an ongoing battle which had caused several more casualties, and by now one of the policemen was in a very serious condition. They therefore called for a back-up ambulance and began a hazardous journey to take the most seriously wounded to hospital, giving artificial resuscitation to the policeman throughout the journey. At the hospital they were requested to go back to the area to collect further wounded and this they did, driving through a hail of missiles and rifle fire. Then they were given a third task which involved going to another area of violence, and this time poor Driver Piggott had to cope with the CS gas being used by the Army. By the time the patients reached hospital, the team was exhausted and in some distress from the gas, but they continued their duty and reported back to Ambulance HQ. It is perhaps no coincidence that A/O Ryan is the son of W. H. Ryan, who had been awarded the BEM for his services to the Brigade in Northern Ireland.

The story of two cadet heroines of the appalling explosion at the Abercorn restaurant will be told in Chapter 10. Now, however, we can pay tribute to two Brigade members who proudly wear the oak leaf of gallantry on the ribbon of the British Empire Medal. Sergeant Haydon Elliot and Mrs Kay Blankley of the HQ Transport Division ran through missiles and shooting in order to reach a youth who had been shot in the abdomen and thigh. They dressed his wounds while still under fire and then carried him some distance to the ambulance, protected only by a riot shield provided by a soldier. Throughout this hazardous ordeal they behaved with absolute calm, total lack of concern for their personal safety and with complete impartiality.

If the pressure on personnel was severe, the strain on the equipment was no less so and the Brigade in Northern Ireland was grateful for the support provided by the Order and Brigade units elsewhere in Britain. Sir William Pike, Chief Commander, was able to provide £2,000 and two ambulances for the hard-pressed Province, testimony to the desire of the whole Brigade to support the brave men and women who bore the brunt of so much violence.

9

A NEW BRITAIN

The Britain which emerged from the Second World War in 1945 bore little resemblance to that of 1939. Important social changes were being made, there was a great feeling of relief that at last the conflict was over and the country attempted to settle back into a peacetime routine in an unsettled and atomic world. From now on man's investment in new technology would increase year by year and a new, more materialistic outlook would emerge. Before the war first aid had been comparatively simple and everyone knew the standards. Now the Brigade was facing a totally new situation requiring new techniques, revised teaching and a fresh look at the broader spectrum of aid to the sick and needy. Public duty would become more demanding and possibly require greater sophistication in approach. Moreover the war had provided the impetus for other organizations to involve themselves with first aid, so St John could no longer claim a unique place in this form of service. Even as a voluntary organization, however, the Brigade was saving the state enormous sums of money, first by carrying out duties which would otherwise have to be done on a wage-earning basis and second by paying for all its own vehicles and equipment, the cost of which was not fully appreciated by a public which still imagined there was some state aid. It was also natural that following six years of war, the Red Cross – the accepted symbol for international voluntary aid – should have become pre-eminent; and equally understandable that the White Cross of St John – playing its supporting role – should have been eclipsed to some extent. Henceforth the concept of joint or coordinated effort with other agencies would be the way ahead, despite some loss of individual freedom.

Within the Order of St John and its Foundations, it was expected that there would be a reduction in numbers as demobilization reunited families and the personnel who had joined for the duration of the war resumed their peacetime occupations. Some wartime Divisions did not survive the transition to peace and were disbanded; others were amalgamated, but in rural areas this was not always practicable. Since it was considered essential to maintain a degree of continuity for the cadets, early efforts were made to retain or recruit suitable young leaders. At the same time it was decided to create a coordinating body in each county and the first St John Council was established in Dorset in December 1945, to be followed in 1946 by Norfolk, Sussex and Devonshire, with Plymouth as a separate 'county'. Yet another practical step was taken in February 1946 when the validity of the Association's Certificate was limited to five years. In the following year a new Brigade nursing post of County Nursing Officer was established, each holder to be a qualified SRN. Meanwhile the Medical Comforts Depots were still providing scarce items of equipment to the needy.

On 8 June 1946 people in their thousands – men, women and children – gathered in London for the official Victory Parade. There were of course victory celebrations all over the country, but here in the capital representatives of Britain and the Commonwealth would give thanks for the end of the war on behalf of all who had taken part. The Brigade was represented officially by thirty-six uniformed members from all parts of Britain and there were also personnel marching with the VADs and JWO, the Civil Defence and the Naval Reserves. But there was a working representation of 4,000 members of all ranks on public duty that day and they handled more than 5,000 casualties, completing 32,000 hours of voluntary duty for this one occasion.

While routine work continued with some degree of normality, the Brigade was still called out to answer emergency calls, as in 1947 when floods in Cambridgeshire and Lincolnshire were extensive and serious. Brigade members were quickly involved in rescuing victims and where the vehicles could not go, the men and women waded waist-deep in icy, muddy torrents to carry stranded people to a makeshift hospital at the Gainsborough Divisional HQ. It was here that a baby girl was born shortly after the mother had been brought to safety. Another baby, born in Wales, brought a mixture of mirth and pride to the Brigade; the beach hut at Barry – manned by the Brigade – was needed urgently and a fine healthy boy was born there. The following year the proud mother returned to the beach hut to introduce her son – Barry St John! These beach huts (or static posts) and road patrols were continued for several years and provided excellent assistance during peak holiday periods. Cobham (Surrey) Ambulance Division was able to meet both commitments by designing a motor cycle and side-car – the latter discarded by the AA – which was painted black with the Brigade badge super-imposed and toured the popular beauty spots.

A year later, the sea around the coast of Cornwall was to witness tragedy when HMS *Warspite* ran aground as she was being taken to the breakers' yard. In gale conditions, the Divisions from Cornwall under the command of Assistant Commissioner Tressider rigged up a breeches buoy and Brigade members swung from the cliffs to work in confined spaces and rescue thirteen men who had been trapped on board. Superintendent Roach and Sergeant Perkins of St Ives played a prominent part in the operation, as they had in rescue work carried out during the previous year; indeed both men had been awarded the meritorious First Aid Certificate during their service. Not all accidents ended in tragedy, however, as one young first-aider discovered when he was tending a man who, with others, had been brought ashore from a stranded vessel. He suddenly whispered urgently to the Superinten-dent, 'I think this man has stopped breathing.' 'Oh no I haven't – hands off!' came a loud and equally urgent response. Such mistakes can also be made by nursing members, one of whom was returning home after having recently passed her first-aid examination, when she saw a small crowd around a man lying face down in flood-water near a man-hole cover. Quickly she knelt beside the man, tenderly felt for a pulse at his neck and began to turn him over prior to resuscitation. The 'patient' suddenly sat up and said, 'I don't know what you are trying to do, miss, but I'm trying to clear this drain!'

*

The National Health Service was created in 1948 under an Act which required local authorities to provide the main ambulance and hospital transport, and this naturally resulted in some discussion regarding the future of voluntary organizations. It had been thought that local health authorities would call on the Brigade to provide ambulance transport, but it would have been unreasonable to expect a voluntary organiz-ation to do so. However, the official St John view at the time was that the Order and its Foundations were not political, that they existed to alleviate suffering and so they would carry out whatever duties were considered necessary. At a Senior Officers' Conference at Hoddesdon, Herts, in June 1947, the point had been made that the local medical officers of health were responsible for providing an effective pro-fessional service and some of them would be wary of employing members of a voluntary organization on work for which they had ultimate responsibility. It would be better for St John to carry out excellently those things which it was permitted to undertake, rather than attempt to spread its commitments. It was perhaps ironic that in 1948 the government experienced a serious shortage of trained hospital nurses and a cry for help went to the BRCS and St John. It was also surprising and disappointing that in late 1949 the State took over all the ambulance transport in Cardiff, first started by the Brigade in 1918, and still an efficient service. At the same time the Medical Comforts Depots were taken over by local authorities. Thus two of the great St John initiatives had now passed entirely into State control; however, if this reduced the scope of Brigade work, it also showed how farsighted the Order had been in those earlier days by creating something lasting of which they could be proud.

It had become clear that the work of the Order could continue only with the aid of physical and financial support from the public. More recruits were needed and existing members were encouraged to stay on to maintain manning levels. It was becoming more difficult to obtain money from a public which tended to accept the presence of Brigade members at football matches without perhaps understanding that the NHS did not cover these duties; the promoters had to arrange for voluntary organizations to provide staff. Nor did the public acknowledge the many other activities which were now required. By the end of 1948 membership had declined to the extent where the drop in numbers became acute – particularly male membership – and there was grave concern at the reduction in the numbers of cadets transferring to the adult ranks. By the end of 1949 it seemed that one of the reasons the volunteers were not coming forward was 'uniform'. Six years of uniform and war meant that the modern youngster was not easily persuaded to join another uniformed organization. There were undoubtedly other and equally valid reasons, but the effect was that by 1950 the Brigade was undertaking considerably more duties with fewer people, resulting in a great increase in the pressure on all members.

On 24 June 1948 the Brigade became the third full Foundation of the Order in Britain, its committee becoming a Standing Committee of the Order and henceforth enjoying the same status as the Association. Its personnel would be very heavily committed during the year as the number of sporting events claimed their share of duty. Apart from the Test Matches and Wimbledon, there were the taxing commitments of the various activities of the Olympic Games; Paignton, Torquay, Henley, Southend, Bisley, Windsor and of course in London. It was a major effort and a great success; hard work, but well worth it. Three years later the Brigade was to assist with first-aid coverage for the Festival of Britain and again there would be many hours of hard but rewarding labour. Although the main element of the Festival took place in London, there were many activities in other parts of the country. In London, however, Commissioner White-Knox had to plan for over twice his normal commitment of nearly half a million voluntary hours of duty, the majority of which would provide coverage for the South Bank site. This site was divided by Hungerford Bridge, with the Red Cross responsible for the Eastern sector and St John for the sector to the West of the bridge. The Brigade also accepted responsibility for the Battersea and Poplar sites. Units from Berkshire, Buckinghamshire, Essex, Hampshire, Hertfordshire and Surrey were invited to assist London District and in addition two members from Malta volunteered. Qualified personnel from almost every County volunteered for specialist duties and this remarkably successful combined operation dealt with over 8,000 visitors who needed treatment of some kind; 3,600 of these had been involved in some physical accident – and this on the South Bank site alone. At Battersea 12,541 cases were treated, over 6,000 of which were due to accidents. But tired and blistered feet presented one of the biggest tasks for the first-aiders and one visitor, having left the Dome of Discovery, came into the St John tent and sighed, 'Now the Dome of Recovery!' These duties were carried out jointly by ambulance and nursing members, one of the first qualified State Registered Nurses to report being Corps Officer Mr Barnes from Accrington. The auxiliary staff felt that they could hardly address him as 'Sister', so they must needs call him 'Brother Barnes', an honourable term in the world of St John. So, after some initial mirth Brothers Barnes, Waterer and Wells became part of the Festival of Britain!

The response of the Brigade to rail accidents has always earned high praise and there are many examples of dogged determination, as well as individual acts of bravery which are ample testimony to this service. Here we can only offer a few examples to indicate the work of members assisting the injured at these disasters. When, on 21 September 1950, the Liverpool to Euston express crashed near Weedon, the men and women of Northampton were quickly at the scene, some nursing members going directly to the local hospital while others helped the men at the crash site. One ambulance member crawled into the wrecked cab to help the trapped driver, who was very seriously injured. The local press were keen to obtain the names of the members, but they chose to remain anonymous and only later was it discovered that it was Sergeant George who had gone into the cab.

Nearly five years later, on Sunday 23 January 1955, the serious train crash at Sutton Coldfield resulted in the Birmingham County Emergency Scheme coming into effect. Immediately members from Birmingham, Sutton Coldfield, Nelson and Mitchells & Butlers Divisions reported to the site and formed themselves into practical teams for first aid, welfare, comfort and rescue. Some nursing members also reported for duty at the casualty section of the hospital. Two ambulances were quickly on the scene with the mobile first-aid dressing station driven by Divisional Officer Sanderson of King's Heath who, together with Divisional Officer Meredith, remained at the scene throughout the night, going into the wreckage to rescue passengers and into the cab to recover the bodies of the driver and fireman. These two, with Divisional Officer Hunt and Privates Dayman and Titmus, who remained on constant duty for 43 hours, were awarded the Brigade's Meritorious Service Certificate.

At the height of the holiday season in 1952 the borders of Devonshire and Somerset were struck by torrential rain and the rivers burst their banks. In Lynmouth and Lynton the swollen waters rushed through the streets, tearing down signs and causing severe damage to housing. On the night of 15/16 August Brigade member Edwin Smith tried desperately to rescue a woman who was being tumbled about by the raging waters, but was himself swept away and drowned. His colleagues, under the leadership of Divisional Superintendent C. A. Durman, brought their ambulance into the town and rescued several people, some of whom were in imminent danger. Privates Richards and Fouracre (whose home had suffered extensive damage) knew the area well and thus went straight to the points of greatest danger to assist holidaymakers to safety. Across the border in Somerset, the Minehead Division was involved with emergency feeding and billeting, first aid for survivors and, inevitably, comfort and welfare. In all these instances the men and women of St John responded magnificently to the emergency calls, their first thoughts being for the care and well-being of others. They gave their time and their skill . . . and one man gave his life.

It was inevitable that the advent of nuclear weapons would cause new fears and present new tasks to those who controlled the emergency services. As one of those services, the Brigade was expected to play its part in Civil Defence and as early as 1948 preparations were made to ensure that the Surgeons and the Association could update their teaching. The Brigade would be trained not only to carry out the instruction but also to lead members of the public and Civil Defence personnel in basic first aid. Rescue parties were to be given special training, provided by the Order and BRCS. A National Hospitals Reserve was set up to support the Civil Defence effort and both the BRCS and St John were requested to recruit personnel. Although the Second World War had passed, there were many smaller wars around the world and it is not surprising to hear that St John members played their part in these. One interesting coincidence reflected back to China at the turn of the century; when the hospital ship *Maine III* was sent to Korea to transport wounded to Japan, in charge of the welfare staff and VADs was Miss Dorothy Haigh who had joined Royton Division in 1934. St John welfare staff also served in the early days of the Malayan emergency, then in Kenya and later in Cyprus. Some came from the UK, but many others were members of the local Association or Brigade.

In 1950 the Home and Overseas sections of the Brigade were amalgamated. Sir James Sleeman – Overseas Commissioner since 1930 – resigned and the unified Brigade was now controlled by Sir Otto Lund, the new Chief Commissioner. James Sleeman's family had strong ties with India and this might well have encouraged the respect for Commonwealth and Empire which was one of the great driving forces in his life. During his twenty years as Chief Commissioner for Overseas, he carried out ten full official tours and saw the membership increase sixfold from 12,000 to 77,000. An engaging extrovert, he was always impeccably dressed in frock-coat with medals, plumed hat and more often than not carried a cane; his neat spare figure and austere bearing were immediately recognizable. He carved the dates and countries of each tour on his cane – constituting a unique record of Brigade service. For the 1935/36 tour this service entailed travelling a total of 51,600 miles and fulfilling over 1,000 separate engagements: no sinecure! In 1950 when change became necessary, Sleeman was already over the age limit and he took the opportunity to resign. The unification at this time was designed to anticipate the creation of overseas Priories of the Order, who would ultimately control their own centres and units independently of London.

On 6 February 1952, the news that King George VI had died numbed the people of Britain. This quiet, good and faithful sovereign had shouldered the severe burdens of his brother's abdication and the full impact of the Second World War. His wife, as Duchess of York and later as Queen Elizabeth, accepted senior office within the Brigade and provided the inspiration for many members of the Nursing Divisions. Now the men and women of the Brigade undertook the sombre duties connected with the King's lying-in-state and funeral, with detachments from many counties taking part. On 15 February well over 2,000 Brigade staff – very many of whom were nursing members – carried out some form of duty. The women of St John had much to be proud of for their record of service over the years was impressive. In 1949 alone the nursing members completed 143,000 separate public duties ranging from assistance at a beach hut to ward duty at Charing Cross Hospital. Many nursing members were involved in welfare duties, industrial first aid and – until these were taken over by the State – the Medical Comforts Depots.

The Coronation of Her Majesty Queen Elizabeth II was scheduled to take place on 2 June 1953. The new Queen would be the sixth Sovereign Head of the Order of St John and the youngest. As preparations for the Coronation progressed, it became clear that this would be the largest public duty yet undertaken, with some 8,294 members involved of which 3,266 came from the counties. One hundred first-aid posts were spaced along the 6¾-mile processional route, with additional dressing-stations at various points. About 4,000 members reported for duty at 5 a.m. and did not stand down until the early evening. Apart from the ceremonies in the capital there were lively celebrations throughout the nation and many local divisions provided the necessary coverage for their neighbours at fêtes, street parties, pageants and parades. For some St John members there was a complete week of light-hearted but important duty; nevertheless, however pleasant the tasks there was still a feeling of immense relief when it was all over and tired feet could be rested.

Public duty on the roads and beaches has been a continuing feature of the St John Ambulance Brigade's work. At Brixton and Southend, an average of nearly 1,500 cases were dealt with during the summer months of 1952 and this was typical of activity throughout the nation. But the Brigade also took to the water whenever the need arose, one of the earliest and most important coastal duties being in connection with the Queen's Coronation when the Fleet was reviewed at Spithead.

Members from the Isle of Wight and Hampshire Divisions established shore-based stations in the normal way, but they also prepared two boats as mobile first-aid posts and cruised amongst the thousands of yachts and motor boats which had thronged to the area. And not in vain, for they treated sixty cases.

As Britain gradually settled into its new mould the social changes wrought during and immediately after the war began to have their effect upon the nation's leisure activities. Many more people took to riding, hill-walking and climbing and of course sailing and 'messing about in boats'. To some of these St John was no newcomer; in Filey the local Division had provided men for the lifeboat as far back as 1926, and as recently as 1975 there were five St John men out of a crew of six. The team made several sea rescues every year and in one year twenty-six people were brought safely to shore – half of these in one week during the height of summer. Elsewhere around the coasts the men of the Brigade were helping to provide a rescue service, and it must be acknowledged that at this stage it was the White Cross belt of the men which undertook the lion's share of the work. Through the sixties and into the seventies, more and more boats crowded the coastal waters and the risk of accidents inevitably increased. In Wales during 1974 there were twenty-five coastal rescues; the following year a boat carrying nine men was caught in a fierce tide-rip, swept against a bridge and dashed to pieces. Some men clung to the pier of the bridge, some tried to hold on to pieces of the boat. County Staff Officer Wilfred Pitman and David Inkman launched a Loughor rescue boat and picked up eight of the men, the ninth being rescued later after a full-scale air and sea search. Even more recently, in 1985, a surfer who had got into difficulties off the Barry coast was saved by St John Ambulance. In Weymouth, Dorset, the Olympic yachting trials during 1977 required first-aid cover and the local Division was part of a joint coordinated service. To be prepared for this type of first aid requires special training which is given at the National Coastal Rescue Centre, Port Talbot. Essex County sent a team of personnel to this centre during 1975; they were worked very hard, expected to do a great deal of pre-course work and then after the course would need to be constantly alert to new opportunities for gaining further special training and experience.

If the seas around our coasts are dangerous, the cliffs are hardly less so and there are similar dangers on the mountains and rock-faces inland. Climbing has become a popular and well organized recreation with its own high standards of training and preparation, but accidents still happen and St John Ambulance has helped many climbers – experts and novices – to safety. A call for help from a cliff or rock-face requires the most careful, courageous and immediate response if the victim is to be recovered without further harm. The Brigade Service in Guernsey in July 1946 was faced with the problem of a youth who had fallen thirty feet on to rocks. As he lay there concussed, with a broken leg and arm and also serious lacerations to the head and body, two teams were rushing to his rescue; the first team lowered a stretcher and rescue equipment from the cliff top, while the second came in by boat, swimming the last few yards and climbing up to the injured man so as to avoid any fragments of rock being dislodged and causing further injury. A similar rescue was performed by the Sidmouth Division in 1950, when a young man had been trapped on a ledge fifty feet from the cliff-top for five hours. Cyril Irish was lowered on two ropes into a gully so as to reach the stranded man; after treating his immediate injuries, he tied him to one of the ropes and accompanied him to the top as the St John team hauled him up.

In the Lake District the Ambleside Ambulance Division was given the title of the Langdale Rescue Squad because of its dedicated work in rescuing people over an area of 200 square miles. The terrain they worked over varied from deep peat bog to difficult rock climbs. Such a task requires detailed knowledge of the ground and of the special equipment which may be necessary; moreover the men have to be physically fit, mentally alert and capable of operating in the worst weather. On one occasion in the early days of the team's existence, a stretcher could not be moved up to the casualty and so he was tied to the back of one member of the team, using the long toggle ropes which formed part of their equipment. This fellow then carried him over broken ground and scree in a long descent to firm ground, where he was tied on to the stretcher using the same toggle rope. Not surprisingly this team earned a formal Vote of Thanks from the Chapter-General for its consistently courageous work.

Although St John Ambulance is not authorized to operate in Scotland, the Chapter-General decided that the Priory of Scotland – as a part of the Venerable Order – should support the concept of a mountain rescue team for the Highlands and in 1967 a grant was made by the Order to help finance the project. A special vehicle with winches, lean-to tents and an appropriate first-aid kit was purchased. Indirectly, therefore, St John is providing a service here as in other parts of Britain.

In Wales a mountain rescue service was sponsored by the Brigade and this now provides some of the finest rescue and first-aid instruction available in the UK. Dr Ieuan Jones of the C. and A. Hospital in Bangor teaches students who come from all over Britain, with special or basic courses being held in Scotland at Fort George, for the RUC and for the RAF stations at Valley and St Athan – as well as in Jersey and of course in Wales, normally at Plas-y-Brenin. Dr J. N. Parry, Commander St John Ambulance for Wales, rightly draws attention to the high standards necessary to achieve success on these courses – it is not enough merely to attend and some courses have suffered high failure rates because Dr Jones and his team are so exacting.

The Derbyshire Peaks area is served by a Mountain Rescue Unit which has brought many people to safety, but there is another reason why Derbyshire should feature in this chapter. The County possesses three mounted Divisions and is only the second St John area in the world to provide first aid on horseback – the first being Fiji! Derwent was the first area to saddle up, followed by the Northern area of the county and finally the Peaks area. These mounted Divisions are expensive to run and require very careful organization, but they do have the marked advantage of speedy movement over difficult terrain and the ability to carry heavier equipment. In Hampshire the large tracts of the New Forest are also patrolled by a St John mounted Division.

As well as providing a service to the holiday public on the hills and beaches, St John Ambulance had for several years arranged for rescue and first-aid craft on rivers and reservoirs. The Thames is patrolled on its upper reaches by Reading (Berkshire) River Division, which in 1969 built its own rescue boat and collected funds for store-rooms and equipment. It was a successful venture first because real assistance was provided for the public, and second because the members found that new and stronger ties evolved from working together. Morale and motivation improved. It was therefore a great shock when their hut and boat were irreparably damaged by vandals. New craft were eventually provided and in a period of four years the Division undertook 300 patrols covering 2,280 hours and dealt with 286 incidents. Weybridge Division also provides a boat for the Thames and for a local sailing club. The lower reaches of the Thames are covered by the Thames Tideway Division of London District, whose personnel in red coveralls with the St John badge on their backs made a colourful addition to the Lord Mayor's Show in 1976.

Rutland Water is one of Britain's largest man-made lakes. Completed in 1976, the reservoir is used for boating and fishing. John Fry, whose son Peter had tragically died in a boating accident, created the Peter Fry Rescue Trust which took the form of a rescue organization managed as a joint venture by the Royal Life Saving Society and St John Ambulance. The two organizations immediately began joint planning and training and purchased boats. Every member was required to hold the Bronze Medallion of the RLSS, to possess a current First-Aid Certificate and belong to either the RLSS or SJAB. After initial training, new members were also required to be proficient in boat-handling and water rescue methods. Ventures such as this are never easy to initiate and great credit is due to Leicestershire County Staff Officers Roy Davenport and John Nuttall, who became involved with administration and organization from the outset. The story continued on 28 October 1977 when a purpose-built rescue centre and HQ was opened by Peter Fry's mother, who was thus able to see that her son was being remembered in the best possible way – by serving the boating public.

So by the mid-1960s the people of Britain were taking advantage of two decades of peace. Their leisure pursuits had become more adventurous and therefore potentially more dangerous, there were many more cars on the road and air travel was becoming commonplace. Increased affluence was beginning to be followed by new problems affecting the social life of Britain. For a while – particularly during the 1950s – the fortunes of the Brigade had improved, but this progress was not being sustained and so there was more to be done but fewer members were coming forward. The pressures of change remained and it was becoming clear that voluntary organizations required to change also and so be in step with modern society.

10
ST JOHN CADETS

In 1903 a group of Brigade members in Sutton-in-Ashfield, Nottingham, formed a 'juvenile unit' for young men aged between 14 and 17 years. They were given a beret, belt and haversack and so began their first-aid training. At one point there were as many as thirty members in this unit, all playing a valuable part in their local Division. The group lasted for several years, but since it was not accompanied by any national initiative it ultimately lapsed and almost twenty years were to pass before the cadet movement of the Brigade was formally instituted.

In March 1922, Brigade Order No. 416 inaugurated the Cadet Branch of the Brigade as we know it today by authorizing the formation of Cadet Divisions 'to afford facilities for juveniles to meet together for instruction in junior and senior first aid and home nursing'. Boys and girls aged 11–16 were in the junior section, and aged 16–18 in the senior section. At the age of 18, those who had obtained the adult first-aid certificate could join the adult Divisions and in this lay the essential difference between the St John cadets and other youth organizations which did not have an adult service commitment. The early uniform for boys was to consist of a black Balmoral cap, grey flannel shirt, black and white tie, black shorts with thin white stripe, grey stockings, belt, haversack and armband. The concept of annual re-examination was envisaged for cadets as well as for the adults.

On 25 May the first Cadet Division to be formed under this order was that of the Gateshead Girl Cadets. In June an Ambulance Cadet Division was formed at Aldershot and a Nursing Division at Shipley in Yorkshire. Other Cadet Divisions were also formed during the remainder of 1922, and of particular note is the formation on the same day – 18 November 1922 – of the Ambulance and Nursing Cadet Divisions at Rochdale in Lancashire, the first area to create the two divisions simultaneously. In fact the Roche cadets, as they were called,

111

proved to be among the most successful Cadet Divisions in Britain. Three years later, the first overseas Cadet Divisions were formed in Bombay, the Ambulance Division on 1st October 1925 and the Nursing Division on 25th October. By this time the Brigade at home could boast of a total of nearly 3,000 cadets, and by 1928 the number had risen to over 4,000 while overseas cadets had increased to 460.

Guidance for cadet behaviour is provided by the 'Cadet Code of Chivalry' and – like the Scout law – the young people are expected to know it and to live by it. The cadets promise to serve God, to be loyal to the Sovereign, observe the mottoes of the Order, help the suffering and be thorough, kind and thoughtful. There has always been a need for incentives for young people and in 1931, the Grand Prior's Badge was instituted as the principal and senior cadet award. The first Grand Prior's Badges were awarded on 17 February 1933 to two boys from Slough – G. Anderson and W. Lloyd – and one to a nursing cadet from Australia, Marion Higgins of Marrickville in New South Wales. A year later the first nursing cadet from Britain, Gladys Dodds (also of Slough) received the Badge and in the same year four boys from Christchurch, New Zealand qualified, to become the first Grand Prior boy cadets overseas. In 1946 New Zealand was to take the lead, with a greater number of cadets who qualified for the Badge than in the whole of the remainder of the Commonwealth. Now, more than fifty years later, this award is still among the most respected of youth badges and those who earn it – and earn it they must – are permitted to continue wearing it as adults. There is no quick and easy route to the Grand Prior's Badge, which requires candidates to qualify in no fewer than twelve proficiency awards, selected from a given total.

The requirements for the proficiency badges are such that high degrees of skill and determination are needed. The rock-climbing syllabus, for example, is not just a matter of theory or undertaking a hill walk; this dangerous subject is treated with the seriousness it deserves. Candidates are expected to have experience of the selection, storage and maintenance of clothing and equipment, the ability to conduct basic rope-work involving belaying, abseiling, the use of carabiniers and descendeurs and climbing with top ropes. Each candidate must actually climb four selected routes and prove that he/she has done preparatory training. Only the highest standards are acceptable for such activities, and the Brigade insists upon meeting those standards whatever the sex of the candidate.

The service of the boys and girls who joined the Cadet Division before 1939 consisted by and large in the provision of routine support to their adult division at local events and on major public duty. Like youngsters everywhere they had high spirits and were not averse to poking a little fun at the system, as when one described a skeleton as a man with his inside out and his outside off! Their training was in the hands of an officer specifically appointed for cadet work and most of the older members had qualified for their adult certificates and transferred at the age of 18.

We have already related how cadets served during the Second World War; when peace returned there were over 32,000 boys and girls ready to continue that service in peace. But the world had moved on and the forms of training and service which were acceptable in 1939 were no longer suitable. There was need for more outdoor activity and greater use of film for instruction purposes. Cornwall took the lead in 1945 by making a film *Cadets of the White Cross* which was loaned to other counties; the same year saw the first issue of a journal specifically for cadets, *The St John Cadet*. Also in 1945, Ebbw Vale Ambulance Cadet Division formed one of the first Parent Associations, which provided a good family and social base as well as a stimulus to further achievement. In the same period, consideration was given to youngsters under the age of eleven being allowed to join the cadets; many had already done so unofficially and Brigade Circular 4 of 1948 regularized this situation with the formation of the junior branch. Special Service Shields for award to those cadets who had completed over 200 hours of voluntary service were also instituted. At the same time planning was begun for a specific cadet competition, the first Cadet Finals being held on 28 November 1947 in London. The Duchess of Kent, Lady Superintendent-in-Chief for Wales, presented winner's trophies to Horsham (Ambulance seniors), Southwick (Ambulance juniors), Weymouth (Nursing seniors) and Ipswich (Nursing juniors). Morale and motivation were already high throughout the movement when in 1948 Princess Margaret became Commandant-in-Chief of the Cadets, a position she held with distinction and real awareness until 1970 when she handed over to her niece Princess Anne.

The period from 1945 to 1950 was therefore one of great progress for the Cadet Branch of the Brigade not only in terms of organization but also with regard to activity. Cadet camps were initiated so that the qualities of self-reliance, self-discipline, teamwork and outdoor skills could all be developed, whilst at the same time everyone could enjoy themselves and have fun. The idea of camping and outdoor training is not new, nor is it unique to St John, but it is an important ingredient of cadet training. Counties have held successful and enjoyable camps for many years, either at the national St John camping site near Bexhill or at various locations of their own choosing. For a long time these camps followed a fairly familiar pattern, but since the end of the Second World War a new spirit of adventure has been generated and camps have become more challenging. One development of this theme is the conduct of survival and rescue courses now held at Woodlands, about ten miles from Birmingham. Cadets from Hornchurch (Essex) who were attending the course were unfortunate to encounter the worst possible weather, and for them the survival phase following a notional air crash seemed very real. The boys and girls had to build shelters and cook food – using debris from the 'crash' – as well as treating crash victims. In pouring rain and driving wind the juniors and cadets got down to work and put up a very creditable performance for this phase. The rescue phase which followed involved incidents created around an obstacle course and here the victims had to be treated and recovered in difficult and potentially dangerous situations. Cadets from Cleveland who were camping on the shores of Ullswater met similar weather, but were able to succeed in all their adventure and rescue activities, including a night exercise to search for and recover casualties following an accident.

The experience gained by the cadets at these camps encourages the development of qualities of endurance, self-reliance and leadership, all of which are needed as adults. There are other avenues, not confined to St John, where these characteristics can be further developed, for example Outward Bound courses, Sail Training expeditions and the Duke of Edinburgh's Award. Outward Bound training is designed to discover the resilience, physical and mental stamina and personal determination of each individual. Most people are not aware of the extent of their own internal reserves and this form of training raises levels of self-confidence as well as enabling members to come to grips with the practical problems of human relationships and communications. Outward Bound courses also qualify successful participants for some aspects of the Duke of Edinburgh's Award and a large number of cadets naturally attempt the three stages: bronze, silver and gold. One of the more satisfactory features of the last decade has been the increase in bids by the Counties to send their cadets on these courses and to take part in adventurous activity. The Sail Training Association's ships *Winston Churchill* and *Malcolm Miller* have provided really valuable training and experience for the older cadets who have joined them as crew.

Competitions with an expedition or adventure background – but combined with the traditional skills of St John Ambulance – were begun early on in the new 'outdoors' phase. In 1970 North Yorkshire's Cadet Staff Officers, John Coward and John Morley began an annual cadet rescue competition and as the years have progressed the tests have become more demanding and the venues more difficult. A great deal is required of the individual and the team in these competitions, which applies as much to the judges as to the cadets, judging having been done with a Brigade officer and a Safety officer attending each event. Selby Nursing Cadets Division has provided casualties for these occasions and support has also come from British Rail, British Telecom and of course from the Association, whose members assist casualties and provide judges. The problems set are realistic and based on actual situations, within the competence of the well-trained and demanding leadership, teamwork, decision-making, physical stamina and first-aid skill. It is not an easy event to organize, nor was it easy to succeed, but everyone who attempted the competition gained greatly from taking part.

The opportunity to use one's training to save life in a real emergency does not arise frequently, but when crises have occurred the cadets have proved fully able to deal with them. Many cadets of all ages and both sexes have received awards for their bravery and in 1947 the 8th United States Air Force stationed in Britain presented a trophy to be awarded annually for gallantry. Betty Matthews of Littlehampton, Sussex, was the first recipient, followed by Jack Harwood of Bodmin, Cornwall. The third was Betty Ives of Andover, Wiltshire: aged only twelve and still learning to swim, she rescued a boy from a gravel pit, cleaned weed from his mouth, gave him artificial respiration and brought him to the shore where adults took over. There is no doubt that but for her courage and skill this boy would certainly have drowned. Many other instances of bravery can of course be cited. In Wales, for example, a student member David Glyn Thomas was working in the Duffryn Rhondda Colliery when a roof-fall occurred, trapping a miner. David hurried to the scene and assisted in preventing further harm to the man, treating those injuries which he could see and remaining with him while a large boulder was moved. After this he completed his first-aid treatment and the man was taken to hospital. We have to bear in mind the conditions under which this work was done to appreciate the real impact of David's quiet bravery.

By 1951, it was necessary to create the grade of 'student member' at the older end of the cadet scale, for those cadets who had gained the adult certificate but were not yet old enough to transfer to the adult division; today the name has been changed to 'Youth Divisions' and in Surrey the Youth Divisions formed a 'youth column' – a kind of St John Emergency Flying Column which owned its own Land-Rover and attended outdoor and adventure events, providing a most valuable first-aid service under tough conditions. As might be expected a significant proportion of these older St John cadets, particularly the girls, opt for careers in medicine or nursing and have generally been very successful.

In 1953 the cadets of the East Coast divisions showed their resolve as well as their skill when heavy rain and mountainous seas caused extensive and severe flooding. The great majority put on their uniforms and reported to their Ambulance Halls without waiting for instructions from their officers. On arrival they were given important if routine tasks dealing with evacuation, child welfare, the sorting and distribution of comforts, messages and the care of the aged and homeless. Vital work was done at a critical period in the relief operation and this was real work – not just something to keep youngsters out of the way; it was also hard work, and sometimes distressing for young people to do the things which had to be done, but they carried out their tasks willingly, efficiently and cheerfully. Some of the older cadets helped the adult Divisions and one – John Price, aged sixteen, from Grays in Essex – spent 144 hours on duty in one week. During this time he personally rescued a man whose eyes had been damaged and later responded to a call from a harassed father who asked him to catch his children as he dropped them from a first-floor window, his ground floor being flooded to a depth of several feet. This done, John took the whole family to a relief centre. All in all he made thirty separate visits to flooded areas, on one occasion carrying a crippled woman down a ladder on his back and placing her in a rowing-boat. He was awarded the American Cup for Gallantry in 1953 and also the Order's Life Saving Medal in Silver.

From Chester in 1955 comes a story of two boys who, while on their way home from a training night, saw a family trapped on the top floor of a burning house. Fred Whitley and Kenneth Rogers immediately sent for the emergency services and entered the house, reaching the

Above: HRH Princess Margaret presents the American Cup for Gallantry to John Price who had won the cup as a Cadet and transferred to his local adult division *(Mirrorpic – Daily Mirror)*

Right: Cadet Joanna Holder at the presentation of her Certificate of Honour

Above: Pilots of the St John Ambulance Air Wing discussing a mission

Right: Kirk Ireton, Derby – St John on horseback, 1977 *(Derbyshire Times, Chesterfield)*

Right: SJAB volunteers bringing out the injured at the Eltham rail disaster. June 1972 *(Associated Newspapers Limited)*

Facing page: Ealing train crash. SJAB members were quickly to the scene to help. 1973 *(The Times)*

Below: The Flying Christine II – Guernsey's 'rescue' boat

AMBULANCE ☩ LAUNCH

HRH The Duke of Gloucester, Grand Prior of the Order of St John

Lady Moyra Browne (Superintendent-in-Chief), Rosemary Bailey
(Chief Nursing Officer) and Helen Gribble (Deputy Chief Nursing
Officer) and Roy Archibald return from inspecting a mine. 1976 *(F*

p: HRH Princess Anne at Avon Tyrrell where St John helps the disabled
...oliday. Franz Stevens (blind), Tom Yendell (thalidomide victim)
...Yvonne Townsend produce the holiday newspaper. 1983 *(Glenys Duke)*

... South Molton Division (Devon) receives the welfare cup for its
... the blizzards of February 1978

stricken family only to discover that the parents were unconscious and one of the four children was lying asphyxiated. The two boys revived the father before returning to bring out the mother who was still unconscious. They then went with the family to hospital and wrote a report of the incident; only then did they return to their own homes. More recently during the tense situation in Northern Ireland, two 15-year-old girl cadets of the Belfast Fourth River Division were the first trained civilians on the scene of the explosion which rocked the Abercorn restaurant. They told the Army unit that they were first-aiders and were promptly given a kit and allowed into the sealed area. These two young girls, Hilary Ferguson and Lee Moore, then treated the victims until the arrival of the official ambulance; the danger might have passed, but the horror remained and they did what they could to help. Hilary said afterwards, 'It was awful. I'll never forget it.' Nor should we forget this and all the other efforts of cadets who, though young, set out to serve mankind not only by these acts of bravery but also through the less spectacular but vital means of giving simple assistance to the public.

It would be easy for cadets to become bound up with their own local organization, but the concept of a national movement of charity is not lost on these young people. The cadets of Gwent and Lancashire, both Ambulance and Nursing divisions, arranged an exchange of visits during 1976. At Easter the lads and lasses from Lancashire visited Wales, and in October the reciprocal visit was made. In the same year the cadets of Cornwall, Devon, Dorset and Somerset gathered for a joint rally at the Royal Marines Training Centre at Lympstone. Older cadets from Plymouth, Sidmouth and St Ives laid on a demonstration of a cliff rescue, highly relevant to those who live near the West Coast cliffs. Cadets from Dorset and Somerset also showed how canoes could be built and then demonstrated their use as inland first-aid boats. Princess Margaret, Grand President of St John Ambulance, visited this camp accompanied by Sir Maurice Dorman who was then Chief Commander; she was impressed by the activity taking place at all age levels and later presented fifty-two Grand Prior's Badges.

However, the idea of getting to know and understand others extends beyond the shores of Britain. In June 1977 more than a hundred cadets from Oxfordshire visited Malta for a ten-day camp and goodwill visit. The same year saw ten young St John members, including cadets, travel across the world to camp as guests of the New Zealand cadets at Wanganui, where in 1927 Edward Gilberd had founded the first Cadet

Division outside Britain. Their fellow guests were from Australia and Fiji, so the British contingent was able not only to obtain valuable experience of the first-aid methods used where distances are considerable and the terrain is rugged, but also – of great importance – gain insight into the 'any weather' concept of training and competitions. The two officers who accompanied this group – James Bond, Staff Officer Training for Essex and Katherine Guilbert of Guernsey – were loud in their praises for the visit and their feelings were echoed by Trevor Dick, Chief Cadet Officer of New Zealand, in a letter subsequently written to Grosvenor Crescent.

Cadets also require some degree of independence in the shape of their own training rooms or HQ, so that in the press of adult activity they are not neglected. Such an HQ was created in Hull after 4,000 voluntary hours of work on a building which required extensive renovation, allied to large-scale fund-raising by the cadets themselves and also the senior Divisions. When on 15 February 1976 the Archbishop of York dedicated the building in the presence of Lord Westbury (then Commander St John Ambulance, Humberside), the boys and girls who had shown the grit to see the project through could feel justly proud of themselves. Rushden Division encouraged this same pride in its cadets by offering them the challenge of making their own sailing dinghy and using it for first-aid and rescue work.

In 1975 it seemed that too few cadets were prepared to transfer to the adult Divisions on reaching the age of 18. There were some valid reasons – exams, job-hunting and first steps at work – all associated with the difficulties of the 15–18-year age bracket. There were also some excuses, but there was another more worrying reason in some Divisions (though not in all): the dull routine nature of adult practice nights. The years which followed confirmed this trend and also pointed to a slow decline in cadet numbers overall. There was clearly a need for the senior officers of St John Ambulance to take stock and stem the flow if its work was to continue, and many meetings and formal conferences addressed themselves to these problems.

In December 1983 a conference of County Staff Officers (Cadets) was held at the Birmingham HQ of St John Ambulance, West Midlands. John Sunderland, then Commander SJA and now Commissioner-in-Chief, welcomed the delegates, who included two HQ Staff Officers with highly relevant experience. Laurie Hawes (Chief Staff Officer) and Jenny Eaves (HQ Staff Officer Cadets) both began their St John service at an early age. Jenny, a member of a St John family, was a junior at the age of eight, then a cadet who received her Grand Prior's Badge from Princess Margaret in 1969. From 1966 to 1983 she competed at the Brigade Finals, being a member of the Preston Combined Division which won the Perrott Shield in 1974, the first combined division to do so. As an adult member she had been involved with both the Association and the Brigade as Secretary, Instructor and Training Manager. In 1982 Jenny was appointed Staff Officer Cadets at HQ, where her experience at the working end is proving invaluable. Laurie's service is no less impressive; joining Gillingham as a cadet in 1944, he later went to Headquarters as a Staff Officer and Assistant Registrar, became Staff Manager in 1974 and in 1976 took over the appointment of Registrar. Such experience is bound to bring benefit to discussion of the cadet training programmes. But cadet experience also plays its part in the field of command; Derek Fenton, formerly of Ealing Division and its Competition Secretary, rose through every rank in the adult Divisions to become Commander of No. 1 (Prince of Wales's) District which is responsible for so many central public duties. Harold Touzeau, now Commander of Guernsey, joined the Brigade as a cadet and has given fifty years of service. Men and women like these who are now in positions of great responsibility will never forget to look to their cadets for responsible service, nor will they withhold their own support from the Cadet Branch.

The convention which restricts St John Ambulance first-aid activity to the English side of the Tweed has not prevented the establishment of a flourishing and hard-working cadet unit in Scotland. The Denny Cadets from Larbert have given such consistently good service to the elderly, disabled and the hospitals in their area that they were given a grant of £1,000 from the Royal Jubilee Trust. Mr D. Watson Law, Supervisor of the cadets, decided that this gift would be used to purchase a projector and screen to assist with the training of handicapped young people. These cadets constitute an extremely fine example of service, well recognized by the Priory of Scotland.

There are no conventions regarding who may and who may not be a St John cadet; physical handicap is no barrier, as was proved by Mandy Truslove of Warwickshire who at one time was unable to walk, but who put in more than 200 voluntary hours to earn the Service Shield. Emergency first-aid has been taught to deaf youngsters who were able to complete much of the training, and also to two blind cadets who passed their examinations. It was not an easy decision for the Commissioner-in-Chief to accept these youngsters as uniformed cadets, since they would always have a limited capability and possibly would not become fully qualified adults. However, the cadets enjoyed their service, made new friends and in the process taught the less handicapped members a few things about determination.

The Cadet Branch is not devoted solely to first aid and outdoor activities: music, drama, authorship and painting are all recognized and encouraged so that there is a broad spectrum of achievement and understanding, not least of the ways in which they fit in to the structure of society. In 1953 an article by the Dean of Westminster was carried in *The Cadet* explaining the significance, solemnity and dignity which lay behind the glitter of the Coronation of the Queen. Barely a month later 1,700 cadets were enjoying the fun of the Coronation Camp at Strubbers in Essex, where they were joined by cadets from the Commonwealth; and the following year the cadets assembled for a rally in Hyde Park. This famous expanse of green was to be the venue for the Golden Jubilee in 1972, where the fiftieth anniversary of the St John Cadets was celebrated in the presence of HRH Princess Anne. The Princess, who devotes so much of her time to the welfare of children, spoke to the cadets as their Commandant-in-Chief, complimenting them on their perseverance and preparedness. Then she announced that the prestigious Albert Schweitzer Prize, presented by the Goethe Foundation of Switzerland for service to humanity, had been awarded to the St John Cadets.

In January 1986, Ringmer (Sussex) Combined Cadet Division and Newton Abbot Nursing Cadet Division went to Adelaide in South Australia for the first Commonwealth Cadet Championship, where they were competing against teams from Australia, Canada, Fiji, Malaysia and Papua New Guinea. Despite the high standards of all the teams, Ringmer carried home the championship – a proud day for all the British cadets.

If the training and development of the St John cadets is to continue to meet these high standards, there will be a continuing need for efficient, effective and well-motivated cadet leaders: men and women whose selection and preparation is of the utmost importance. The Brigade has always acknowledged its debt to cadet officers, whose work involves a great degree of personal responsibility, and it is only natural that considerable emphasis is laid on their training. The first residential camp for cadet leaders took place during 1942, when the number of Cadet Divisions had begun to show a marked increase. By 1955 the subjects being covered at a leaders' course included 'The Social and

Psychological Needs of Youth', 'Teaching Methods', 'Hospital Work', 'Leadership' and of course routine matters such as regulations, correspondence and insurance, all of which must be studied if the cadet is to be looked after properly and allowed to develop his or her full potential. Today cadet leadership is just as important – perhaps even more so – in a society where violence, divisiveness and prejudices are rife and 'kicks' offer an easy alternative to sustained and self-disciplined service. The modern concepts of leadership training, where age and rank are of less importance than commitment and competence, are bringing forward young men and women who attend such events as the Outward Bound 12-day course for those whose work prevents them from taking the longer training. In this way younger leaders are being prepared for their vitally important role as cadet officers. The cadets need support from their adult partners and from the public because they remain a vital investment in the future of St John; not only are they citizens of St John, they are the future citizens of Britain.

Many officers of the Brigade, including several who started their service as cadets, have acknowledged that St John 'sort of runs in the family' and one of the most commendable aspects of St John Ambulance is its family spirit. First it is a family of colleagues, all of whom serve with the same aim, and second it contains so many members whose families have served the Brigade and the Order for many years. In fact there are few charitable and voluntary organizations which can claim such a strong family tradition – one which embraces men, women and youngsters from all walks of life. Lord Scarbrough was a most dedicated Sub-Prior of the Order for two decades from 1923 to 1943; his daughter, Lady Serena James, was President of a County and a Division for forty years from 1940 to 1980; his grand-daughter, Lady Westbury, has served as a County President and is now Superintendent-in-Chief with a total of thirty-three years of service, while her husband Lord Westbury has served in various appointments, including Commander St John Ambulance Humberside, since 1967; finally their son, Lord Scarbrough's great-grandson, is himself a member of the Order of St John. This represents family service totalling more than one hundred years.

Such a depth of continuity is equally applicable to families whose service has been entirely within the Brigade. George Creech and his wife Mary from Avon completed over 100 years of joint service and had the pleasure of seeing their two sons gain the Grand Prior's Badge and go on to become officers in the Brigade. Then their two grandsons joined the cadets, so that before 1983 – when George and Mary retired – their family had completed 160 years of Brigade service, with three generations serving at the same time and four grades of Order membership represented by the adults. In 1954 the Derham family of Burnley, Lancashire, could also boast of three generations serving at the same time. Florence Broughton of Northampton could claim a family link going back to 1905 when her father had joined the Brigade. She herself retired in 1975 after fifty-one years of service, but had watched with pride her daughter and four grandchildren serving in the Towcester Combined Division; their combined service would total 217 years! Bristol can be proud of its Bookham family, who all decided to take up first aid after a son lost an eye and had to fight for his life. That was in 1978 and now there are seven members of the family serving; in 1984 they completed over 3,000 hours of duty between them.

These and other families in all parts of Britain are carrying on the wonderful St John tradition which provides a focus for loyalty and motivation as well as much needed continuity. Even without the ties of blood, however, there is in the best St John Divisions a family atmosphere which is encouraged by both lay and medical members. Social changes have underlined the need for a stable environment within St John Ambulance and this has coincided with the nursing members having increased influence in Brigade affairs.

11
THE PROFESSIONAL DIMENSION

Early in the Order's search for humanitarian work in Britain, its leaders wished to involve women in the field of auxiliary nursing. It was as long ago as 1873 when a paper was read on St John's Day suggesting that steps be taken to provide nursing training, but after consultation with teaching hospitals and a public meeting no progress was made. However, the seed had been sown and when the Association was formed in 1877 there were many women supporters; indeed the whole ambulance concept was criticized as being 'an ephemeral female fashion'! How wrong this long dead critic was, for women have been working alongside their male colleagues for the whole of the Brigade's history, establishing their own tradition of quiet commitment and competence in the good times and the bad. The contribution of nursing members to the overall achievements of the St John Ambulance Brigade has been of the very greatest importance.

The first nursing corps or guild was formed in Oldham on 15 September 1885, under the guidance of Dr and Mrs Thompson and Miss Barstow. Their aim was the provision of invalid comforts and food for the sick poor by the establishment of a depot and a soup kitchen. Other corps or guilds quickly followed Oldham's example: Ravensthorpe (Yorkshire), Leicester, Richmond (Surrey) and Hull provided women members to look after the sick in specific areas, thus anticipating to some extent the concepts of home nursing and Medical Comforts Depots. They maintained this commitment over the years and Mrs Laverack, Superintendent of the Hull Division, became the first woman to be awarded the Service Medal of the Order which was presented to her in 1901. In 1890 London's first Nursing Corps was formed by Miss Blye Bourke and Dr A. C. Tunstall as a Children's Home Nursing Guild and was later to become No. 1 (Stoke Newington) Nursing Division of London District. These women carried out over 500 visits to the 'sick poor' of Bethnal Green within their first year and made countless loans of sick-room items from their Depot. By now Guernsey and Oxford had also formed Nursing Corps and there was an increased awareness of the need for some district-based nursing capability. Training was arranged at St John House, Worcester and many women – including a large proportion from the working class – trained for certificates in cottage and maternity nursing.

A busy and important year for nursing members was 1893. First the St John's Gate Nursing Division was founded by Mrs Agnes Calvin Lines, Miss Blye Bourke and Mrs Church Brasier, supported by James Cantlie; Mrs Church Brasier became its first Superintendent. Second, a nursing uniform designed by Mrs Calvin Lines and Miss Blye Bourke was worn on public duty with the men in April and later at the Royal Wedding by the 22 nurses on duty. Third, this same uniform was worn when a detachment of nurses led by Mrs Stuart Wardell demonstrated first aid and nursing at the Royal Review in the presence of Queen Victoria, who recorded that this was extremely well done and most useful. Finally, 1893 saw a proposal that a nursing course should be available for men, using the women's syllabus. In the following year the Wellingborough Corps established the first Ambulance Hall, setting an example to the whole of Britain. They appointed a trained nurse, Mrs Pickering, to lead the women's section, thus anticipating the appointment of 'nursing officers' at the various organizational levels in the Brigade. The remaining years of the nineteenth century saw further increases in the nursing membership of the Brigade, so that when the Boer War began there were some 1,250 women out of a total Brigade strength approaching 9,000. Their distinctive long black dresses with white bibbed apron and collar were topped by a black straw bonnet with white organdie frills and tapes and from their waists they hung the reticule which held their personal first-aid kit and scissors. For inclement weather, they wore a black cloak with shoulder cape displaying the St John Ambulance badge on the right shoulder.

On 21 February 1911, Lady Perrott was appointed to the new post of Lady Superintendent-in-Chief of Nursing Corps and Divisions in the Brigade. She was no stranger to the work of St John for her husband, Sir Herbert Perrott, had been Chief Secretary of the Association for over thirty years. One of her first tasks was to arrange for specific nursing attachments to London and provincial hospitals so as to provide up-to-date training and replace the courses previously held at St John House, Worcester. Under the inspired leadership of Lady Perrott the

Nursing Divisions flourished and in 1912, 2,000 out of a total membership of 4,600 members were on parade at the Royal Review at Hyde Park. In the following year, 200 nursing officers assembled for an important conference at 'The Gate'. In 1914 the nursing members went to war as VADs either in home hospitals or overseas, including service with the St John Ambulance Brigade Hospital in Étaples; it was here that Sister Bain was killed during the German bombing in May 1918. During the period of the war, well over 9,000 nursing members served in some capacity.

The years from 1920 to 1939 were divided into a period of crisis and economic depression which was followed by a few years of comparative stability. The Nursing Divisions were delighted when in 1922 Lady Perrott presented an impressive competition shield in memory of her husband and this remains the principal competition award for nursing members to the present day. It immediately provided an incentive for improved performance and a rallying point for them, maintaining morale during the years of the Depression. By 1931 there were 579 Nursing Divisions with a membership of some 13,000 and during the years leading up to the Second World War the women members of the Brigade undertook more and more responsibility; this was a period when few women went out to work, so they could devote some time to the Medical Comforts Depots and to service at the beach first-aid huts. They continued to attend on public duty in uniform and were also doing a great deal of work such as hospital duty and visiting the sick at home in addition to their normal Brigade functions. The Nursing Divisions were beginning to make a significant impact on the Brigade and were gaining more and more influence at all levels, but this development was overshadowed by crisis in 1939 when war came.

The work of the nursing members during the war of 1939–1945 – either as part of the Joint War Organization or in an independent capacity with their home divisions – has already been summarized in an earlier chapter. In all, 31,000 St John women helped in a wide variety of ways to pull Britain through.

The end of the Second World War brought a degree of reluctance to continue in uniformed service, but the Nursing Divisions appear to have retained their members somewhat better than the men. In 1949, nursing members carried out over 143,000 separate duties, most of which would have required two or more hours of work. The womenfolk of Britain were not yet going to work outside home to the extent that they do now, so were still available to perform the normal duties.

However, already there were signs of change, due first to a national shortfall in trained professional nurses and second to increasing awareness of the welfare requirements of the country. The National Health Bill – which brought in the National Health Service – required changes in policy because of State management. The inevitable result of these pressures was increased work for the nursing members, who now attended hospitals on a regular basis, undertook duty in support of the NHS professional nurses and increased their local visiting and welfare work for infants, orthopaedic clinics and elderly patients at home. The Nursing Divisions in the late 1940s and early 1950s were good recruiting areas for professional nursing, but they were also involved in the running of comforts depots, blood transfusion centres and industrial first aid. Lady Louis Mountbatten, Superintendent-in-Chief in 1950, was able to claim that the 'quiet, unobtrusive, voluntary service rendered by the nursing personnel throughout the Commonwealth entails much self-sacrifice and is worthy of all praise'.

There is a sense of continuity and stability in the nursing ranks of the Brigade, exemplified by the fact that over a period of seventy-five years the present Superintendent-in-Chief, Lady Westbury, is only the sixth to hold this post. Lady Perrott, whose inspiring and charming leadership had placed the nursing members in the eye of the public, held the appointment throughout the First World War and the years of the Depression into the period of consolidation which preceded the Second War. In 1939 her failing health and advancing years demanded that she should seek more rest and Mrs Lorna St John Atkinson was appointed to succeed her. Regrettably, however, this dedicated and popular woman of whom so much was expected was stricken by illness and died in July 1942.

The person chosen to lead the nursing members through the Second World War was Lady Louis Mountbatten, later Countess Mountbatten of Burma but invariably known as 'Lady Louis' by those who had known her previously. Her commitment to the sick and wounded during the war is a legend and she did not spare herself; in all her travels she sought out those who were responsible for helping the suffering and satisfied herself that everything possible was being done for their well-being. She possessed not only that charm and charisma which drew people instinctively towards her, but also the capacity for attention to detail which meant that nothing would be forgotten and the determination to see a problem through to a solution – not to mention a memory for names which was awe-inspiring! No wonder that from the most senior Commissioner to the most junior nursing member, she was instantly respected and admired. She represented the care, the smile and the grit of the nursing members of the Brigade in one of their finest hours. When the war was over she continued to travel both at home and overseas to further the aims of St John, and even when Vicereine of India she found time for St John work. When Lady Mountbatten died in Jesselton in 1960 during a tour of the Far East, the Order and the Nursing Divisions of the Brigade lost a leader of world stature. It was fitting that her coffin should be draped with the flag of the Order and borne by members of St John as it began its journey back to Britain.

Marjorie Countess of Brecknock had served in the ATS during the war and in 1946 she joined the Brigade, becoming HQ Staff Officer to her cousin Lady Mountbatten and later Deputy Comptroller for overseas matters. By 1960 she had already acquired sixteen years of HQ experience and was fully familiar with the policies of Lady Mountbatten. She was therefore a natural successor and for the ten years between 1960 and 1970 she held the post of Superintendent-in-Chief. Travelling throughout the Commonwealth, she earned a reputation as an ambassador for the Brigade and also for the Order as a whole. It was perhaps hardly surprising that when she resigned from this busy position she should be invited to become Chief President; when she finally retired from this office in 1984, Lady Brecknock had spent thirty-seven years in the Brigade at National HQ.

In 1970 Lady Moyra Browne was appointed Superintendent-in-Chief after twenty years in the Brigade. She had joined Craig's Court Nursing Division in 1938 as an 'ambulance sister', as nursing members were then called. In 1939 she took up full-time nursing, working in hospitals in Chichester and London and eventually qualifying as an SEN. When the war ended she joined Grosvenor Crescent as Staff Officer to the Chief Officer Nursing Cadets. Family commitments took her away from the Brigade for a while, but in 1964 she rejoined, first as Staff Officer to Lady Brecknock and then as Deputy Superintendent-in-Chief. The hallmark of her service was her contribution to the everyday work at Headquarters in addition to normal visits to Brigade functions at home and overseas, praising and criticizing where appropriate. She initiated the St John Year of Nursing in 1980, which provided the Brigade with ongoing assets including three annual sponsored nursing bursaries and a marked increase in the number of male members taking the nursing certificate. Lady Moyra will be remembered for her initiative and courage when a bomb exploded in a London restaurant in

127

1975. She immediately went to the aid of the victims and probably saved the life of a man when she discovered and removed from the back of his throat a fragment of what had once been a fork; it had been blasted there by the force of the explosion. For thirteen years Lady Moyra led the nursing divisions, but she was the first Superintendent-in-Chief to be designated Deputy Commissioner-in-Chief as well. Thus the present-day practice of women in the Brigade filling appointments hitherto reserved to men was carried a stage further. She handed over to Lady Westbury in 1983.

The present Superintendent-in-Chief and Deputy Commissioner-in-Chief is a member of a family whose service to St John began with her grandfather, the Earl of Scarbrough, who was Sub-Prior of the Order from 1923 to 1943. Lady Westbury became Vice-President of East Riding, Yorkshire in 1954 and her first official task was to welcome Lady Mountbatten to Filey where she opened a new HQ on what she described as 'a magical day, never to be forgotten'. In 1971 Lady Westbury was appointed County President of Humberside, her husband being the County Commander St John Ambulance. Two days after taking up the post she was already busy – visiting Thrapston Quadrilateral Division to present the 97th Grand Prior's Badge won by a cadet. This one division had 100 members and had been run by Superintendent Miss Tiney for twenty years. Having been involved in hospital management for eleven years, it was natural that Lady Westbury would wish to see nursing personnel obtain real experience and she was delighted when the Royal Navy and Royal Air Force agreed to take members for two weeks' training in their hospitals at Plymouth, Portsmouth and Ely – a great privilege.

The Superintendent-in-Chief depends upon the Chief Nursing Officer of the Brigade for professional advice and again St John has been fortunate in the quality and commitment of the women who have held this important post. The first CNO, Miss Noreen Hamilton, qualified at Westminster Hospital and joined the Westminster Division in 1930. In 1949 she was head of the National Hospital Service Reserve prior to being appointed CNO in 1952. In 1960 she handed over to Miss Lucy Duff-Grant, who had trained at St Thomas's Hospital. Miss Duff-Grant later became President of the Royal College of Nursing and was CNO until 1965, when she handed over to Dame Barbara Cozens, a former Matron-in-Chief of Queen Alexandra's Royal Army Nursing Corps who marked her tenure of office by her travels to meet the local members. In 1972 Miss Rosemary Bailey took over as CNO and has already held the post for longer than any of her three predecessors. She joined the Crystal Palace Division in 1955, taught at the Royal College of Midwives and has been particularly interested in training. The workload of the CNO has now greatly increased and Miss Helen Gribble has been appointed Deputy CNO.

The modern nursing members have all the dedication of their predecessors – and they need it, for they have to operate in a very much more difficult environment. They are always ready to relieve hard-pressed hospital staff. In Launceston, Cornwall, three young women started a nursing division and in its very early days the local hospital needed urgent help, being short-staffed due to an outbreak of Asian flu. The surgeon remarked that he had never known St John refuse any aid to the sick and the hospital matron telephoned Christine Best at 6 p.m. that night, asking for someone who could report for duty at 9 a.m. the following morning and for cover to be provided every day for two weeks. Christine took the first duty, reporting in uniform prompt at 9 o'clock, then she arranged reliefs from amongst eight nursing members and between them they helped to keep the hospital going for two critical weeks. A similar situation arose in Wales, where the Cardiff Castle Division was seeking nursing experience at Cardiff General Hospital when the staff and patients were struck down by the flu. The Matron was heard to say, 'Thank goodness the St John are coming in tonight!' Yet another instance of hospital help comes from South-East London where a disastrous fire claimed the lives of twelve teenagers and caused a further thirty casualties, mostly with serious burns. The local hospital was short-staffed and Divisional Nursing Officer Miss H. Wheeldon arranged a St John rota of 54 nursing members, including the latest recruit. Between them they completed 270 valuable hours of duty, giving real help to the hospital and its patients.

There are many instances of individual bravery and skill in the story of the women members of the Brigade, but two must suffice for this account. In 1957, on Sunday 7 June, nursing member Edith Collins (Secretary of Wandsworth and Southfield Division) had just reported for duty at Battersea Park when she was informed that a fairground employee had been struck by one of the coaches of the 'Big Dipper' and was lying on the track 40 feet above the ground. Miss Collins first called an ambulance, then climbed up to him and, depite her precarious position, was able to treat the fractured femur which she correctly diagnosed. She then waited with the injured man until a Neil Robert-son stretcher was sent up. This single-handed demonstration of bravery and skill attracted praise from the police and professional ambulance men. Courage and skill of a different kind was shown by Mrs J. Abraham of Exmouth who stopped a fight between rival gangs of youths who had terrified visitors to Budleigh Salterton. She then assisted a handicapped girl who – unable to move – had been trapped on the beach and was in great distress. Finally she tended to the wounds of those gang members who had been unable to leave the scene. She acted quickly, calmly and correctly when others near the scene did nothing and she was quite properly commended by the Commissioner. What is interesting is that she did not give her name; it was not until the father of the handicapped girl wrote to thank the Commander SJA Devon that Mrs Abraham was traced.

It has often been said that a sense of humour is a necessary part of a nurse's character and those in St John are not without this great asset. When the next to come forward during a blood donor session had the surname of Stone, the nursing member on duty smiled at him and said, 'Well – we can but try!' The nursing members of Weymouth were faced with the need to use their triangular bandages to improvise a bathing costume when a young woman complained, from the safety of the waves, that her bikini had been carried away by the tide. Such incidents may have brought temporary amusement, but there is always a need for a good-humoured approach to patients and their problems: willingness to learn deaf and dumb language; keeping food hot for patients whose illness makes them slow eaters – in short, having patience with the patients.

Since 1980, the St John Year of Nursing, when nursing members went to Jerusalem and Rome and also remained in the public eye in Britain, the women have been extremely busy. Their membership has remained strong, while the Ambulance Branch has found difficulty in recruiting. Southend (Essex), for example, raised its nursing strength from three to thirty-four in a period of three years. Now that many more men are qualifying for the nursing certificate, the old distinction between the Ambulance Division and the Nursing Division is fading. Men are proving to be attentive nurses and the women are taking on more administrative tasks. In the Combined Division where skills are not related to sex, the joint efforts of men and women in working together are proving to be an effective answer to modern requirements. The nursing skills required by the Brigade are additional to the basic first-aid requirements and it is not easy for volunteers to reach the required standards without the help of qualified medical officers.

The Order of St John has always owed a great deal to the dedication of its medical officers – now known in the Brigade as 'surgeons' – who like the lay members are all volunteers. Indeed, in the early days of the Association the work of the medical profession was an essential ingredient of success. The Surgeon of a Corps, the first title for local units of the Brigade, was the titular senior member of his division and responsible for running it. He dealt with the training syllabus and was expected to support the divisional superintendent – lay leader of the unit – in creating a unit spirit and furthering the general well-being of the division. This concept of medical responsibility allied to teamwork existed at all levels of the Brigade to the topmost appointment of Medical-Officer-in-Chief.

Two prominent medical men who were closely involved in the initial formation of the Brigade, Sir William MacCormac and Samuel Osborn, were to play important roles in its development. William MacCormac, a large imposing figure, had been involved with the Anglo-American Ambulance Unit and Hospital in 1870: as President of the Royal College of Surgeons and Chief Surgeon of the Brigade, he volunteered for service in South Africa during the Boer War. Appointed Medical-Officer-in-Chief in 1896, he was the first to hold this appointment and in the same year Sam Osborn was appointed Chief Surgeon of the No. I. Metropolitan District. Osborn, like Mac-Cormac, had been part of the Brigade from the beginning and had been in medical charge of the fifty men who carried out the Brigade's first public duty at Queen Victoria's Jubilee in 1887. He also went to South Africa as medical officer of the Van Alen Hospital and was attached to the Household Cavalry for some time. Osborn was a practical first-aider as well as a doctor and did much to consolidate the definition of first aid so as to separate this from remedial assistance. A third pioneer also warrants mention; the first Corps Surgeon of the first London registered unit – No. I. St John's Gate Corps, registered in 1887 – was a Dr A. Symons Eccles who in 1893 presented the first competition trophy to the Brigade, a silver cup which is still awarded today to the runners-up at the Brigade Final competition for Ambulance Divisions.

In 1930, Dr Ella Webb of Dublin became the first woman to be appointed as a divisional surgeon; she had already shown both courage and dedication in 1916 during the riots in Ireland. Within a few years other women were appointed, so that by the time of the 1937 Review there were seven on parade. The period of the 1930s saw increases in the ranks of surgeons in the same way as in the remainder of the

Brigade, and at the same time the nature of the appointment of Chief Surgeon was changed. Until 1931, the post had been held by highly placed medical members of the Order of St John, who had not always worked previously with the Brigade, but on 24 November 1931 Colonel Clarence Isidore Ellis, CMG, TD, took over from Sir William Bennett, KCVO, who had held office since 1915. Ellis had begun his service with the Brigade as a Divisional Surgeon in Torquay and had held other medical appointments as well as being a Commissioner, where he had gained experience of Brigade administration. In 1932 Nigel Corbet Fletcher was appointed Assistant Surgeon-in-Chief; known as 'NCF', he had written in the *St John Gazette* and an earlier journal called *First Aid*, answering the questions of readers and commenting on the work of Brigade units and individuals. A tall man who had played rugby for Cambridge and England, he brought to the Association and Brigade the tenacity and directness of his playing days. NCF's two great memorials are first, his book on the history of the Association and Brigade, and second the Annual National Medical Conference. Add to this his constant contributions to the *Gazette* and it is possible to assess how much time and effort this man devoted to St John's charitable work. He believed that very high standards should be demanded of the Brigade's medical staff and that they must 'remain efficient in the same way as other members of the Brigade'. In his view, there was a difference between those duties which are required and those which are expected. In the first category came divisional practices and training (twelve times in the year), responsibility for training and attendance at the annual inspection. But surgeons were also expected to attend public duty in uniform and also attend divisional working and social meetings.

It was perhaps inevitable that NCF would become Surgeon-in-Chief and indeed he took over from Ellis in June 1936. Among his first tasks was to convene the first Brigade Medical Conference, which was held at St John's Gate on 10 October 1936 and attended by 29 of the 54 Brigade Surgeons. Although its agenda was simple by modern standards, it closed with a resolution that this should become an annual event; thus an important initiative had been taken. The second Conference assembled in 1937, when a telegram wishing success to the delegates was addressed to 'Cordite Fletcher'! This explosive character retired from the Brigade in 1950 and died on 21 December 1951, being succeeded by his Deputy F. H. Edwards who regrettably died within a year of his appointment whilst attending the year's Medical Conference. Major A. C. White-Knox, CBE, MC, MB, ChB then took over and also held the post of Principal Medical Officer of the Association, the only doctor to hold both positions. During the War he was summoned to Buckingham Palace to give a course of lectures on first aid to King George VI and Queen Elizabeth (now the Queen Mother). He and his deputy Dr Marcus Scott (later to succeed him) wrote the first joint *First Aid Manual* for the Association, the St Andrew's Association and the BRCS. Space does not permit of a full account of his work for St John, but mention should be made of a little book he published in 1952 titled *First Aid Competitions and Casualty Make-up*, compiled to standardize procedures throughout the St John world.

One of the many ventures undertaken by Dr Marcus Scott following his appointment as Surgeon-in-Chief was the formation of the Medical Board on 29 February 1968; the first Chairman was Sir Hedley Atkins, a past President of the Royal College of Surgeons.

In 1937 the Brigade once again broke new ground when a series of television demonstrations was presented from Alexandra Palace between 8 January and 19 February. NCF, P. G. Darvil-Smith and W. C. Bentall gave instruction on first aid at home, in the factory and at sporting functions. Then in March of that year, A. C. White-Knox spoke on the radio about first-aid training. Major White-Knox took over NCF's role as commentator in the *Gazette* as well as being Surgeon-in-Chief, earning himself the unofficial title of the most knowledgeable first-aider in the UK. In the New Year Honours list of 1961, he was awarded the CBE for his work on behalf of St John. William Bentall had been appointed in 1935 to coordinate ARP training throughout the Brigade and in 1936 became Deputy Surgeon-in-Chief. There were teams of energetic men such as these operating throughout the country and the number of doctors who joined the Brigade increased so that, by early 1939, NCF could report that the medical strength had never been higher: 2,715 Surgeons were involved in the Brigade. Of equal importance was the fact that most of these were fully integrated into their divisions, playing a full part in all activities. It was small wonder that morale in the Brigade was high at that time. By August 1939 some of the Surgeons were being called up for war service, while others who could not join the Forces filled the gaps in various divisions for the duration of the war. The end of the Second World War saw the need for further social change and the creation of the National Health Service. Despite increased workloads and the difficulties of working under the new systems, the medical profession maintained its interest in the Brigade – there were 216 new appointments in 1949, bringing the total number of Surgeons to 3,486.

The names of Brigade Surgeons feature in the lists of Brigade men and women who have been awarded medals and certificates for gallantry or devotion to duty. Divisional Surgeon J. S. McKay was called to Markham Colliery at 3.30 a.m. on 10 May 1938, following an explosion. Though he was under no obligation to descend into the shaft, he did so and assumed control of the underground rescue operation, going into the most dangerous areas, examining casualties and treating them until he was himself overcome by fumes. He collapsed and was only discovered when another rescue worker heard him groan. Brought to the surface, he was taken to Chesterfield Hospital where he was detained for three days. He was awarded the Life Saving Medal of the Order of St John in Gold.

In 1967 Dr Colin Dawson, then Area Surgeon of South-East Area, London District, was awarded the Life Saving Medal of the Order of St John in Bronze for his work at the Hither Green train crash. He had been a Divisional Surgeon in Orpington since 1954 and later became District Surgeon of London. Dr Dawson was at home when the telephone call came that there had been a crash at Hither Green; he promptly put on his uniform and drove to the scene, to be greeted by the police who waved him through to park with the emergency vehicles. Rescue work could not proceed until a doctor had established whether or not one trapped man was in fact dead, so that if he was still alive a rescue could be attempted. Dr Dawson crawled alone into the tangled wreckage and remained exposed to great danger for twenty minutes while he examined the victim and regrettably pronounced him dead. He then remained at the scene as the rescue work began. Another St John man, Area Nursing Officer Harold Bugg, was also awarded the Bronze Life Saving Medal for his dedicated service on that occasion. In 1975, the Royal Humane Society awarded its parchment to Colonel Robert Ollerenshaw, Surgeon-in-Chief of the Brigade, for his part in the rescue of two men from a quarry. There are many other members of the medical profession whose example of bravery has been acknowledged within the Brigade, whether officially recognized or not, but we have space here only for these few examples.

Many medical men had accepted the dual role of medical adviser and executive officer, combining the duties of Surgeon with those of a Commissioner. This has undoubtedly bound them closer to the Brigade layman; no longer is the Surgeon a uniformed figurehead – despite the somewhat archaic rank, he is expected to be fully conversant with modern medicine, emergency methods and training. Some, like Robert Percival – County Surgeon and later Commander St John Ambulance for Kent – have been asked to travel to Commonwealth countries to train the local St John instructors there. Robert Percival and J. J. (James) Bond, Area Superintendent of London, were sent to Nigeria to teach and advise on St John Ambulance organization and administration. Although such missions are not strictly medical in character, they could not be attempted without the authoritative presence of qualified doctors.

The Surgeon-in-Chief is the senior medical authority and also the officer responsible for maintaining cohesion amongst all the Brigade's qualified medical officers. He and his staff maintain the essential links between the Brigade and the Association on medical matters, and also discuss medical and nursing matters with the Chief Nursing Officer who, with her deputy, is always invited to attend the Surgeon-in-Chief's monthly staff meetings.

The present holder of this highest medical office is Dr J. Claverhouse Graham, who joined the Brigade in 1952 as a Divisional Surgeon and was promoted to HQ staff as Assistant Surgeon-in-Chief in 1967. In 1971 he was appointed Deputy Surgeon-in-Chief to Colonel Ollerenshaw, and among many other duties was responsible for the heavy task of collating the tests for Brigade Final competitions for some years. He was also for some time chairman of the organizing committee for the annual Surgeons' and Nursing Officers' Conference. In 1974 the Grand Prior appointed him Surgeon-in-Chief and he was made a Knight of Grace in the Order of St John in 1973. This was followed by the award of the OBE in the New Year Honours in January 1982.

Dr Graham has discussions with leading teaching hospitals, with his County Surgeons and the medical staffs of overseas organizations. In addition he deals with the important matters of equipment, assessing requirements, studying trials reports and finally selecting the items most suited to the needs of the modern Brigade.

Brigade Surgeons, at whatever level they serve, have to be very conscious of the pressures on the modern Brigade and the need to maintain the very highest standards. The legal requirements of certification, with the consequent insurance coverage, make it essential that every first-aider is fully aware of the serious responsibility which he or she will shoulder when a crisis comes. There can be no room for second-rate equipment nor second-class training and St John must count itself fortunate in being able to rely upon such dedicated professional medical personnel, for their work is central to the success of St John Ambulance. They are the teachers and guides, guardians of the Brigade's tradecraft and, as such, they play a most prominent part in all aspects of training.

12
TRAINING AND COMPETITIONS

Since 1877 the central theme of the Association and later the Brigade had been the training of lay people to carry out emergency aid. Indeed, the whole purpose behind the early St John initiatives was to prepare citizens to help each other when accidents occur. There had always been a need for qualified doctors to teach the medical subjects and lay instructors to deal with the practical aspects of first aid. It must be stressed that, apart from one abortive effort to arrange 3-month hospital courses, all St John training is geared to practical first aid; there is no room for half-measures and no place for those who seek to stray outside the bounds of first aid. Those who wish to practise as first-aiders in the Brigade accept a serious responsibility and the public expects them to be fully trained and thoroughly competent to deal with any emergency. Peter Shepherd's concept of 'a few plain rules' remains valid, particularly for young people. There can be only one standard – the highest. No second class is possible where life may be at risk and this is why from the earliest days the Brigade has insisted on annual requalification for all its members. To meet the standards of today the original idea of six 'lectures' would be totally inadequate; training must be continuous, up-to-date, realistic and practical. The quality of the training is almost wholly dependent on the knowledge, skill and enthusiasm of the instructors, so they too must be trained to do their job properly.

It was natural that the Brigade should model some of its original training on the Army. It was after all a form of Army reserve. The camps of instruction also had a military flavour, but however under-standable this may have been, there were people – including some members of the Brigade – who criticized this leaning towards the military. Differences of opinion occurred which nearly led to the disbandment of some units, but Church Brasier and his friends persuaded members to keep going. Gradually the military flavour was diminished and specific training schedules were designed for mining areas and closed divisions such as the railway companies, who placed emphasis on their own particular needs. The programmes became more relevant to meet new skills which had been identified to meet changing circumstances, and the instructors were constantly attending updating courses. There was no doubt that the Association and Brigade were determined to provide the best possible instruction and George Hebb of New Mills, Cheshire, who spent over 45 years as a railway ambulance member, reflected that the instructor who dealt with their ARP first-aid training was a 'perfectionist – his name may escape me after all these years, but his training *never*!' The manuals produced by the Association have made a long-term international impact. 'Shepherd's Book' has been translated into most of the world's languages, a catalyst which has resulted in a greater spread of understanding, influencing first-aid training worldwide. In Wales the need for up-to-date manuals led to the provision of a special manual *First Aid in Mines*, while cooperation with the Royal Life Saving Society on methods of artificial respiration ensured that standard 'drills' were taught for this vital aspect of emergency aid.

Following the Second World War, training was eased from the rut into which it had sunk during the war years and as the 1950s gave way to the 1960s, so a more professional approach could be detected in Brigade training. It was however several years later, in 1973, when the first British St John training convention was held at Mychett near Aldershot, with the aim of ensuring that a variety of new training ideas were discussed with those who would put them into practice. Then followed the second training convention, held at Canterbury and attended by the County Training Officers of England, Wales and Northern Ireland, together with delegates from the Commonwealth and West Germany. One of the more interesting if noisy parts of this convention was a visit to Brands Hatch racing track where Dr J. W. Prout, County Surgeon for Kent, explained the organization of first aid and the treatment of race casualties. In August 1975 a group of British officers attended a combined training camp as guests of the Johanniter-Unfall-Hilfe in Germany.

The training of young adults is crucial to the efficiency and continuity of divisions and in some respects this is an extension of cadet training, for the younger adults require challenge, fitness and experience in decision-making as well as skills training. When, therefore, the

Commissioner-in-Chief, Major-General Desmond Gordon, proposed an adventure theme for young adults, there was no lack of support for the schemes which followed. Thirty-eight young St John men boarded the Sail Training Association's *Malcolm Miller* on 29 February 1976 for the first voyage to be crewed entirely by the Brigade. Sir Maurice Dorman, the Chief Commander, saw them hoist the St John flag to the top of the mast before setting off for two weeks' hard work as sailors. In June that year an all-girl crew repeated the venture, sailing from Grimsby where Lady Moyra Browne, Superintendent-in-Chief and Lord Westbury, Commander Humberside, wished them 'bon voyage'. The girls, in white T-shirts with a line drawing of their ship, looked a fine bunch of seafarers as they manned the rigging for the ship's return to Southampton.

We have already seen how cadets can enter for the Duke of Edinburgh's Award. Whilst the younger members will work for the Bronze or Silver sections, the adults up to the age of twenty-five will more than likely be attempting to earn the difficult Gold Award which is presented personally by Prince Philip. This is a training scheme for everyone, therefore St John has two roles to play: first in offering its training to those people of other organizations who need first aid, nursing or child care for their projects, and second, making sure that the standards of their own candidates are good enough for this demanding and highly relevant award. In 1985, over 600 St John people between the ages of 14 and 25 were attempting the various stages of the Award – proof enough that it has captured the imagination of members.

Year in and year out, decade after decade, the manuals of St John Ambulance have been opened in Ambulance Halls throughout Britain. For a long while the Association was the sole teaching authority, but this is no longer the case. Practice nights have changed along with the requirements of the manual, but there has always been insistence on the correct assessment of priorities, a sympathetic approach and a quick but purposeful display of first-aid skill. Whatever the year, whatever the circumstance, casualties will still require to be treated according to the severity of their injuries and the possible danger to life. As the years have passed so new methods have evolved, perhaps to be replaced in time by others as improved equipment becomes available or medical science advances. Today's manual and teaching is approved by St John Ambulance, St Andrew's Ambulance Association and the British Red Cross Society, which also applies to *First Aid and Caring for the Sick*, a home nursing manual. There is also a book mainly for children and cadets which was produced by St John Ambulance in 1983, entitled *The Essentials of First Aid*. This reduces some of the more complex aspects of first aid to language which youngsters can understand and indeed it has become popularly known as 'the ABC of first aid': A – Keep the Airway open; B – Check Breathing and if necessary apply mouth-to-mouth ventilation and C – check the Circulation and if stopped apply external chest compression; then deal with severe bleeding. These are life-saving measures and the saving of life is the very essence of first-aid training. That it works is proved by the experience of Mrs Brighton, who had just passed a first-aid course for which this book was essential reading. On the day of her final test she attended a wrestling match where a 16-stone man collapsed. She applied mouth-to-mouth ventilation and chest compression for over five minutes while an ambulance was called. The man recovered and another life was saved.

Apart from the standard training associated with first aid and nursing qualifications, additional training is needed for public duty of a specialized nature. This type of training, however, is only really effective if the right personnel have been selected. When, in 1970, the Buckingham St John Ambulance discussed safety and first aid with the local auto-cross clubs, it soon became clear that a Special Duty unit would be needed at the various race meetings. The Clubs decided to raise funds for a purpose-built vehicle and St John began the process of calling for volunteers and arranging a selection course. The unit's training was supervised by Dr Margaret Gillison (County Surgeon) and Miss Nancy Sale (County Training Officer) who held a driving and physical fitness selection day at Beaconsfield. It was a rough, demanding day and many failed to qualify for the new unit, but the one nursing member who entered passed with flying colours. Following this, the specialized training began with fire-fighting, forced entry into crashed cars, safety precautions and advanced first-aid instruction, involving treatment of patients in awkward positions, use of airways and the Beaufort stretcher. By the end of 1970 about twenty men and women were undergoing the training. The generosity of Lord Camoys in donating a Land-Rover to St John Ambulance gave the unit the opportunity to try out equipment which could be taken to the various sites and also facilitated further driving training in difficult terrain. On the very first duty at an auto-cross, the team concerned was due to present a demonstration of its capability, but fate intervened when at the very start of the day a car overturned. This was for real! The team was at the crash in seven seconds and the driver was successfully removed from the car and taken by St John Ambulance to Wycombe General Hospital. Since then the team has attended many events, proving the value of good selection and thorough training.

Training for emergencies has been undertaken in every St John County, with situations varying from a serious rail crash or an explosion in a power station to a simulated terrorist attack which caused severe casualties. All of these emergencies provide the opportunity for lessons of control, coordination and cooperation with the Police, BRCS, WRVS, Central Electricity Generating Board and of course local authority ambulance services. Since the modern county emergency services require a coordinated response to any disaster, such joint training is invaluable and will also allow the St John units to play their part in any national emergency.

As the pioneer organization for first-aid instruction, the Association was also largely responsible for the impetus given to competitions. In 1880 George Hutton began to use competitive testing as a form of training during his 'Ambulance Crusades' in the North. For several years competitions remained local affairs, but in 1890 the first Brigade Annual Camp was held, with first-aid competitions as a feature of the programme. In 1893 the Great Eastern and Caledonian Railways set up an annual competition amongst their centres, and in the same year the first of the important Brigade trophies was presented – the Symons Eccles Cup, given by the Chief Surgeon of London District in commemoration of the Brigade's duty at the wedding of the then Duke of York and Princess Mary.

On 6 May 1897, the St John Ambulance Association instituted three separate competitions to commemorate Queen Victoria's Diamond Jubilee: a General Competition open to all Association centres, a Railway Competition open to the regional railway centres; and a Brigade Competition open to all Corps and Divisions of the Brigade. The General Competition was not repeated, but the Railway and Brigade Competitions continued. Although a Brigade Competition had been staged at camps since 1893, the year 1897 marks its origin as a separate and important highlight of the Brigade's year. This was also the year in which Sir Thomas Dewar, Sheriff of London, presented a shield for competition among the Corps and Divisions of the Brigade, also in commemoration of the Diamond Jubilee. This shield became the principal award at the Brigade Competition, and in the following year the Symons Eccles Cup was awarded to the runners-up, which is still the case today.

The first competitions had been clumsy and ineffective by modern standards, a card showing the patient's injuries being hung around the neck of a volunteer who then subjected himself to the ministrations of the enthusiasts! It was not long before some small degree of realism became part of the competition. In 1899 the first attempts at realistic staging took place at King's Cross for the Inter-Railway competition, when the contest was given a natural flavour, being based on a rail accident. Further improvements were subsequently made until in 1905 the Association produced the first marking sheets for the Railways competition; later that same year the injuries cards were removed, requiring competitors to find out for themselves the injuries sustained by the patients. These experiments in realism proved successful and in 1909 the rules were amended to include the phrase 'to deal with cases under conditions of actual emergency' and detailed marking sheets setting out the sequence of action for each victim were formally instituted. Thus the Railway Centres and Divisions paved the way for subsequent improvements. In 1923 the Brigade staged a very realistic lift accident as the team test for the men's final (the Dewar Shield) and from then on realism would become a major part of all Brigade competitions, involving sound effects, casualty simulation and stage 'props', not to mention a great deal of stage management. In 1926 film was used for the first time to indicate the background to the incident; then time limits were imposed, based on medical advice. As the standard of training increased, so the competitions at all levels were themselves improved and broadened in scope to stretch the competitors. Detailed marking sheets and careful briefing of 'actors' and judges became ever more important as the degree of realism improved. The men and women who took part enjoyed themselves but also took it seriously, and when only a few marks could make the difference between taking home a trophy and returning empty-handed, the need for fair, sympathetic and consistent judging was clear.

Competitions had been discontinued during the First World War, but were restarted in 1920, by which time women were playing a much more important part in Brigade affairs. In December 1921 Lady Ethel Perrott, wife of Sir Herbert Perrott and Superintendent-in-Chief of Nursing Divisions, presented a large shield for award to the Champion Nursing Division of the Brigade, which was first won by Dublin Headquarters in 1922. This magnificent trophy is still highly prized by the Nursing Divisions, who train hard for the privilege of competing for it. In 1926 the readers of the journal *First Aid* showed their appreciation of the work of Nigel Corbet-Fletcher by giving him a fine silver cup. This he presented in turn to the Brigade where it was used as the runners-up prize in the Nursing Final; the first division to be awarded the cup was Liverpool, who went on to win the Perrott Shield in 1927.

The men were not to be outdone by this sudden surge of feminine competitiveness. In 1926 Charles Trimble, who had played such a vital role in mobilizing No. 4 District in 1899 and commanding the Brigade Hospital in 1916, commemorated 31 years as a Brigade Commissioner by presenting a shield for award as an individual prize in the Ambulance Division Finals. Two years later, on 23 February 1928, Dr F. E. de B. Pim presented a very fine cup for the Ambulance members of the Police Forces in England, Wales and the Isle of Man, the first winners being Lancashire Constabulary. The nursing members later obtained another very attractive trophy, when in 1943 Mr Oliver Golding presented a statuette of a St John nurse in uniform as an award for home nursing. Although competitions had been suspended during the 1939–1945 War, this was an appropriate prize to be presented at a time when St John women were playing a vital role in nursing. Mr Golding's statuette was much admired; sculpted by Sir William Reid-Dick, it was exhibited at the Royal Academy in 1943.

The resumption of competitions following the Second World War occurred in 1947, when the Brigade Finals were held in the Victoria Hall, Bloomsbury. It was also in November 1947 that the first Cadet National Competitions took place, the prizes being presented by the Duchess of Kent. For both ambulance and nursing cadets there were senior and junior classes; the winners on this first occasion were Horsham seniors and Southwick juniors for the boys, while Weymouth seniors and Ipswich juniors took the girls' trophies. The major ambulance cadet trophy is the cup presented by A. C. White-Knox while the principal prize for the nursing cadets is Lady Dunbar-Nasmith's cup, both presented in 1947. There are of course runners-up trophies for the cadets too: Lady Mountbatten's cup for the girls presented by Lady Louis herself in 1949, and the Schooling cup for the boys. In addition there are cups for individual performance and for specific tasks such as bedmaking. Standards have become higher and the tests more competitive, but whether they win or lose cadets are very proud to have taken part in the Brigade Finals.

The term 'Brigade Finals' trips easily off the lips, but for those who organize the final of the national competitions of the St John Ambulance Brigade, it represents the culmination of many months of labour. For the competitors it means giving up time to prepare for Divisional, Area, County and Regional Competitions which become progressively more difficult. Each Division is eligible to put forward a team to take part in an Area Competition where, although most competing units have probably met each other as friends or at joint duties, rivalry exists and there is still a keen desire to win. Standards of presentation and time-keeping are high, with stewards appointed to oversee the various support tasks which are necessary. Casualty simulation and make-up feature in this, the first stage of the national competition, just as they will in the remaining stages. At County level, interest in the competition takes a slightly different form, reflecting the administrative and social importance of the British County system – more guests are invited, judges and time-keepers are appointed from a broader geographic base and so the interest widens and each team's experience is greater, win or lose. The winners will go forward to represent their County at Regional Competitions, at which stage – because of the greater distances to travel – the costs of each team are higher, requiring fund-raising or direct support from the County and Division. The twelve Regional Finals must be held in time for tests to be written, stage sets prepared and programmes printed for the Brigade Finals held in July of each year. On the day of the Finals, some 1,500 spectators will gather at Croydon, eager to watch the best first-aiders in the Brigade displaying their knowledge and skill. The teams of judges will conscientiously mark the good points and the bad with respect to each individual and team performance. There is constant activity for competitors, stage managers, Casualty Union members and judges. The importance of the occasion reaches everyone – a point lost here, a silly mistake there, will surely offset a good performance elsewhere. Concentration is total and when in the evening the trophies are awarded, tiredness descends on those who, whether competitor or worker, have given so much of themselves on this one day. Speaking after the Grand Prior's Competition in 1985, the Duke of Gloucester said that in these first-aid competitions there were really no losers; in his opinion everyone gained in some way, not least the public from the improved general capability, since the first-aider was the one person who could really help those in trouble.

From 1922 until 1948, the work of preparing stage sets and 'incidents' was undertaken by Mr Joe Grossman and John Maxwell. As the years passed this team experienced at first hand the changing nature of competitions and the extent to which realism had become an important ingredient of the Finals. Joe Grossman had joined the Brigade in 1907 and was soon involved in competition work; indeed, it was largely due to his initiative that films began to be used in 1926. He died in January 1949, respected as a loyal, dependable friend of the Order and having played an important role in the life of the Brigade. George Craft took over the mantle of competition manager until his retirement in 1966, then handing over to David Hallard who is the current manager. It is the manager's task to write scripts for the scenarios set by the medical officers, arrange for time-keepers, lay and medical judges, stewards and make-up teams to be present and also to ensure that scenery suitable for the setting is available. In addition it is his responsibility to prepare the trophies for display in the hall. At one time the scenery was stored in Elstree Studios, but when the film company encountered financial difficulties, David Hallard was forced to find alternative facilities for constructing, painting and storing the many complex sets. Thanks to the generosity of British Rail, Port of London Authority and later the Central Electricity Generating Board, it has been possible to keep the work going, but the poor manager has a two-hour drive each way to work on the sets. For the Brigade Finals, he has to prepare four large sets for the team tests and twenty smaller sets for the individual tests. No competition, whether at Divisional level or the Finals, can take place without willing helpers back-stage: props men, tea ladies, ushers and cleaners are all as much part of the competition as the other members of this busy team which will number some seventy people.

On 20 November 1950 the Central Hall in London played host to a new and important first-aid competition for men. The Duke of Gloucester, Grand Prior of the Order of St John, was there to present a new trophy which he had authorized as the prize for a first-aid competition between the winning teams of certain national organizations. In that first year seven such bodies took part, among them the Brigade, and the winning team at each of the finals went forward to compete for 'The Grand Prior's'. The actual test was set in a fairground, where the Associated British Picture Corporation had prepared a background with swings, tents and film 'extras'. The magnificent trophy of a mounted knight was won by Brighton Police SJAB, a closed division of the Brigade and winners of the Dewar Shield. It is of interest that leading up to the appearance of these seven teams of four men at the Central Hall, over 1,000 teams had taken part in various

145

stages of their respective competitions and something approaching 10,000 people had been involved in different ways. In 1952, Horsham Nursing Division presented another prize for nursing members along the same lines as the Grand Prior's, and this was first won by Palmers Green.

The principle of competitions has its supporters and detractors, and there has always been a risk that they might be viewed as an end in themselves. However, it is indisputable that through the medium of the competitions there is benefit to teaching, testing and teamwork and overall standards are bound to improve. Eloquent proof of this is an incident at a colliery in the West Riding of Yorkshire, when an open works train in a coal seam went out of control and many casualties were caused, some very serious. Four St John men (Messrs Round, Yoxall, Hyde and Thomas) who were on the shift provided 'excellent first aid arrangements with efficiency and calmness' and were awarded Certificates of Merit. These same four men had been runners-up in the competition for the Grand Prior's Trophy!

13
PUBLIC DUTY

The term 'Public Duty' has been a part of the Brigade's vocabulary from the earliest days, indeed from the first public duty carried out by St John personnel at the Lord Mayor's Show in 1886, the year before the Brigade was officially formed. Since the first official Brigade duty at the Diamond Jubilee on 21 June 1887, members have always been prepared by training and commitment to put on their uniform and undertake whatever duties they may be asked to perform. For many years these duties were rather stereotyped, requiring an almost automatic, mechanical response; now, however, a public duty can be a heavy responsibility for the officers who organize it and a great challenge for those who undertake it. Depending upon the task and location, the extent and nature of the assistance required can stretch the personal skills of members to their limits, with a greater diversity of injuries, sometimes in an environment which brings personal danger and organizational stress. The range of duty is as wide as the needs of the public; if the authorities – national or local – have a requirement for first-aid cover, the Brigade is there to provide it. Unfortunately, however, this is sometimes taken for granted.

The great state occasions and Royal ceremonial still involve many participants and attract more and more spectators. Her Majesty the Queen's Birthday Parade, the State Opening of Parliament, Royal garden parties at Buckingham Palace – and those personal occasions which for the Royal family are more public than private – all call for Brigade support. The wedding of the then Princess Elizabeth to Prince Philip on 20 November 1947 involved 1,000 St John personnel as well as nearly a hundred members of BRCS. Between them they treated over 2,500 cases, some fifty of whom were stretcher cases, and for the first time St John stretcher squads were on duty in Westminster Abbey. On 29 July 1981 the Prince of Wales married Lady Diana Spencer at St Paul's Cathedral and again the Brigade was on duty. Prince Charles and the new Princess of Wales subsequently sent a message of thanks to

147

General Peter Leuchars, Chief Commander: 'Please convey our warmest thanks to all those concerned for their hard work and assistance at today's ceremonies. We deeply appreciate all your efforts on our behalf.' Those efforts involved a great deal of detailed planning, coordination with the Red Cross and police and some sacrifice of time by those who volunteered for the duty.

Windsor, Ascot and Hampton Court all attract many visitors during the summer months, providing Divisional Superintendents with quite a problem with public duty rosters. During the mid 1970s 'Uncle Jim' Glass – Superintendent of Windsor's Ambulance Division – was confronted by an increase in duties at the Castle: the Garter Ceremony in St George's Chapel, polo on Smith's Lawn – these occasions require as many adults and cadets as possible just at the time when members want to go on holiday. At Hampton Court in one week during the summer of 1975 the local Division, Teddington, dealt with a very wide range of casualties from a lost child to a most serious case of drug abuse. Elsewhere in Britain the summer influx of tourists adds to the public duty roster, each division having to manage its own jigsaw of personnel availability. The great ceremonies, together with national occasions and events such as the Festival of Britain, are mostly coordinated by London (Prince of Wales's) District who invite representatives from the Counties to assist. This is necessary to ensure that everyone is aware of his or her responsibilities and is fully prepared for them. Districts, Counties and Divisions accept responsibility for duties undertaken at their respective levels and each has a public duty officer whose task it is to coordinate between units, check that there are sufficient trained men and women available with up-to-date qualifications, liaise with police and hospitals, arrange a record system and deal with such matters as equipment, transport and insurance cover. Planning for the location of aid posts, the siting of a control point and whether or not to put out foot patrols in large crowds will depend upon the specific circumstances of each duty. Detailed reconnaissance is necessary if the officer in charge is to give an effective briefing and exercise control. Good communications have been proved essential so that a quick response is possible. All this is progress much beyond the public duty of yesteryear, but one thing remains the same – if the first-aiders make a mistake, the consequences could be tragic. It is for this reason that the Brigade insists on regular training and annual requalifications, thereby providing the public with greater confidence in voluntary first aid.

Public Duty

Nowadays there are duties connected with our modern world which have brought great recognition to the Brigade, both collectively and individually. Some of these, which we now accept as normal, could never have been dreamed of in the early days of the Brigade. For example, could Church Brasier have foreseen the pop festivals with thousands of young people converging on a single field? Could Ethel Perrott have imagined the Notting Hill Carnival? Could Furley have believed that a day would come when a mobile treatment vehicle would be first used at a London Marathon at a staggering cost of £48,000?

When pop groups arrived on the musical scene, their style of music and the tendency to treat the top performers as cult figures led to packed concerts at suitable theatres, cinemas or halls, and in open spaces such as Hyde Park. More often than not these occasions were complete 'sell-outs', many fans being forced to wait outside the building in the hope of merely seeing their musical idols. One such concert was held in a cinema in London, where the atmosphere generated by the pulse of the music, the noise of fans keyed-up with anticipation and the claustrophobic, almost airless hall led to a number of casualties, mainly from fainting. Such was the intense concentration of the audience that some victims were not noticed and in addition the young people began to press forward towards the stage. Members of the Brigade had already dealt with a number of casualties, others were requiring treatment and any further pressure from the audience would have caused more. The Brigade senior officer in charge, Derek Fenton, therefore requested that the concert should be halted temporarily so that the area near the stage could be cleared to save life and prevent further injury. However, some lessons have to be learned the hard way; less than a week later the same concert was being repeated in Oxford, where the local Division faced the same sort of problem but with fewer resources available to deal with it.

Mass demonstrations, involving thousands of people marching or gathering in a restricted space, have always presented fearsome problems for first-aiders. In recent years the increasing frequency of such demonstrations, the number of participants and the appetite for violence have all seemed to grow, multiplying the difficulties and dangers which face the police and emergency services. One of the most demanding of public duties at demonstrations was that in Grosvenor Square in 1968. It occurred outside the American Embassy and was brought about by the American involvement in the Vietnam War.

149

Although a type of duty never previously performed by St John, the then Public Duty Officer of London (Prince of Wales's) District, Derek Fenton, immediately offered medical assistance to the police which was readily accepted. While St John worked in co-operation with the police, they always remained entirely independent and strictly neutral when dealing with casualties arising from members of the police and public alike. Despite the fact that Brigade radio communication was non-existent, liaison was maintained from the outset by various other means. Only 48 hours' notice was given, yet four mobile units from London and Surrey; ten ambulances; doctors, nursing officers and more than sixty members were all in position well before the arrival of the protesters.

The preparations included the siting of equipment and ambulances in side streets so that they would not be hemmed in the square with no exit route to the local hospitals. In the event this proved to be a wise precaution because of the intensity of the violence. At one stage during the most violent period, a man lay seriously injured in the midst of the crowd and the senior St John officer in the area went in with a first-aid kit to treat him and take him to safety. He had no idea how the people would react, for some had become very excited and volatile, but in the event a path was cleared and the victim was safely evacuated. There were over 400 casualties to police and demonstrators and 115 of these had to be taken to the neighbourhood hospitals. It is worth noting that there was never a shortage of volunteers, particularly from amongst the younger members who also accepted unhesitatingly the necessity for strict discipline.

In situations such as these, the members of St John became aware that their uniform could give them certain privileges which are denied to others: a safe passage to treat victims, a degree of protection for their first-aid posts and some personal safety. Sadly, however, even this limited security was later to be abused, when members on duty were deliberately attacked. In the press of the crowds and in poor light it was often difficult to distinguish between the St John officers and the police, but this was rectified by the issue of a Brigade Order in March 1975 which requested that all officers attending a duty should wear the White Cross belt and haversack; thus the familiar symbol of service to others would stand out clearly. The then Commander-in-Chief, Major General Desmond Gordon, was often seen so dressed. What would have happened if St John had not been there? Would anyone else have carried out these difficult duties? How much would it have cost to provide coverage from municipal ambulance services? These are fair questions to pose wherever public duty is undertaken by men and women who have devoted time and energy to the acquisition of skills enabling them to offer service to the public, and then give more of their time so as to put those skills into practice. It may be that honest answers would give cause for concern.

The 'pop festival' is a more recent development in the musical world, combining the idea of a concert with an outdoor holiday atmosphere. In the early 1970s, Essex County was faced with a request to provide first-aid cover for a pop festival at Weedon near Clacton, to be effective from 8 a.m. on the Saturday to 1 p.m. on the Sunday. These were of course the timings of the actual festival, and presumably the period covered by insurance on behalf of the organizers. However, the St John members knew that many visitors would begin to arrive much earlier and would leave well after the concerts had ended; they were also aware that accidents in crowded areas have a habit of occurring outside official performance times. So in the event 35 nursing members and 40 ambulance members from 12 separate Divisions reported for a duty which began at 6 a.m. on Friday and ended at 6 a.m. on the following Monday, a total of 60 hours' continuous duty in shifts of eight. Most members spent more than 20 hours on duty during that weekend and some went straight back to work afterwards, having only returned home to change on Monday morning. This was a difficult duty, made more demanding by the menacing behaviour of some ruffians who started a fight, causing casualties, and were themselves later 'beaten-up' by stewards. The result: one fractured skull, five serious head and face wounds and many less serious injuries – this of course in addition to the many 'routine' injuries and ailments associated with such gatherings. In June 1971 Amesbury Division (Wiltshire) faced the daunting problems of dealing with the pop festival at Stonehenge where the one disaster which everyone dreaded – fire – became a reality, causing many casualties some of whom had very serious burns. The St John teams dealt with 370 people, 23 of whom were admitted to hospital.

At the Knebworth pop concerts, Hertfordshire St John units work with the local Red Cross, the Samaritans and Release to deal with the many and varied casualties. The Divisions of Hampshire and Surrey provide coverage for the festival at Blackbushe Aerodrome and in 1978 the St John teams were faced with two potentially serious developments here: first, some of the medical arrangements which had been

151

laid on did not materialize and second, although 100,000 people were expected over 200,000 turned up – and this was described by the organizers as 'a picnic'. The extra strain on the Brigade was considerable; 1,500 people were treated by 100 Brigade members on duty. A disturbing aspect of the modern pop scene has been the appearance of drug-related casualties. At one concert, a person had taken an overdose of intravenous heroin, while another had taken too much LSD. The appearance of drugs which are being sold and used by quite young people who are temporarily removed from parental discipline is a worrying aspect of the events. Many patients have come into the St John tents with sickness brought on by drug abuse, requiring a combination of first aid and social service. However, the St John men and women are there to serve, not to judge, and the service of David Nobbs and the Amesbury Division certainly saved one life and alleviated the suffering of many others.

When we think of the word 'carnival', we imagine a happy-go-lucky crowd, colourful costumes, dancing, laughter and music. On most occasions this has been the situation at the Notting Hill Carnival, but regrettably not always; there have been several times when rioting and mindless violence claimed many casualties and members of the Brigade on public duty worked under highly adverse conditions and amidst great personal danger. London has unfortunately become a more violent place and, as the capital city, it is the venue for many demonstrations which may themselves be a cause for further violence. On all these occasions the professional and voluntary medical services would be severely stretched if St John mobile units did not treat minor cases on the spot. The Brigade in London usually calls for assistance from the Home Counties for the major duties and in 1976 Caterham, Ash Vale and Weybridge provided either ambulances or mobile first-aid posts to assist at the carnival. By 10 a.m. on Bank Holiday Monday Commissioner Derek Fenton had deployed six mobile first-aid posts, eight ambulances with five surgeons, six experienced SRNs and ninety Brigade members. In the afternoon rioting began; missiles were being thrown at police and the ambulances and from 4.30 p.m. to nearly midnight this violence continued. All the Brigade's ambulances were continuously on the move collecting and ferrying casualties. On one occasion the Commissioner asked for police outriders to escort serious cases and such was the violence that one of these escorts was himself injured and taken to hospital. Three ambulances were damaged, though fortunately no Brigade members were injured. Just after midnight the Brigade was stood down after fourteen continuous hours of duty, the most exacting so far undertaken. Nearly 400 people had been injured, many of them police, and 114 cases taken to hospital. Sir Robert Mark, Commissioner of the Metropolitan Police, wrote an official 'Thank you' in police orders:

> To the Volunteers of the St John Ambulance Brigade we express our profound admiration and gratitude for their selfless devotion in the face of considerable danger to which they exposed themselves in the service of police and public.

Ray Pennock of Weybridge provides an example of this devotion. A member of Weybridge Division for 16 years, he was on duty at Notting Hill for thirteen hours continuously at the 1976 carnival. The *Review* which reported the award of his BEM tells the story:

> Despite physical danger and the fact that his post was inundated with casualties, his devotion to duty, calm disposition and quiet sense of humour were a steadying influence on all who worked with him in such testing circumstances.

In 1977 every part of the United Kingdom except Scotland had contingents on duty for the Jubilee celebrations of the Queen and Prince Philip. The value of the national organization was also demonstrated during the occasion of the visit of His Holiness Pope John Paul II to this country in 1982. From the outset, St John was represented on the national co-ordinating committee by the Deputy Commissioner for London, John Gerrard. Over a period of fifteen months they considered and prepared forty different programmes before the event actually took place. Well-attended services and meetings in London, Coventry, Liverpool, Manchester, York and Cardiff involved the major deployment of Brigade units and personnel. Such was the pace of the programme that it was necessary to make separate arrangements at every location visited, which in London involved covering five venues at the same time; during the two days of the visit to the capital, all resources were used.

The morning of Sunday 21 April 1985, anniversary of the Queen's actual birthday, saw over 20,000 men and women converge on Greenwich. People of widely varying age groups, from all walks of life and from many different nations – some near professionals, others novices, some disabled in wheelchairs – all had but one aim: to enter and complete the fifth London Marathon. They would run 26 miles across London to finish at Westminster Bridge and the St John Ambulance would be on duty to look after them. This important public duty is coordinated by No. 1 (Prince of Wales's) District assisted by units from Kent, Sussex and Surrey, and requires a major detailed briefing prior to the event for all station and sector commanders. Location of HQ, radio communications, organization of sectors and their staffs, position of ambulances and mobile posts, foot patrols, reserve stores of foil and woollen blankets, segregation and documentation of casualties – all these factors are covered in a thorough explanation of the day's responsibilities. Finally Dr Dan Peddoe, himself a marathon runner, spoke of the stress and pressure on the runners and reminded an intent audience of the need for great care being taken in order to avoid serious damage.

By 7.30 a.m. on 'M' Day, 1,100 St John men and women, spruce and smart in uniform, were reporting to their appointed places in the capital and along the route. The race programme described them as the 'A' (for Ambulance) Team. Leslie Webb, Commissioner of London's Eastern Area, was responsible for 'E' Sector which included the Isle of Dogs with its notorious cobblestone mile, which the runners are pleased to see behind them. Here London's new mobile first-aid post, EM 1, was deployed: a magnificently appointed vehicle with up-to-date first-aid and resuscitation equipment provided at a cost of £48,000. Sylvia Buxton, Assistant Area Nursing Officer and in charge of the vehicle, could well feel proud when members of the public stopped to admire this splendid new facility which had been provided solely by the members of St John, their friends and supporters without one single penny of government grant. At station 14, tucked into a side street with good access to main roads, the Weybridge Division prepared for the first runners. Their mobile first-aid post, LD 69, had been a tour coach but with a great deal of work they had converted the interior to provide a facility which had already seen good service. Less than a year later Weybridge had not only purchased a new 'mobile' to rival EM 1, but had also completed the building of a new HQ. Now, however, Steve Smith the Superintendent was anxious to see that his team was ready. Ray and Kate Pennock and the burly Moran triplets, assisted by cadets from London, made their final checks and waited for the leading runners.

It was not long before the first casualties arrived, calling out, 'Quick

154

– got anything for cramp?', 'Deep heat, can't stop' or 'Can anyone do anything for these——blisters?' Some just staggered in and slumped into a chair to be kept warm and massaged until they were ready to continue, whilst others were put into 'Vaseline alley' for aching muscles to be rubbed. One obviously tired runner who would not be able to continue gasped, 'I'm cream-crackered!' as he fell into the arms of an understanding nursing member, and this duly appeared on his casualty card! Throughout that day 3,800 people needed treatment and of those only six were sent to hospital to be discharged within 24 hours. In fact, most were home before Derek Fenton, John Gerrard and Bert Willis at radio control could stand down. There was no doubt that the White Cross belt proved itself no less dedicated than the runners. Dr Peddoe records his praise by saying that, 'St John in London provide the best medical service to marathons in the whole world.' Of course marathon runs take place all over Britain; in Merseyside in 1983 over 500 St John personnel, including cadets, were on duty for the Liverpool marathon. Commissioner J. E. Cook deployed thirty vehicles to support this event and although there were 350 casualties, only two were sent to hospital for minor treatment. It says much for the organization of the facilities and the briefing of St John staff that such events can be held with so few major casualties. Detailed planning, teamwork, good control and individual skill and sympathy are the keys to success. The records from Merseyside's first-aid tent give some idea of how busy such places can become.

Football matches are yet another sphere of activity for St John members. When Millwall played Luton Town in March 1985, Tony Jarvis and the South Bedfordshire Area Brigade were on duty. Violence erupted and the White Cross belt was soon in action treating stab wounds and cuts caused by missiles (in one case a £1 coin had been filed to a sharp edge!). Imagine the horror when Fred Cauldwell, a uniformed member on duty then nearing retirement, was knocked to the ground and broke his wrist. A few minutes later when Derek Pratt, a keen young ambulance member, was kneeling to help someone in trouble, he was viciously and deliberately kicked in the back; as a result he required medical treatment and lost time from his work. On the same day, but in another part of the ground, a nursing member who was walking from the first-aid room to the pitch was kicked in the head by supporters in the stand. Fortunately she was not a tall lady and only suffered the indignity of losing her hat and the shock of the blow, but she could quite easily have suffered a severe injury. The service of the

Brigade at that game was considered worthy of a St John Certificate of Commendation to the Area as a whole – the first time this had ever been awarded – and a letter of commendation from the Bedfordshire police.

This kind of service is also necessary when genuine accidents happen at matches as in Worcestershire on 11 December 1982 when the local team was drawn in a cup-tie playing at home. A barrier gave way during the game and members of the crowd were injured, some falling to the ground to be trapped amongst poles and advertising hoardings. There was chaos, but the police and St John personnel restored some sort of order and managed to convey casualties to the first-aid posts or hospital. This was not national news and there was no outcry about violence, but to those who were injured Brian Chadd and the men and women of Worcester were quiet heroes of the day.

On Saturday 11 May 1985, events at two football grounds in Britain stunned a population already shocked by the behaviour of British fans in Brussels. In Birmingham the home team was playing against Leeds and members from Nelson Transport Combined Division, Queensway Combined Division, Yardley Quadrilateral Division and Winchester House Division were on duty. When the home team scored just before half-time violence erupted; coins, bricks and metal bars were thrown and many fans invaded the pitch. The first casualties, some very serious, were caused amongst the police force, and later amongst the rival fans. Within a period of about forty minutes about a hundred casualties were caused and further St John personnel were requested. When the game ended another battle broke out; a wall collapsed and when Nursing Member Diane Buckle rushed forward to help a trapped youth she was immediately knocked to the ground, beaten and kicked by rival supporters. She was taken to hospital where she was detained, suffering from very severe bruising. Superintendent Dave Belcher and the St John staff dealt with over two hundred injured people, taking more than fifty of them to hospital, but even while this was going on the assaults continued and the ambulance was stoned as it began to leave the ground. At the Bradford football stadium, horror took a different form – a raging inferno which engulfed a complete stand, causing fifty deaths and many injuries.

When the Popplewell Inquiry was subsequently set up, many suggestions put forward by St John were published as recommendations. As a result, many of the licensing authorities are including the statutory requirement of an adequate first-aid post with recommended numbers of personnel in the licences issued to football clubs.

Duties performed at motor racing circuits, motor-cycle races or hill climbs can be very demanding because the speed of the event means that any accident is likely to be serious. Leicestershire had consistently provided first-aid cover for the Mallory Park racing track and as the needs of the situation changed, so did the resources available. There was a bond between the St John personnel and the racing fraternity – competitors and organizers alike – which made the duty pleasant but no less efficient. Many famous names have been assisted by the St John teams which included cadets, and it was a proud moment when J. L. King, Cadet Division, was presented with a trophy by Barry Sheene, world champion motorcyclist whose skill, courage and determination are themselves an inspiration to young people. When in 1982 Mallory Park was forced to close, the comradeship between the riders and St John did not end and the Leicestershire teams joined with those from Derbyshire in supporting Donington track which had opened in 1977. But 1977 also witnessed a serious accident to a St John member. Cadet Pauline Rivers of Radstock Nursing Cadet Division was seriously injured at a motor-cycle scramble when she was hit by one of the bikes. She was taken to hospital for an emergency operation but later went on to gain her Grand Prior's Badge.

Farningham Division in Kent has been the local first-aid team for Brands Hatch for many years. On 7 December 1980 Len Berry, the Divisional Superintendent, and his staff were surprised and delighted to hear that the circuit had decided to show their appreciation by devoting one race meeting to St John Ambulance. The idea was that a proportion of the money taken at side-shows and off-track events would be donated to the local Division. This practical demonstration of gratitude and goodwill served to strengthen the commitment of divisional members who know that their service is appreciated.

Brigade members are sometimes asked to volunteer for joint duty overseas. In 1975, the Sovereign Military Order invited SJA (as a Foundation of the Venerable Order) to work alongside SMOM members providing first-aid during the nine busiest weeks of Holy Year in Rome. Teams of surgeons, qualified nurses, nursing and ambulance members were marshalled and undertook duties for specific weeks. Lancashire's County Surgeon, Dr P. J. Wren, represented the Order of St John, while Sheila Puckle of London and Robert Percival of Kent were two of the senior officers. This was a very arduous task, with forty casualties during the two-hour Papal audience, but it was also rewarding in the sense of being a joint service to people who had travelled long

157

distances to be in Rome at that particular time. A joint duty of a very different character took place in Canada, when twenty young SJA members teamed up with Canadian St John for the Commonwealth Games in 1978. The combined contingents were kept very busy; there were many occasions when they were under real pressure and only too pleased to be able to return to the monastery where they were staying. They had gained valuable experience and proved that the St John family spans the globe.

Public duty means being on duty and therefore on call for the whole period of the duty. Very often a host of minor ailments is dealt with, passing virtually unnoticed and therefore not fully recorded. However, the very presence of a trained and experienced first-aid team is of vital concern to organizers who need insurance cover, and also to competitors who are glad of the assurance that trained men and women are at hand. Those who have not undertaken such duties might reflect on what it means to voluntarily give up a part of a week-end (sometimes a complete week-end) and accept the high degree of responsibility which accompanies first aid at the various forms of public duty. It is not a 'picnic', nor a way of getting free tickets as some doubters have suggested, but a genuine responsibility for which specific training and careful organization are necessary.

Many duties are completed with no major casualties and little call on the volunteers, but as we have seen modern sports actually do result in serious casualties requiring instant and effective action. Two Cornishmen on public duty at a motor-cycle scramble in May 1985 faced such an accident when a rider had fallen; the man following him had to swerve over a dangerous jump to avoid hitting him, his own bike went out of control and he was thrown to the ground. Gently Terry Penharwood removed the man's crash helmet and Malcom Bent applied artificial ventilation – mouth-to-mouth resuscitation – and restored the rider's breathing. When the young man recovered, he said, 'I am damned lucky SJA were there – if they hadn't been, I wouldn't be here now; they were magic.' Another life had been saved, which in itself is worth the many thousands of hours spent on public duty. It is better to be fully trained and not needed than to be urgently required yet unable to respond.

14
CARE IN THE COMMUNITY

There has always been an element of welfare in the work of the Brigade, inevitable in any movement which has 'service' as its aim. During and after the Second World War this aspect of St John work assumed greater importance, with welfare teams being sent to Malaya, Greece and Cyprus under the Joint War Organization. At home, too, the need for welfare work increased and today it is a vital and much appreciated form of St John's service to the community. 'Care in the community' has attracted many people to St John where they become either Brigade members or auxiliaries who, whether uniformed or not, are dedicated wearers of the St John emblem. In 1941 when the National Old People's Welfare Committee was created as part of the National Council of Social Service, the Brigade was represented in this new venture along with other charitable organizations. Almost immediately the Brigade's preparatory work of previous years assumed great importance and in particular, the Medical Comforts Depots were able to provide much needed equipment to old people. In Norfolk several divisions began to organize clubs and summer outings for old people; at Dartford in Kent the local division organized a Darby and Joan Club in their HQ, while in Cheshire and Lancashire Brigade members including cadets did shopping, took pensioners to collect their money, raised cash to purchase wheel-chairs and generally tried to make things easier for the aged.

At the end of the Second World War, service families began to be sent to join the new Occupation Forces in Germany and Tilbury Docks became the scene of bustle and activity with thousands of women and children waiting for military ferries. In this melée St John members did sterling work operating a port welfare service. Soon civil shipping lines took over the job, but they asked some St John women to continue their work and before the requirement ended they had served well over 200 ships, putting in over 8,000 duty hours, with an average of six members looking after each ship. In 1947 the Whitstable Nursing Division heard a lecture about the importance of homes for the aged; Mrs Papworth (the Superintendent) and her members immediately put a deposit on a house in Tankerton and a St John Home was born. The bedrooms were quickly in use and the nursing members and cadets gave the venture their total support. Although at first the home was barely able to keep its head above water financially, it was maintained so well that the patients felt comfortable and very much at ease; it remains a valued facility for those in need, who include former senior nursing members of the Brigade.

In 1947 Princess Elizabeth and the Duke of Edinburgh received a most unusual but very practical wedding gift from the cadets of Bexhill, Sussex, who adopted four old ladies and pledged to look after them – this pledge was their present. During 1949 and the early years of the 1950s St John welfare work was increasing. The joint St John and BRCS Service Hospitals Welfare Committee Conference in 1949 drew attention to the increasing requirement for welfare work both in hospital and during convalescence, but at this time there were only 114 trained welfare officers employed by the committee. Although a distinct development, directed at hospitals, this conference demonstrated clearly that more auxiliary volunteer workers would be needed in the future. Some divisions – particularly those where nursing members were in the majority – were already reaching beyond first aid into a form of local community welfare service, assisting the health authority and district nurses, shopping for the elderly and arranging outings. At Halesowen, Worcestershire, the Divisional Christmas party for the blind had become a popular event; in Kent, 'Operation Enterprise' in 1954 saw members reporting at 5 a.m. to assist polio victims on to a ferry for a day trip to France, and at 7 p.m. they carried their frail passengers back to their homes. In Dorset the county St John Council had been assisting the elderly on a regular basis since 1949; five years later the value of consistent support with a degree of continuity had become greatly appreciated in the community as a whole, by officials, relatives and neighbours as well as by those who benefited directly.

Joint welfare operations with BRCS continued wherever the need arose. The violence in Cyprus in 1963 and 1964 led to the establishment of a Joint Relief Commission led by John Coles, with 26 volunteers drawn equally from the Red Cross and St John. The JRC's main task was to assess the most urgent and serious needs of a divided population, then to take whatever action was necessary to provide medical aid, shelter, food, clothing and transport. It was essential that the relief measures were applied with the strictest impartiality where they were most needed. Coles divided the Commission into teams of two volunteers, usually one Red Cross and one St John; only when he gave an unqualified guarantee that there would be no smuggling and no firearms, was he allowed to operate. Robert Percival of Kent, a St John Surgeon for ten years, was teamed with Joan Wiggal of the Red Cross and these two were shot at as they were travelling to a duty; fortunately they were not hit. Other members of the team may not have heard shots fired in anger but were only too aware of the frustrations in that environment. After five months it became clear that the voluntary organizations had done all they could and it was now time for the United Nations to take responsibility.

As the years passed, the need for national welfare work of varying kinds became more evident. There were more elderly people in the population; young women were working by day and needed some form of day nursery for their children; and the needs of the physically and mentally handicapped were more pressing. Finally, society itself was changing, the pendulum of permissiveness swinging further outwards and bringing more problems for the hard-pressed social services. There was hardly a Division of the Brigade in Britain which was not active in some way, but many of the projects went unrecorded. Welfare, however, is not simply a matter of pushing a wheel-chair, making a cup of tea or doing the shopping; patients and the elderly need reliable advice about local authority or national regulations as well as a sympathetic and patient listener when they have problems – whether these are real or imagined. The task of voluntary welfare personnel was far more responsible than many imagined: quite unlike first aid as it was originally understood, but vital human aid none the less.

In 1972 the Secretary of State for Social Services (then Sir Keith Joseph) invited various voluntary organizations to meet him and expressed the view that 'Care in the Community' was the greatest need of the day. As a result of this, St John was asked to increase still further the amount of work it was doing in this field. Doubt was expressed in some Counties as to whether this would be possible without jeopardizing what was then considered the Brigade's main function – first aid. However, from that time onwards more and more work of this kind was attempted and also properly recorded for the first time. It was then that Sir Keith Joseph presented St John with a trophy for welfare, to encourage and develop this type of practical work within the community.

It is not easy to assess who should receive an award for real, practical welfare work, which by its very nature relies on teamwork and requires a long-term approach to the needs of either individuals or the community as a whole. Those who judge the projects do so on the basis of initial reports, interim progress reports and a final report showing the degree of success achieved. A short-list of projects is produced and a team of judges visits the divisions concerned with them. In 1975 the village of Bere Alston in Devon was proud to learn that their Combined Division was the first unit to win the new Welfare Award for a project which provided real help to the elderly, involved other welfare and social organizations and took account of care in emergencies. The judges felt that this project had 'contributed immeasurably to the quality of life of the whole community'. In the same year, Birmingham Post Office Division planned a project to assist the handicapped and in particular those suffering from multiple sclerosis; four members of the division gave up a week of their holidays to care for patients and the scheme was highly commended. In 1976, Birmingham won the Welfare Trophy for consistently successful and practical aid over two years.

The story of Highworth Division in Wiltshire illustrates the kind of commitment which is now generated within St John to meet the needs of social service. The Highworth White Cross Club is one of the Brigade's modern success stories, successful because it meets the genuine needs of a complete community, and in particular of the disabled and handicapped who are the true members. The Club is the result of a St John initiative and is still sponsored by the Division but involves other charitable organizations, church wives' clubs, Girl Guides and naturally the social service committee for the local council. The activities of the handicapped members are carefully planned so that they derive real value and experience the satisfaction of some form of achievement. The cadets of the Division made a wooden seat which has been presented to the club; members were taken to Longleat for a special visit and other St John Divisions provided helpers for the day. Finally, in order to raise funds a Highworth man entered the London Marathon. This is a real-life welfare project which earned the Division the Keith Joseph Welfare Award. But the Northern counties have also played their part in welfare – in 1977, the Queen's Jubilee year,

Skelmersdale Quadrilateral Division in Lancashire was awarded the trophy for its commitment to the elderly, housebound and lonely members in their community. Skelmersdale has continued and extended this project into the 1980s, despite difficulties which others would find insurmountable. They face one of the highest percentages of unemployment, have no ambulance or 'unit' transport other than their superintendent's car and do not have their own HQ. The cadets of the Division travel weekly to Liverpool's wholesale market to buy fruit and vegetables, which they then sell to the pensioners of the area for the wholesale price. This Division brings help to families who really need it, in an area where social service is of great importance.

For many years, members of St John have assisted disabled people who wished to go on the pilgrimage to Lourdes. One man who made twenty of these journeys as a stretcher-bearer was Herbert McGuire of Middleton. Some of these visits were at the initiative of a Division or County, whilst others were made in cooperation with the Sovereign Military Order. In 1976, as part of a joint venture, a team of attendants and nurses from several counties in Britain worked closely with the Sovereign Order on this important welfare task, a task which has as much to do with faith as it has with physical well-being and which continues to the present day.

In July 1975 Bath City Division was engaged in an exchange of visits between groups of disabled people from France and Britain. Early one morning the members arrived at the Cheshire Foundation Home to dress and assist the disabled travellers, taking them – together with their wheel-chairs and specialized nursing requirements – to Bristol Airport, whence they flew to Bordeaux for a two-week holiday. Then the team drove on to Southampton to collect a group of French patients who were taken back to the Cheshire Home in Bath. Two weeks later, after their normal summer duties, they did the reverse journeys. It has always been in the nature of St John people to take the initiative rather than waiting for someone else to point out that there is a job to be done, and to be involved in welfare is to be a social worker with all the responsibilities that fall on the shoulders of those who try to help the less fortunate in their community. From Wellingborough comes a story of five years of such quiet, unobtrusive but immensely valuable service. An elderly lady suffering from glaucoma and being also very arthritic, required eyedrops twice daily. For five years members of the division attended her at home, Christmas and Bank Holidays included, and did not miss a day. 'The St John Ambulance has been marvellous,' was the thanks of a most grateful patient who could not administer her own relief measures.

In 1981, the International Year of the Disabled, Lady Elizabeth Godsal, Joan Packham and a group of St John members of Berkshire County decided to plan a disabled holiday for 1982. With the help of the Enterprise Units of Berkshire and Oxfordshire, and contacts made with potential helpers, the venture took shape and on 11 September 1982 a mixed group of 32 disabled and 34 young St John members set off in a coach for a trial 'holiday' at Avon Tyrrell in the New Forest. It was a tremendous success with everyone becoming fully involved; not least Jim Mitchell, the coach driver, sports organizer and welfare worker combined. Originally meant to be a 'one-off', this proved so successful that it was decided to plan another similar holiday in 1983. Hampshire County agreed to combine with Berkshire, and Avon Tyrrell was again booked for a week. Lady Elizabeth Godsal, County Superintendent for Berkshire and Mrs Glenys Duke, County Superintendent for Hampshire, provided the organizing keystone and members of St John set out to raise cash to cover 77 holidaymakers for one week at £100 per person. Each person attending would pay £30 towards the cost; the remainder came from sponsored walks and swims, half-marathons and other sports, together with generous donations from companies, Round Table and Rotary. On 17 September the second holiday began, with members from Hampshire, Berkshire and Oxfordshire taking part and doing most of the work; this welded teams together and allowed the handicapped to play their part as best they could. Many visits were included in their first programmes, including the Royal Navy at Portsmouth, Nelson's HMS *Victory* and a performance of the musical 'Annie'. Major-General Peter Leuchars, Chief Commander, visited the camp and was impressed by the commitment and the obvious enjoyment of all who took part.

This St John holiday for the disabled has been arranged every year since that first 'one-off' trial and is now a valued regular fixture, designed not only for enjoyment but also to provide open-air activities for the disabled which they would not otherwise be able to attempt. The St John members who attend have a hard-working and challenging but enjoyable holiday too. In September 1985, Princess Anne visited Avon Tyrrell and watched disabled holidaymakers canoeing, building rope bridges, swimming and publishing the holiday newspaper the *Tribune*, which is edited and printed by the handicapped. They reported the visit of the Princess and the staff presented her with a framed copy of the edition. Let those who wrote in the *Tribune* tell their story: 'I could not have come to Avon Tyrrell without the help of St John Ambulance. They are the best friends I have ever had,' a blind girl reports, 'I brought my guide dog Kaye, I have become more independent . . .'; a helper writes, 'I find the combination of a holiday and helping disabled people very rewarding. . . .' After one holiday, as a practical sign of appreciation to all the helpers, Ken Billington of Hampshire laid on a special 'thank you day' at the site. It *is* good to be appreciated – and St John volunteers are no different from others in this respect.

Mary Neville-Kaye, the Brigade's Chief Welfare Officer and herself an experienced Superintendent at both Divisional and District level, has no doubt that concern for the handicapped and the underprivileged will call for yet more help from the Order and that welfare work will increase. She is also convinced that the cadets have a vital role to play, assisting others and at the same time gaining in experience themselves. In addition, some divisions are arranging overnight accommodation for relatives who need relief from the burden of caring for loved ones; the term 'caring for the carers' is an apt description of this task. Many people have joined St John as auxiliaries in order to do this work; they do not want to wear uniform or guarantee regular weekly attendance, but they share a desire to serve the community. Help for the handicapped is not a mechanical response; the type of help needed varies with the person and the degree and nature of the handicap. A caring and interested approach, backed by patience and persistence and a willingness to tackle the perhaps less pleasant aspects of personal attention – this is the requirement. Today many handicapped people live longer than heretofore; they have the same needs as others and feel the same hopes, but they suffer the frustrations and indignity imposed by their situation. St John members can provide the care and interest which will add colour to drab lives and bring a spark of friendship to people who need it most. None of this help can be provided without money and it is pointless to hide the fact that St John needs constant injections of cash to run such projects as those at Avon Tyrrell and Lourdes as well as the local schemes which are becoming more important facets of St John work.

15
IN THE AIR

On 1 May 1985 at the Banqueting Hall in Whitehall, Her Majesty the Queen, accompanied by Prince Philip, presented the Britannia Trophy to the St John Ambulance Air Wing. This supremely important award is given for the most meritorious performance in the air; among previous holders are Alcock and Brown, Sheila Scott and John Cunningham, so the Air Wing as a unit was sharing honour with some of the greatest names in aviation. St John Ambulance coordinates the work of two vitally important forms of service in the air. The carriage of patients with qualified air attendants is the responsibility of the Aeromedical Service, while the transfer of transplant tissue and surgical transplant teams is the function of the St John Air Wing. The work of the Order and Brigade in the air which led to this recognition of the Air Wing is an essential part of this story.

The first step was taken on 6 April 1924 when a cardiac patient was flown from Paris to Croydon escorted by Charles Green, a St John member of the Invalid Transport Corps. The tickets for this flight are now displayed in the museum and rightly so, for the success of this first flight was to lead to other developments. In 1934 the first Air Duties Ambulance Division was established in Ipswich under Divisional Surgeon Malcom McEwan, to deal primarily with casualties arising as a result of aeroplane accidents. The members had begun training in 1933 and did not officially form the unit until all had received instruction on burns, fire fighting and surgical nursing. They then did their first duty at Mildenhall for the start of the UK-to-Australia air race in 1934. We must remember that this St John service was designed to assist on the ground, but the BRCS and St Andrew's Ambulance had already carried or escorted patients by air. However, in 1937 St John personnel joined with the BRCS in an air evacuation exercise, but then

166

came the war and by the time peace returned there were new requirements and new aircraft.

In 1947 the St John Counties of Somerset and Berkshire became involved in air escort duties and sought ways of obtaining the specialist training required for in-flight escort and nursing duty. Somerset successfully dealt with a number of serious cases from Weston-super-Mare, while Berkshire assisted in the move of a patient from Switzerland to London. In 1953, air attendant courses were started by the Association with the assistance of British European Airways, and a textbook was produced. In 1954 the first air attendant duty following the reintroduction of a specialist air attendant appointment was undertaken by Sergeant R. J. Baker of Ealing, who collected a seriously ill casualty and escorted him to Cyprus, returning home after 60 hours' absence. The following year Mrs A. M. Woolston of Brixton took patients to Jersey and Amsterdam, and Mrs Smellie of Essex escorted a helpless patient to Germany. Then in 1956 came the important airlift of Hungarian refugees from Austria to the UK, a joint operation with the BRCS under the aegis of the International Red Cross. Among the St John personnel who played a prominent part in this evacuation was Derek Clark, a former cadet of Southwick Division who joined St John's Gate Division whilst studying to be a dentist in London. In the days before Christmas 1956 Derek reported to Blackbushe Airport for two air journeys to Austria and made one road and ship journey in February 1957, in all spending 150 hours of actual duty covering over 5,000 miles. In 1958 he escorted the first stretcher case outside Europe via Aden to British Somaliland. 1956 had also seen the air attendants in Egypt at the request of the Foreign Office following the Suez crisis, collecting British patients from hospitals and returning with them in a Dan Air chartered aircraft. Since then the Air Attendant Service has been used by major airlines, travel agencies, education authorities, the Foreign and Commonwealth Office and by the St John Air Wing when flying a patient. There is also a direct affiliation to the AA, in that the AA can provide insurance cover for holidaymakers to be returned to the UK in an aircraft of the St John Air Ambulance in case of accident or illness.

Many of the air attendants achieved a measure of distinction because of their preparedness to travel and their competence during the flights, some of which lasted many hours. Frank Murkin travelled to Africa and America several times and to Australia twice. He vividly recalls one duty which took him to 'the pens', the area beneath Heathrow Airport where illegal immigrants are questioned. Here he was asked to accompany an epileptic and mentally retarded youth to his home country, but on arrival the boy's family were reluctant to receive him back. We can only imagine Frank's concern – even anguish – as he turned towards the aircraft for an immediate return journey, not knowing what reception his patient would receive. On another occasion he was sent to Zaire to bring back two wounded British mercenaries. Their delight at seeing him was something he would always remember – whatever their situation and background, they needed help and St John was there to provide it. Arthur Weston, who made several flights to Kuwait, was often asked for by name because of his sympathetic approach in the air. These are just two of many who had given St John Aeromedical Service such a good name.

Even further scope for service in the air arose with urgent carriage of organs for transplants, blood, drugs and of course surgical teams and patients who require special transport. During 1971 surgeons at the London Hospital were concerned at the lack of good transport facilities for kidneys which became available for transplant. Following correspondence in *Flight* a group of pilots met to discuss options with two officers of the Metropolitan Police. The inevitable committee was formed and Squadron leader H. G. Pattison, DFC, became its chairman. At the same time the President and Superintendent of the St Margaret's Division, Epping, P. G. Bowen and R. A. Peedle, were seeking ways of using light aircraft for modern ambulance work. Meanwhile the Department of Health, which had not initially been convinced of the role for volunteer pilots, was collating information on patients requiring kidney transplants. The biggest area of concern was the short 'life' of a kidney once it has been removed from a donor; it is necessary to have a reliable, flexible, fast form of transport permanently available. In November 1971 the first mission was flown when a kidney was transported form Heathrow to Nancy in France. This trial journey provided several valuable lessons for the future and proved that the concept was workable. A National Organ Matching and Distribution Service was set up at Bristol and this – now known as UK Transplant Service (UKT) – assumed responsibility for the movement of transplant tissue. By the end of 1971 a suggestion by the Brigade and some volunteer pilots that they could work together and meet the requirements proved acceptable, and on 2 February 1972 the St John Ambulance Air Wing was inaugurated.

The nucleus of the new organization was formed around a Flight

Control Centre at St Margaret's Hospital, Epping. Pat Bowen was a war-time Royal Air Force Officer now employed as hospital administrator, and St John Area Commissioner for Western Essex; R. A. Peedle was Divisional Superintendent of Epping Combined Division, based on St Margaret's Hospital. These two – together with former RAF Wing Commander H. H. (Harry) Drummond, H. G. Pattison and Mrs Betty Bowman – became the founders of the Wing. Pattison recruited the pilots and Drummond established the Control Centre, immediately starting the lengthy process of selecting and training fifteen volunteer flight controllers. D. A. Anderson was appointed treasurer, becoming the third principal executive officer of the new Wing.

Towards the end of 1972 St John Air Wing was asked if it could fly a severely-injured boy from the South of France to Stoke Mandeville Hospital. An appeal was made for funds to cover the cost of the flight and within fifteen minutes the money had been pledged. Rapid arrangements were made and an Islander aircraft with St John air attendant on board took off for Montpellier. Whilst the flight was in progress the RAF station at Benson was contacted and agreed to open its runway during the night. The aircraft landed at 1 a.m. and the patient was safely admitted to Stoke Mandeville before 2 a.m. So began a new dimension to the St John air effort, the Air Ambulance Service, with Derek Clark as one of the founders. The new service required trained personnel, in-flight equipment and the ability to charter appropriate aircraft for the carriage of seriously-ill patients or those whose condition made it difficult for scheduled flights to accept them. This new development provided greater flexibility because smaller airfields could be used, closer to a receiving hospital. Aircraft have been chartered from Thurston Aviation (the Islander) and McAlpine (HS 125) for air ambulance flights, while the AA has received so many requests within its insurance cover that one of its aircraft has been converted to an air ambulance and used on several 'aero-med' flights. Cardiac cases were carried in a Cessna Golden Eagle which can fly at 11,000 ft with sea-level cabin pressure. By 1974 intensive care was possible in flight, and a little girl in a coma was safely carried from Palma to Norwich using this equipment.

The two forms of air activity – air attendance and air ambulance – were combined in 1974 to form the St John Aeromedical Service, since when the staff in the operations room at St John Ambulance HQ have been on duty 24 hours a day, 365 days a year, ready to receive calls for help. The Aeromedical Operations Room is staffed by qualified nursing personnel who have a list of some two hundred doctors and nurses, all volunteers who are prepared to travel at a moment's notice when free to do so. The Operations Room is able to contact medical specialists, consultants and hospitals as well as all the major airlines and – crucially important – air transport companies who arrange the air ambulances. Aeromedical Services maintain sets of in-flight medical equipment to convert aircraft into air ambulances at five separate airports, where the equipment is regularly serviced and maintained at a constant state of readiness by teams of dedicated volunteers. Some idea of the value and popularity of the Aeromedical Service can be gained from the figures for duty flights: 44 cases in 1975, 94 in 1976 and over 100 in 1977, rising to more than 200 cases by 1983. This does not include the road transport duty or sea escorts.

During 1984 the Aeromedical Services undertook 761 operations, a significant increase over previous years, mainly in scheduled flights. Increased operating costs, mainly due to the cost of fuel, caused a decrease in air ambulance flights. The most dramatic case of the year – and one which again broke new ground – concerned the repatriation of six Hong Kong Chinese crewmen whose ship had been hit by an Exocet missile in the Persian Gulf. It was necessary for the controllers to charter a neutral Swiss aircraft and medical team and arrange a fighter escort for the flight into the war zone.

The first action on receipt of a call is to contact the doctor handling the case in order to discuss the patient's condition and so decide how best to arrange transport and care. One important aspect of this first call is the ability to ask detailed questions regarding the patient and so identify the medical requirements: for example, whether or not the patient can travel sitting up or will need a stretcher. Then the complex question of tickets is tackled, together with such problems as changing flights, re-routing and the provision of road ambulances and hospital beds. Cases have been dealt with from as far away as China, Australia, New Zealand, Korea and Brazil as well as within Europe. It is a complicated piece of medical and travel organization, involving teamwork between the operational staff and the medical personnel undertaking the duty.

The team now handles an average of some 600 cases each year and in addition provides road ambulances to meet a further 200 patients a year. Some of the patients, particularly those who have been injured in accidents, require careful and specialized in-flight nursing and attention to equipment such as monitoring tracheotomy or drainage tubes or intravenous infusions. Some psychiatric patients need 24-hour attention, a tiring and distressing task for attendants. There have been several occasions when these volunteers have had to deal with two or three patients in one aircraft. Meanwhile there is more to do in the control room, for each patient's condition and the progress of the flight are matters of the gravest concern to anxious relatives and friends. They are grateful for the phone calls which tell them that the plane has taken off, landed safely and finally: 'You can phone the hospital now – he's there.' We do not need much imagination to see what comfort this brings; it is part of the caring attitude of the modern St John Ambulance.

Meanwhile, the new St John Air Wing was pressing ahead and by the end of 1972 could call on nearly a hundred qualified volunteer pilots with access to some sixty aircraft of various types. They had already completed 27 missions, covering over 16,000 miles, and had been on 'standby' for a further 38 occasions. The pilots were formed into ten 'Groups' each led by a group co-ordinator, and there were also unattached pilots all over the UK. H. G. (Pat) Pattison and Harry Drummond played important roles in setting up an organization and establishing the procedures necessary for putting a plane in the air one hour after the control centre had received a request. It is the Wing's great pride that since that first day they have never failed to answer a call for help – no matter when or where, and whatever the weather. Only one mission has failed to meet the strict medical time schedules and that was due to fog closing the airfield some twenty minutes before the plane's estimated time of arrival. Despite the voluntary nature of the duty and the unusual call-out time there has been only one accident, but even so the kidney arrived in time and the crew were uninjured. Within a year air traffic controllers in Europe were becoming accustomed to the duty Air Wing controller's voice: 'This is the St John Ambulance Air Wing – we have an emergency medical flight.' Airports would reschedule traffic to provide clear landing or take-off for St John, some airfields would remain open specifically to receive a flight, and police would be on hand to escort the road ambulance at speed. This cannot just happen; it is the product of sound organization, flexible planning and the unstinting cooperation of many agencies.

The volunteer pilots who are the core of the Air Wing are auxiliaries of St John; their dedication and the support of their families is crucial to the success of the concept. Because many calls for help come in at night, pilots have to be prepared to travel to a closed airfield, push their own plane to its taxi point and take off in what may be appalling conditions. Their mission has only begun; the destination may be anywhere in Europe and there have been several flights to Belfast where urgent operations awaited the arrival of plasma or a kidney. There is no guarantee that an airfield will be open and the risks of being diverted have to be catered for. This of course reduces the chance of timely arrival and so the St John pilots are prepared to take off and land when others might abort or divert. In 1973 two pilots from Newcastle Aero Club accepted a mission to Denmark, a journey of 650 miles. Their club fuelled the plane and parked it on the apron. The controller at Epping notified Coventry (the donor airfield) and an airfield in Denmark that the mission was approved and as darkness fell, this particular emergency flight got under way. In Denmark surgeons began the operation which would involve the kidney now over the North Sea. On landing, eager hands grasped the life-saving box 'Kidney for Transplant' and a high-speed convoy rushed it to the hospital. The pilots locked the aircraft, went with guides to a hotel and slept until roused for their return journey, landing at Newcastle 20 hours and 1,400 miles later. They did not then know if the operation had been successful, but one spoke for both when he said, 'I hope so, though; I really do hope so.'

The St John Air Wing is not a male preserve; there are women pilots and air controllers who have played an important part in the Wing's development. Some of the women controllers are members of St John Ambulance, while others have auxiliary status; indeed it was a woman controller, Heather Bowman – a Brigade member since the age of eight – who faced the difficult task of controlling two kidney flights to different destinations at the same time. Women pilots too have faced their share of discomfort and danger: Mrs Pamela Howard of Southampton, whose husband has travelled with her as crew member, and Dr Mary Storrier who, despite walking with the aid of a stick because of polio, has flown several missions including some to Belfast during times of great tension.

During the period between Christmas 1977 and New Year 1978, the Air Wing undertook a mission every night for seven nights, flying nearly 4,000 miles in gale-force winds and dealing with 16 different airfields. In 1984 the St John Air Wing continued its support of the Department of Health with a most active year and a significantly increased capability, due to the use of helicopters as well as jet and turbo-prop aircraft. During the year the Wing flew 91 missions, almost double the figure for 1983. This included 29 foreign flights to Europe, 44 missions carrying heart transplant teams, 16 carrying liver transplant teams, one pancreas team and eight patients. In addition, thirty kidneys were transported from donor to transplant hospitals. The Wing has established biennial meetings with the staff of the UK Transplant Centre, a useful forum for discussion of priorities and procedures, while at the Flight Control Centre at St Margaret's Hospital, Epping, the controllers ensure that those procedures are put into practice.

At 0920 hrs on 24 April 1984, a provisional mission was requested to collect an eleven-year-old boy who was at Lourdes with a school party and return him to London for a kidney transplant at Guy's Hospital. At 12.15 the medical tests had been completed, the mission was confirmed and assigned the number K5663. The Air Wing had already made its preparations through Ted Girdler who arranged for a Golden Eagle aircraft, with its pilot Christopher Lawrence, who was already at Stuttgart with the aircraft to take on the flight. Lawrence flew to Tarbes, collected the boy and flew directly back to Heathrow, his turn-round time at Tarbes being only just over thirty minutes! At nine o'clock that evening the plane landed, to be met by a taxi with police escort so that the young patient could clear the airport quickly. Such is the cooperation and goodwill shown to St John by the British Airports Authority, but their generosity was to go further when they waived all normal airport handling charges.

By the end of 1984 the Wing had flown 683 missions, covering 312,381 miles and involving 2,522 flying hours. More recently it has been faced with missions which have involved much more than simply organizing an aircraft and pilot. On 12 January 1985 at 0255 hrs, Heather Bowman received a call alerting her to a request from Harefield Hospital for a team of three to go to Berlin with their equipment. They were required at the Stegelitz Hospital at 1200 hrs and precise timings were critical. By 0335 hrs Captain Brian Bedford and William Fleming of IDS were standing by the Citation aircraft, it now being necessary for Bedford to obtain clearance to travel along the air corridor through East Germany to Berlin. The mission having been confirmed and allocated the number K6434, all was now ready and waiting for the result of tests which would determine whether the transplant operation could go ahead. Just after 8 a.m. Ron Crawford took over control and meanwhile, whilst the team were on the way to Heathrow, clearances were being obtained – though not without

173

several delays – from the Berlin Air Safety Centre. At 0953 hrs the flight took off from Heathrow, landing at Tempelhof at 1200 hrs. About an hour later the team left Berlin for the return journey and just before 1600 hrs the aircraft landed at Heathrow. Immediately a call was put through to Harefield so that the surgical teams could have the maximum warning, and just before 1700 hrs Harefield telephoned Ron Crawford thanking the Wing for all their help. The two controllers had covered a total of fifteen hours for a flight time of just over four hours.

On 19 April 1985 mission K6689, with Eric Thurston at the controls of a Beech King Air 200, took off on a flight from Stansted to Heathrow to Innsbruck and return. This time Betty Bowman was controlling from her home and within ten minutes of receiving the first call the aircraft and pilot had been contacted and confirmed. Eric Thurston brought the aircraft to Heathrow, picked up the team and set off on an eight-hour round trip for a total of five hours' flying time. For these and other similar flights the controllers require to make some 25–35 telephone calls to hospitals, pilots, co-pilots, air traffic controllers, embassies and foreign airfields. The logs which they maintain reflect the great detail necessary for these missions of mercy. It is therefore easy to understand why the most successful heart surgeons travel to emergency cases using the St John Air Wing.

Today policy for the Air Wing is decided by a committee at St John Ambulance Headquarters chaired by the Commissioner-in-Chief, but the Wing requires special treatment and a degree of autonomy because of its national character. Its 165 pilots have access to 120 planes; they are reimbursed for any actual expense and given an allowance of £20 per hour of flying, which is needed to keep an aircraft in service in these expensive times. They receive nothing for their time; they are true volunteers in the very highest traditions of St John. These pilots, the St John controllers, mechanics, hospital staff and police are all part of a vital team and so are their families – one wife's comment proves this: 'It does mean that we have to be on call most nights, but I think it's worth it.' The fourteen Flight Controllers are also on call a great deal – they receive the first call for help, select and contact the pilots, alert airfields, deal with weather forecasts, customs clearances, refuelling, police liaison and of course crew briefing. Then they prepare and maintain the detailed log of the whole mission from call-out to final return landing.

The Air Wing presents two trophies for outstanding contributions to its work: the Pooley Sword of Honour for the most outstanding contribution to the service by a pilot during the preceding year; and the

Howard House trophy for the most effective effort by an Air Controller in the same period. However, it was now to be singled out for a truly great honour in its own right. The three men who sat together in the Banqueting Hall on 1 May 1985 represented all the skills of the Air Wing. We have already talked of Pat Bowen and H. G. Pattison; the third was Bill Bailey, a pilot who had then flown over sixty missions for the Wing. It was appropriate that the senior flight controller, air operations coordinator and a pilot of a unique voluntary service should together go forward to receive the Britannia Trophy on behalf of St John Ambulance Air Wing:

> For outstanding service to humanity for
> transporting by air over 700 heart and
> liver transplants and accompanying medical
> staff by 165 voluntary private pilots
> since its inauguration in 1972.

16
THE MODERN BRIGADE

In choosing to write about the modern Brigade, where should one start? So many of its activities are affected more by circumstances than by time and the selection of some arbitrary date would not appear to be appropriate. Already in dealing with public duties and welfare work the constraints of the calendar have been avoided in order to discuss and record progress. Social changes in Britain during the 1960s and into the 1970s do, however, provide us with a reasonable starting point, for these were the years when young people asserted themselves more forcefully, old values were questioned and a materialistic and more selfish view was taken of the individual's rights and freedoms. Some of these changes offended the more elderly in the community, and indeed some were judged even then to be harmful. They appeared to strike at family unity, parental control, self-discipline, corporate loyalty and social responsibility – all sound planks in the structure of earlier decades, in which the Brigade had flourished. Government policy regarding first-aid training and an increasingly violent environment also had their effect and the latter has been discussed in earlier chapters. Interest in all this, however, centres only in presenting a background against which can be seen the effect upon the Brigade's organization, strength, motivation and image, and its role in a future society.

The changing social climate led to questions being asked. Could the Association and Brigade remain separate? Did the public understand the difference? Indeed, did the public see St John as a relevant, contributing part of future society; for without public support, what would be its future? When the answers had been provided another question arose – would the Order be sufficiently determined to put into effect any changes which might be necessary? Within the Association and Brigade the comradeship of earlier years could be maintained despite there being fewer people, but their important and onerous duties would continue. These would not be easy years; they offered what would possibly be the greatest challenge since the war. However, the future of St John would depend on the personalities of the present just as much as it had depended on the pioneers of the past.

In July 1967, following meetings of a working party chaired by Mr N. McClintock, Secretary-General, a memorandum regarding the integration of the Association and Brigade was circulated to the Chapter-General of the Order, Priories, Counties and the senior officers of the Association and Brigade. Hitherto these had been independent Foundations of the Order, each with its own task; the Association taught first aid, as it had done since 1877, whilst the Brigade undertook practical duties as the uniformed 'arm' of St John. But what had been good enough for the first half of the twentieth century might not necessarily meet the demands and responsibilities of modern Britain. Duplication of effort, confusion in the minds of the public, financial difficulties and the pressures of maintaining effective recruitment for the Brigade were all seen as valid reasons for seeking some degree of rationalization within the St John family. Comments were returned to the Chapter-General and by the end of 1967 it was clear that a merger was not only possible but desirable.

There were of course those for whom any change would automatically be a wrong move, but the majority could see the benefit of integration at all levels. Some centres of the Association believed that they represented not only the senior Foundation but also the true aim of the Ambulance movement: to teach first aid to as many people as possible. Some Brigade members held the view that they provided the service to the public which best expressed the great motto of the Order of St John – *Pro Utilitate Hominum*; they argued that while one man could teach several pupils to an arranged time-table, many men and women were required to give up their time regularly and take additional responsibilities in carrying out public duty. The fear was also expressed that one Foundation would be absorbed into the other – that some kind of take-over bid would occur. The truth was, of course, that both functions were equally and vitally necessary and their coordination would be of lasting benefit to the public which both sought to serve. It was therefore necessary to convince members of both Foundations that these proposals represented real progress, and this could only be achieved by persuasion rather than the issue of anything which remotely resembled an 'order'.

On 28 February 1968 the question was discussed by the Chapter-General of the Order. The general concept of unification was accepted and the authority to put it into effect – General Memorandum No. 1 – was published the following day. At first the head of St John Ambulance was to be designated 'Director-General' and would be assisted by a Deputy Director-General; one of these two officers would have responsibility for the Brigade. The first two nominees were Sir Philip Southwell as Director-General and Sir William Pike as Deputy and Commissioner-in-Chief of the Brigade. National Headquarters were already some way down the road towards integration and the policy of merger at County level was agreed for the English counties, but Chapter-General did not wish them to be pressed into a merger before they were ready. St John Councils in the counties were invited to support the concept, acting as a unifying influence. When the merger was first announced there were still some counties which had neither a council nor an Association branch, but by the time the merger was complete all counties had both.

It would not be simply a matter for the Order to rule upon, even though the Grand Prior had approved in principle; Chapter-General was obliged to discuss several matters regarding the statutes of the Order and the questions of legal responsibility and finance as well as the more domestic views within the Foundations.

After considerable and deep discussion, the Chapter-General accepted that the separate objects and purposes of the Association and Brigade remained and the two were being joined together without changing the responsibilities of either body. The resolution then proposed and accepted was:

> That administrative steps be taken to achieve a merger between the St John Ambulance Association and the St John Ambulance Brigade, with the title 'St John Ambulance Association and Brigade' or shortly 'St John Ambulance'.

This was duly recorded in the minutes of Chapter-General and signed by Lord Wakehurst, Lord Prior, on 15 May 1968.

*

It was decided that for a variety of reasons it would be unwise to force the pace of integration in the early stages. Members of both Foundations needed time to get used to the idea and the potential problems of the Order's statutes required to be reviewed as progress was made.

Some Counties and Divisions responded well, but others were content to take their time about implementing the proposals. The merger did not affect St John overseas; individual national authorities would make their own decisions. In August 1968 General Memorandum No. 3 informed the Counties that the degree of flexibility originally permitted could further confuse the public and a new structure was being promulgated for County level organizations. Each county would be headed by a Commander St John Ambulance, who could either appoint two deputies – one each for Association and Brigade matters – or accept one of these roles himself, thereby requiring a deputy for the other function. The Commander SJA for a County was the senior executive officer of the County, a point made in General Memorandum No. 4 of 15 October 1968. The titles of the senior officers at National HQ required amendment to match the County organization, and in 1970 the post of Chief Commander was instituted, but combining with it that of Commissioner-in-Chief of the Brigade. The first holder of this new appointment was Sir William Pike, with Sir Hugh Stephenson as Director-General of the Association.

In 1971 Sir William Pike issued General Memorandum No. 8, in which he drew attention to the need to quicken the pace of amalgamation. The Foundation Conference of 1970 had made it clear that the members expected a lead to be given if the merger was to be effective. The policy to be followed in 1971 therefore had the aim of:

The unification of the former Association and Brigade Foundations into a single Foundation to be so organized as to provide an increasingly efficient and better understood service to the public.

The shorter title 'St John Ambulance' would be used as the normal and formal title of the Foundation, but the terms 'Association' and 'Brigade' would be retained to denote respectively the training function and the organization and duties of the uniformed members. By 1973 the Chief Commander's appointment no longer carried with it a second post; a separate Commissioner-in-Chief was appointed for the Brigade branch, while the Director-General controlled the Association branch.

The operational units of the Ambulance would continue to be Centres and Divisions, but some centres instructed people over a wider area than that given to a uniformed division. It was essential, therefore, that a controlling or coordinating authority should be available at either local or some intermediate level, but not necessarily at both. Where possible, Association and Brigade areas of responsibility should coincide. It was accepted that the local working levels would vary around the country and no time limit was placed on their merger, but counties were requested to complete their unification by St John's Day, 1971. So far as funds were concerned, the memorandum recognized that local units needed money for their own specific tasks, but the basic principle was expressed that where it was possible to administer a joint fund, this should be done. Brigade and Association regulations were then amended to take account of the merger.

When, in 1975, Lt-General Sir William Pike retired from the post of Chief Commander, he had spent eight busy years in the two most senior posts of the new St John Ambulance. From 1967 to 1973 he was Commissioner-in-Chief, handing that post over to Major-General Desmond Gordon. He also became the first Chief Commander in 1969, therefore holding both appointments for four years. The merger had not only demanded tact, discretion and a sympathetic understanding of the overall work of the Association and Brigade; it also required a degree of firmness and wise leadership and St John was fortunate that Sir William Pike was at the helm to provide this combination of sympathy and steel at a critical period. The Order was also fortunate in having as his successor Sir Maurice Dorman, who had been the Almoner since 1971 and was Chairman of the Joint Committee of the Red Cross and St John. Sir Maurice was later to hold the appointment of Lord Prior of the Order of St John.

The 'new look' St John Ambulance was expected to minimize the risks of confusion, allow for more effective coordination and use of resources and project a single image which the public could understand and support. The creation of County Headquarters to be shared by both branches did much to encourage this. The whole St John family was now to be involved in making the new organization effective; County Presidents and the County St John Councils were geared to fund-raising, as they had always been, but they were now to find a more direct role in the development of the new Foundation. The single Foundation and simplified organization were expected to bring advantages in terms of morale, training, recruiting, coordination and economy. By 1970 St John Ambulance owned over 650 ambulances and many of its units owned their own headquarters building, together with a great deal of equipment, some of it used for training and some for operational duty. All this needs finance if it is to be properly maintained and replaced when it has run its course, or when significant new equipments arrive on the scene. The presidents at every level accept as one of their roles that of fund-raising for St John Ambulance, so that these requirements can be purchased. It is therefore relevant to consider the ways in which the presidents have been able to work.

At national level the Grand President of St John Ambulance is HRH The Princess Margaret, who thus maintains the Royal family's link with every aspect of the Order's activity. The Chief President is Mrs Harold Phillips, who chairs the Annual Presidents' Conference, an important meeting at which all levels of St John Ambulance are represented, where problems can be aired and the wide variety of tasks which fall to presidents can be fully discussed. London District's President is now the Duke of Westminster who, since taking office in 1983, has devoted a great deal of his time to meeting Brigade members at training and on public duty. Every County has its President and Deputy or Vice-Presidents for specific functions.

From the earliest days of the Association there have been 'titular heads' or presidents of its 'Centres', the first being appointed for Canterbury in 1878. A year later, HRH The Duke of Edinburgh and HRH Prince Leopold took office as Presidents of the Ashford and Oxford Centres respectively. Then in 1885 HRH Princess Christian became President of the Isle of Wight Centre and HRH Princess Beatrice accepted the Presidency of the Mayfair District of the Metropolitan Centre. In 1889 HRH The Prince of Wales agreed to become President of the Association as a whole. Presidents of Brigade units seem to have been appointed after the 1914–1918 War, being first mentioned in the General Regulations of 1924. Today, after many changes in the detailed regulations, the Presidents of the combined St John Ambulance are expected to be 'persons of influence', a phrase first used to describe them in 1896! Presidents and Vice-Presidents are appointed for every level of St John Ambulance organization from national to divisional. Each is a working member of St John Ambulance, albeit not a first-aider and without executive responsibility, but with a wide-ranging portfolio of tasks which bring lasting benefit to the work, status and morale of the units.

At one time it was thought that the absence of executive authority was a disadvantage, preventing a President from getting things done. As the years have passed, however, it has been seen that the independence given to Presidents permits them to operate where the need is greatest, using their influence in the community to obtain the best results. For a long while Presidents were not expected to wear uniform, but in 1951 authority was given for them to wear the normal uniform with plain buttons and specially designed gorget patches and Presidential badge. In 1952 the first written guidance was provided for Presidents in the shape of *The President's Handbook*, prepared by Lady Dunbar-Nasmith.

It is not easy to summarize the work of the Presidents because it is so varied, and what may be important at one level might be placed in a position of lesser priority in another. However, one of the most vital tasks at every level is publicity; here Presidents are able to use their influence and their contacts to stress the voluntary nature of the Brigade's work, to make its contribution to society more widely understood and to emphasize local successes as well as local needs. By attending the St John Council, Presidents at County level are able to keep aware of all that is going on and so assist in ensuring that there is a common accepted goal. Because of their local knowledge, Presidents are also able to approach suitable doctors and qualified nurses who can assist the Brigade; they can indicate men and women whose skills or character make them suitable instructors or Brigade officers; they can identify and help to obtain sites for camps or training. The fund-raising role has already been indicated and, though not an overriding task, its importance lies in the fact that whilst every penny is of value, the cost of even simple items is measured in tens or hundreds of pounds and the more specialized equipment in terms of thousands of pounds. Presidents have shown the flexibility, initiative and financial understanding to generate the best response from the public and so enable St John Ambulance to be properly equipped.

Within the units of the Brigade, the President can play an important role in welfare and morale, becoming a guide, counsellor and friend to the Superintendents. The cadets, who need a smooth transition to the adult Divisions, will also feature prominently in a President's work. By creating and maintaining interest in the training and welfare of the cadets the President once again eases the burden of the Brigade officers. Overall, the experience and local knowledge of the President is greatly valued at every level; for their dedication to St John is no less than that of their executive colleagues.

The function of Presidents has changed over the years, as they now undertake a far greater role in promoting the efficiency, welfare and expansion of St John Ambulance and help to secure the recognition of the work it performs. Although the office of President still carries no administrative commitment or executive authority, it is by no means a titular position. Indeed, it is largely on account of their neutral duties that they are able to provide unbiased support and advice in their particular spheres of influence.

Whilst reorganization has helped with coordination and economy of resources, it has not and cannot dispense with the need for financial support. St John Ambulance voluntarily gives its time to the public and deserves, in return, some token of the community's awareness and gratitude. But it is not enough simply to state this; the British public requires to be satisfied first, that it understands and accepts what St John means and second, that St John has a genuine need of financial help. Some people have formed the impression that the Order is a rich and aristocratic institution, well able to look after itself. What is not generally understood is that the very limited support provided by the government is restricted in its application and cannot possibly meet the many needs of the Ambulance. At a time when both national and individual resources have been reduced, the amount of money available to support the many voluntary charities in Britain would itself be limited. The British public has not understood that the great work of St John in Britain and in Jerusalem involved very heavy annual operating costs. It would perhaps be incorrect to compare these costs with those of a commercial enterprise doing the same work, but quite clearly they would be gigantic. Nor did people outside the Order appreciate the truly remarkable contribution of working men and women to the work of St John Ambulance at all levels.

In many respects the reorganization and rationalization of St John Ambulance activity has paved the way for closer, more practical ties between the various departments of the Order. Unfortunately, however, the quickening pace of integration coincided with the beginning of a fall in adult male membership which, though at first localized, later spread to most counties. There was some compensation in the form of increased recruiting of women and girl cadets, but although in 1974 the overall strength of the Brigade had shown an increase, the overall signs were ominous. The difficulty of recruiting men persisted; by the end of 1977 the fall in Ambulance members was increasing, with fewer younger replacements coming forward. This of course was a sad blow, because the White Cross belt of the Ambulance member had been the symbol of the Brigade for virtually all its early life. The men who had served in the Ambulance divisions had done the heavy work, provided the stretcher-bearers and also the escorts in the days before the nursing members achieved any prominence. It was the men who answered that first call to duty with the Armed Forces; the men who responded when first aid became essential in factories, mines and railways. In later years, the men formed the nucleus of several special duties teams which were formed to deal with mountain and sea rescue. It was the men who had carried their King during his illness, brought safety to people whose lives were in danger, held the Divisions together by their leadership in the days when it was unfashionable (dare one say unthinkable?) to have a woman Superintendent. The men had been the hub of the Brigade for many years and the fact that in this account there is no chapter devoted specifically to them means simply that their White Cross belt has played a prominent part in all aspects of the Brigade's history – it is not possible to separate the men from the central theme of the Brigade's work.

Why was it difficult in the 1970s to encourage men to join and cadets to transfer to the Ambulance Divisions? Many different answers to this question have been given, some of which should form a part of this study. Some of the older members felt that the Brigade had become somewhat complacent, that there was nothing much for it to do now that municipal ambulance departments were so well established. The National Health Service was looking after people and did not need volunteers. There had been so many duties or days of being 'on call' when nothing drastic happened, and if something did happen the advice was to call an ambulance and do nothing. It was almost like telling a special constable to call the police when in trouble! Surely, the arguments ran, St John Ambulance training meant a little more than this.

Other reasons for the shortfall included the feeling that there had been too much tampering with the organization and the uniform, leaving the men in particular with the feeling that their chosen volunteer outlet had become somewhat unstable and lacking in direction. The role of traditional first aid service did not fit neatly into a modern society which needed sympathy rather than splints; welfare work was becoming more important and women were better able to cope with this. Some believed that the international nature of Red Cross work inevitably led the public to support the BRCS to the exclusion of St John; if there was to be a form of voluntary medical-cum-welfare organization, let it be just one, and let that be the Red Cross. Further reasons, which did not find their way into the pages of reports or the *Review*, concerned the lack of challenge for young men and some failure in leadership at all levels.

None of these reasons was a complete answer to the question, nor could they stand up to detailed analysis on their own. Taken together, however, it was possible to see elements of them all in the various perceptions around the country. There were of course other factors connected with the changes in society and the response to discipline: the appearance of an even wider range of leisure activities which brought about a reluctance to give time to practical voluntary work. Some steps had already been taken during the 1970s to provide a more flexible Brigade organization with no sex discrimination: the establishment of Combined Divisions in which men and women were equal members, doing the same work and attending the same duties. The men were expected to be proficient in the skills of the nursing manual, just as they were at first aid. Later came the Quadrilateral Division, a unit of four sections – Ambulance, Nursing, Cadet Ambulance and Cadet Nursing – all supervised by one Divisional Superintendent who might be male or female. The first Quadrilateral Division to be registered was New Cross, London, on 1 January 1969.

Meanwhile the British public – in particular, the organizers of fêtes, horse shows, football matches, marathons and suchlike – and the officers of the police forces, responsible for good order, all saw the need for more and more duty. By the end of 1980 the number of duties required of the Brigade had increased significantly just at the very time of the steepest fall in male membership. There was, however, progress in many aspects of the Brigade's work, not least in the revival of a number of Divisions whose fortunes had flagged. It is a feature of voluntary organizations that units will wax and wane, often as a direct reaction to the quality of local leadership. In Derbyshire, the first mounted Division in Britain was formed with a veterinary surgeon as well as a Divisional Surgeon and twenty-three members including cadets. Another horsed Division was formed to cover the New Forest and further Divisions were created in Derbyshire, including a band in which some of the buglers were girls.

Silver bands are not new to St John and as far back as the 1920s, some Divisions formed small bugle bands with varying degrees of success. In 1951 Southport formed its band by taking over the instruments of a defunct special constabulary band. Southwark formed a band in 1954, which had some years of success and some of stagnation, but in 1968 it was revived with a different balance of instruments, girls were permitted to join and training was formalized. At the same time the members were all expected to hold a first-aid certificate and be

Brigade members or auxiliaries and in 1976 six holders of the Grand Prior's Badge were amongst its members. This band has had the distinction of playing beside the Central Band of the Royal Air Force and, in the Queen's Jubilee year 1977, of playing at the Royal Tournament and in the forecourt of Buckingham Palace – the first time a youth band had been accorded such an honour. In June each year the adult and cadet contingents at the St John's Day Ceremony are led by St John bands; 1976 saw the West Midlands lead the adults and Southwark the cadets. At 5.30 a.m. on 25 June 1983, a very special band in Somerset was preparing for the honour of leading the St John's Day parade; the girls of St Audries School Nursing Cadet Division Band formed up on parade at Paternoster Square at 11.30 a.m. and marched to St Paul's Cathedral escorted by mounted policemen. Two years later they played at the Royal Tournament and at both events they attracted a great deal of interest and acclaim – their average age was 10½ years.

Several bands have been formed during recent years; Derbyshire, Basingstoke, Hull, Romsey, Surrey County, Sussex Knights of Southwick, Weymouth, Wilnicote and Wadebridge – which played on St John's Day 1985 – all have silver bands. Some of the colliery divisions have fine bands, whilst Accrington boasts a pipe band! St John bands have become so popular that a Band Federation has been formed and joint training is now held so that all can gain knowledge and experience. Roly Gillam, the Federation's chairman, travels extensively to visit bands and assist them with preparation. There seems to be a desire not only to be good musicians but to look good on parade – an attitude which can have a wider impact on Brigade activities.

However, events which would have an even greater and more immediate impact upon the whole future of St John Ambulance were already taking place at national level. Early in 1982 the Market Opinion Research International (MORI) opinion poll organization was commissioned to consider the public's attitude to St John: first, its awareness of St John; second, its willingness to donate; and third, its preparedness to join St John Ambulance. MORI carried out its normal method of selecting a fair representation of the public, covering over 2,000 interviews and 172 sampling points in Britain. In addition, ten men and ten women were invited to take part in a studio discussion of a questionnaire about St John. The publication of MORI's report in August 1982 provided a very interesting view of the public's interest in St John Ambulance, but it was a rather sombre and depressing statement which raised a number of critical questions. The first important point was the realization that about two-thirds of the population had given money to one or more charities, but that of these very few were active participants. Nearly three-quarters of Britain's population felt unable to find time to help charities on a regular basis and this is in itself a rather sobering fact. St John was among the least well-known charities, but its association with first aid was generally acknowledged.

Not surprisingly, many people were prepared to support a caring organization or one which provides a vital community service, and both of these are central to the principles of St John work. However, the public's view of St John Ambulance was affected by the wearing of uniform and its quasi-military organization; these were characteristics which proved less acceptable to those interviewed. A small but significant percentage of the sample believed that St John was a part of the National Health Service. Comparatively few people were aware of St John's ancient origin, or that it maintains a modern hospital in Jerusalem and provides a modern air transport service for transplant organs as well as patients. Few people realized that a cadet branch existed. The general impression given to the public was apparently that of a caring but rather old-fashioned and formal organization whose uniform could be a disincentive to both support and recruitment.

The low level of awareness of St John's work was rather surprising and depressing, given that some form of St John activity had been carried on in Britain for more than a hundred years. But if this was rather worrying, the leadership of the Order and its Foundations could take heart from the assessment that over 60 per cent of those questioned believed that St John had a good reputation. If, then, St John Ambulance was generally admired and accepted as a caring organization, it should be able to encourage support by making the public much more aware of the diversity of St John work, the voluntary nature of the membership and the validity of the first-aid and nursing qualifications. This was MORI's great lesson to St John – go out and let people know more about you; until they know, they cannot be expected to support.

Any report of this nature is bound to stir up interest and encourage debate. Many pens were taken up to write to the *St John Review*, criticizing or supporting MORI's findings. This is not the place to attempt a blow-by-blow account of all this correspondence, but it is perhaps a suitable vehicle for summarizing the most widely held views within St John itself. The first and almost unanimous opinion was that the aims and achievements of St John Ambulance should be more widely publicized. A second, generally held view was that the structure required some modernization, with greater flexibility and greater responsibility for women members. The question of uniform attracted much comment; the military style was unpopular, the possible confusion with police uniform was unfortunate and the fuss made of rank badges was unnecessary. Some pointed out that the presentation of the uniform by its wearer could do much to influence the public for good or ill, while others drew attention to the need for high training standards and to attract public support by displaying competent volunteers. There were of course many who could have come to these conclusions without the aid of MORI. But whatever the views of the individual, it was now up to the National Headquarters to draw the lessons and apply the remedies which would bring St John Ambulance to increased public attention with an improved image and so attract both manpower and money.

This in itself would be no easy task, but St John was not given the opportunity to deal with it in isolation, for first-aid training had also come under the microscope and forthcoming important developments were about to affect all levels of the Brigade. In 1982 the government – through the Health and Safety Executive – introduced new first-aid regulations following criticisms from industry and elsewhere that standards had dropped. Analysis had demonstrated that the adult first-aid course contained too much material for the sixteen hours' teaching. It was decided that for a given work force, a specific proportion of their members should receive first-aid training and be expected to qualify by gaining a statutory certificate. A 'First Aid at Work (FAW)' training package was introduced by St John Ambulance, but its introduction was not universally welcomed; it seemed to many St John members that their authorized joint manual was more than sufficient for the training required and provided effective guidance for first aid everywhere.

What the new teaching attempted to do was to differentiate between the needs of first aid in places of work and those of St John personnel on public duty. The new statutory course was designed to be taught over a period of four days – 24 actual working hours – using the manual as a reference book but not as a teaching medium, and it was introduced following a trial coordinated by National Headquarters under the direction of Chief Commander, Major-General Peter Leuchars. The BRCS on the other hand decided to teach directly from the manual in the allotted time of 24 hours. Teaching methods had changed and it was generally felt that some former techniques were outdated, therefore the government introduced new regulations dealing with the certification of instructors. The Brigade First Aid Certificates issued before 1 July 1982 would remain valid only until their date expired, after which each member would be required to requalify under the new system. Because of the statutory requirement, it would not be possible for members to give first aid and remain covered by insurance unless they had requalified. To qualify for public duty, the Brigade member now had to undertake a further ten hours' training. However, irrespective of personal views, the 'First Aid at Work' regulations had been made, they were now law and St John Ambulance had accepted them as such.

The pressures of 1982 and 1983 were serious, affecting the long-term survival of St John Ambulance, and good practicable solutions were needed as a matter of urgency. It was therefore very fortunate that there was such a strong team at No. 1 Grosvenor Crescent, men and women of experience who were determined to get things done. The Chief Commander, had already served as Deputy Commissioner-in-Chief and Commissioner-in-Chief and was therefore well aware of the background to the MORI report and the 'First Aid at Work' package. He was now responsible for both branches of SJA and clearly both would be affected by the decision taken. The Commissioner-in-Chief, Major-General Sir John Younger, had been Deputy Commissioner for London District from 1978 to 1980 and thus had first-hand experience of the Brigade's contact with the public; he was to bear specific responsibility for recommending changes and putting them into effect. His constant barrage of ideas, most of which originated 'in the bath', kept a willing staff even more willing to see that nettles were grasped. Donald Seymour, Director-General of the Association Branch, Lady Moyra Browne, Superintendent-in-Chief, and her successor Lady Westbury were all involved in deciding upon the coordinated response.

That response involves greater acceptance of the merger, total acceptance and implementation of the statutory certificate, provision of new-style uniforms and a major publicity campaign designed to make the public more aware of St John. At the same time, the national HQ was seeking a practical and meaningful role for younger members who required the challenge of constant action combined with the satisfaction which comes from achievement. This would be particularly crucial for rural divisions, where young people would want to become involved in real first aid or realistic practice. The absence of worthwhile action tended to drive them away; young people are easily bored by inactivity and this problem would clearly challenge leaders at all levels.

*

Having already considered the merger and the statutory First Aid Certificate, we must now look at two other developments: uniform and publicity. There had for some time been a feeling that too much attention was being paid to matters of dress at the expense of practical work. To be fair, this criticism had been voiced at various times in the past, but it had always been accepted that uniform was necessary. Now the feelings within the Brigade were supported by the MORI poll, which had indicated that the wearing of uniform could be a disincentive to both support and recruitment. There were a number of valid objections to the design of the Brigade uniform: first, it was too much like that of the police at first glance; second, its rank badges were too military in nature; third, there was insufficient flexibility regarding the occasions when uniforms would be worn; and finally, so far as women members were concerned, it was slightly outmoded. These were good reasons for seeking a change and a working party was therefore set up to design a whole new range of uniforms which would meet existing criticism and provide flexibility through a mix-and-match capability.

The new uniforms were made from materials which clearly differed from those of the police. There were fewer trimmings, badges were to be of cloth rather than metal and – of some importance – they would be less expensive than the previous patterns. Simplification of style and adornment was a high priority of the working party, as was the quality of outdoor protection. Of course uniformity would still be required and the point was firmly made by national HQ that all members were to be dressed alike for any given duty. The grey nursing dress for women members would henceforth be worn with sleeves rolled up and protected by elbow 'frillies', whilst the nursing tunic for men which was introduced in 1980 would remain. Special duty uniforms were introduced, with considerable flexibility in selecting the items to be worn. Badges of rank would all be worn on the shoulder and, as in the past, qualified medical practitioners would wear theirs on a red background while qualified nurses wore their badges on a grey background. The St John badge at the shoulder was the single cross; the lion and unicorn had been removed, to the annoyance of some members. One part of the uniform stays and rightly so – the White Cross belt of the men. This, more than any other single symbol, represents the Brigade in action.

The final aspect of the response to MORI involved the mounting of a publicity campaign: something striking and, if necessary, controversial; something which could not be ignored and would generate comment and discussion. The Public Affairs Department, under the chairmanship of Lord Westbury, sought the advice of Saatchi and Saatchi, who agreed to help with the problems of image and publicity. At the same time it was decided that the sponsors of events should be encouraged to make proper acknowledgement of St John Ambulance by increased donations and the provision of advertising space. The space would then be used for a standard advertisement, so ensuring that every unit was reacting to a coordinated SJA plan. Finally, Lord Westbury made two important points when launching the campaign: first, that every member of the Brigade is a 'public relations officer' and must take every opportunity to promote the Brigade; and second, that more young volunteers are necessary if the Brigade is to survive. This vitally important campaign is still under way and it is not possible to predict what results will come from it. Moreover, one thing is certain and that is the continuing requirement for trained first-aiders, nurses, escorts and welfare workers in the modern community. St John has shown clearly that it has developed the skill, dedication and experience to tackle this wide variety of tasks.

It is perhaps tempting to see these changes simply as a reaction to MORI, but for some time there had been a desire to divorce the Brigade from its military style ranks and adjust its organization. MORI had confirmed the need for change and National Headquarters was now taking its first steps to apply remedies which will have a lasting effect on the future of St John Ambulance in Britain. It would be a grave tragedy if St John could not now attract the physical and financial support of the British public and so continue to play a leading community role after a century of service to mankind. Proof that the Brigade was capable of continuing this support, irrespective of creed, colour or political background, was demonstrated during the national ambulance emergency at the end of 1978, during terrorist incidents and as part of emergency training.

One of the ugliest features of modern life is the advent of terrorism with its indiscriminate slaughter. We have seen the response of Brigade personnel in Ulster, but mainland Britain has also been subjected to terrorist attack and once again St John members have distinguished themselves by their devotion. In Birmingham on 21 November 1974, two bombs exploded in the city. Mrs S. M. Rushton and Valerie Willis, who were on duty, went immediately to the Central Hotel which was being used as a casualty collection centre and assisted in the treatment of 60 victims. Then they went to the site of the explosion to give further assistance to many people who were dazed and still in a state of shock. Terrorists have also struck at innocent passengers, as on 5 August 1973 when Mr B. R. Lathwell of No. 1 Vauxhall Division, Luton, was waiting for an aircraft at Athens airport when terrorists attacked. His action that day won him the praise and thanks of his fellow passengers and the Life Saving Medal of the Order of St John in silver: 'In recognition of first aid rendered under conditions of great personal danger when several of his fellow passengers were wounded during a terrorist attack.'

The increase in violence and the many advances in technology can lead to situations where the potential casualty level is high. Major emergencies have been defined as those in which living casualties number fifty or more, while a major disaster is an incident with a high death rate. The rail crashes at Eltham (when Brigade men were on the scene within four minutes) and Ealing; the Flixborough explosion; serious sporting incidents and violent demonstrations – all these fall into the category of civil emergency. The Divisions and County staffs of the SJA have taken part in exercises to train for emergency duty involving immediate assessment of the overall casualties, selection of priorities, coordination and cooperation with other services, and communications. In 1974 Chester laid on a disaster exercise involving a power station explosion; Dorset's exercise involved a terrorist attack on a fuel dump in which units of the Army, Fire Brigade and Police took part. County Surgeon W. A. L. Tucker organized and directed the 300 St John members who were being exercised, while officers from the County Emergency Planning Team were on hand to advise and criticize.

The capabilities of a good civil emergency team are precisely those which would come into play for Civil Defence and from 1948 until the Civil Defence Corps was disbanded members of both the Association and the Brigade took part in civil defence training. The requirement for trained, motivated, well-led rescue and first-aid teams continues.

On Saturday 18 November 1978 at about 3.30 p.m. the St John Ambulance Area Transport Officer for Coventry, George Bradley, received a telephone call informing him that from 5 p.m. that day the West Midlands Ambulance Service would no longer operate and asking if St John could meet essential emergency calls. As it happened all the Coventry ambulances of the Brigade were assembled for a tea-party which was being given for the handicapped and elderly residents and Bradley was therefore able to confirm that St John could help. He immediately contacted Ted Cross, who was to be the ambulance staff officer in charge, and Chris Poole, who would assist. The three men organized an operations HQ and provided 24-hour coverage from the very beginning of the ambulance emergency. As the pressure mounted during the following days, some radios failed and the Brigade enlisted the help of RAYNET amateur radio operators whose contribution was invaluable in maintaining essential communications. Brigade men and women came on duty straight from work and remained on stand-by throughout the night. No call was refused and each ambulance was staffed by driver, escort and nurse – 'just like old times' according to one Brigade veteran. As the emergency became more protracted, retired members provided welcome and efficient relief. On Tuesday 5 December 1978 the emergency ended; the Brigade had provided cover for 17 days, using 115 personnel, answering 316 emergency calls and completing 4,600 hours of duty.

In January and February of 1979, the London Ambulance Service suspended duty and the Brigade in the capital and the Home Counties provided 51 ambulances and over 1,000 members to serve the London public. 750 members were detailed to accompany police vehicles; where trouble was expected, police accompanied the Brigade ambulances, while Brigade liaison officers took up duty at New Scotland Yard. In fact little trouble was experienced, because SJA was serving mankind, not acting as an arm of government. In Northumbria during the same period, St John Ambulance provided five ambulances for emergency duties within the space of an hour. These duties in support of the public at a time of tension in the professional ambulance services were undertaken as an emergency function designed to provide a basic service, not in any partisan sense.

Support for the community has always required an effective supplies system, capable of responding quickly and with flexibility to a wide variety of demands.

One of the original aims of the Association was the provision of first-aid handbooks, splints, bandages and stretchers. These were the main items stocked in the Stores Depot which opened on 15 May 1879 under the direction of John Furley. Later W. H. Morgan, a contemporary of Furley's, took over this work which, over the years, provided an even greater variety of equipment to the Association and Brigade at home and overseas. In 1950 the department became subject to central administration and its name was changed to St John Supplies Department. In 1961 Priory House was made available and it is from here that Brian Rockell, the present Director of Supplies, meets the needs of the St John fraternity world-wide. His staff of 28 deal with Brigade uniforms, a complete range of first-aid kits designed to exacting specifications plus other items needed for first-aid rooms, nursing requirements and of course training manuals and teaching material. While the principal object is to provide supplies for St John, there are many requests from other organizations who value the high standard of workmanship and the efficient service of the department. Those who serve here have met some extraordinary demands, but one they could only smile at – a division had requested fifty St John Flashers! After a suitable amount of leg-pulling the Divisional Superintendent received the correct item.

If Supplies Department can be relied upon for the smaller items, who will supply the high-cost items such as ambulances? The question has but one answer – the men and women of St John, through fund-raising and from donations made by generous well-wishers. From the early days when a stretcher was slung between two tricycles, St John has provided its own transport and, with the sole exception of wartime ambulances issued after 1945, continues to do so. At the same time the members continue to invent or modify existing material to suit their particular requirements. Area Superintendent Hukin of Sheffield designed a lightweight, two-wheeled, one-man stretcher trolley for use in confined spaces or when trained manpower was limited. Holt Division, Norfolk, converted an old caravan into a very smart towable first-aid post with a special door for wheel-chair access. London Transport Corps designed and constructed a mobile first-aid post from a Bedford bus chassis and equipped it with two-way radio, oxygen equipment and a 30-gallon water tank. These self-help or DIY measures are cost-effective, saving a great deal of money which can be spent on other items. Unfortunately, DIY is not always possible and many divisions have had to find the funds to purchase ambulances or 'Mobiles', the name now given to the large mobile first-aid posts. The cost of these vehicles today is phenomenal; more expensive than some housing.

Housing too is necessary for the progress of the modern Brigade. Some of the Ambulance Halls of the Brigade's early years have now gone, to be replaced by more modern buildings. Designs have changed to meet changes in structure and training, but the need for buildings has continued and with it the need for money and effort on the part of members. Basingstoke Division rescued an old building which was due for demolition and in the three years from 1971 to 1974 converted it into an HQ. In 1975 Harrow Division purchased a building and designed its interior so that different social activities could take place; cadet and adult training rooms, offices, stores and a garage were incorporated into the design. Stevenage Division raised £17,000- and then put in 8,000 hours of labour in addition to normal public duty. Cleveland Division has provided a practical outdoor training centre with excellent, if simple, facilities for visitors. These are some examples of work which is going on all the time.

The HQ is still the focal point for controlling public duty by the uniformed staff and training programmes of the Association Branch. It is a meeting place for work and social events, providing an invaluable base for comradeship. It was therefore a matter of great pride to London (Prince of Wales's) District when Her Majesty the Queen agreed to open the new District Headquarters at 63 York Street. The HQ was to be known as Edwina Mountbatten House in memory of 'Lady Louis', whose dedication to the suffering took her to every part of the globe in peace and in war, mostly as the Superintendent-in-Chief of St John Nursing Divisions. Appropriately the Countess Patricia Mountbatten, eldest daughter of Lord and Lady Mountbatten, was present at the ceremony.

At 3 p.m. on Thursday 11 December 1980, the Queen's car arrived at the building amid the delighted cheers and shouts of local schoolchildren. The Royal Standard was broken at the flagpole above the entrance, Her Majesty was greeted by local dignitaries and then HRH The Grand Prior introduced her to Group Captain Pirie, Chairman of the St John Council, who had done a great deal towards the creation of the new HQ. A guard of honour formed by ambulance and nursing members lined the route to the dais where the official opening ceremony was to take place. The Lord Prior, Sir Maurice Dorman, a former Chief Commander, presented senior officers of National HQ and the Queen then unveiled the plaque in green Cumberland slate with the following inscription:

Edwina Mountbatten House
Headquarters
St John Ambulance Greater London
opened by
Her Majesty the Queen
11th December 1980

The Queen was presented with a bouquet by Cadet Sergeant Heather Burgess, holder of the Grand Prior's Badge, and then toured the building to see all the aspects of St John work done in London. Colonel Lewis, Commander SJA London, introduced the Commissioner Derek Fenton and his staff who showed the Queen displays of Brigade work on land, on the river with the Thames Tideway Rescue Division and in the air with the Aeromedical Service and Air Wing. Group Captain John Mason, General Manager of the Association and Stan Aylott, the Chief Instructor, explained their work. After the formal tours Her Majesty joined the members for tea, signed the Visitors' Book and with a first-aid kit presented by Miss Doreen Sainsbury, concluded her visit with a 'walkabout' amongst the members. It is not often that the Sovereign Head of the Order can find the time in a busy schedule to make such a visit, but Her Majesty clearly enjoyed her tour and thanked those responsible for the project in general and the presentations on the day. Those who were there were privileged to represent the Brigade in London. Those who were not can draw inspiration from the Private Secretary's letter to the Chairman of the St John Council: 'You will have seen for yourself how interested the Queen was in her tour and she has asked me to say that she was greatly impressed by everything.'

*

In 1983, a happy development took place for those who had devoted their lives to St John but had reached retirement age or had to resign for other reasons. On St John's Day 1983, the St John Fellowship was formed.

Previously, the Foundations of the Order of St John had never had an 'Old Comrades Association', although a number of clubs and groups of former members had long existed in some counties. For many members, however – particularly Brigade members who had found an entire social life in the comradeship of their Division – the moment of retirement meant the loss of the main source of satisfaction and enjoyment in their lives. One Nursing Member with over 30 years' service said, 'When I left my last meeting, I came out of the building and felt entirely cut off . . .'

The objects of the St John Fellowship are:

a. To enable former members to keep in touch with St John and with each other.
b. To form local Branches which will arrange meetings, social events and other activities as desired by members.
c. To help former members in need, especially the housebound and those in hospital or residential homes who would appreciate visits and outings.
d. To support the activities of the Foundations of the Order.

After three years, all these aims have been fulfilled. By 1 May 1986, there are 55 Branches in UK and – an exciting achievement – two in Australia, with much interest growing in Canada and other parts of the Commonwealth. Branches are usually based on a local Divisional or other St John headquarters, and meet there once a month for talks, demonstrations, fund-raising schemes and the organization of many activities for St John and other community projects. The most successful Branches are those which are easily accessible to members in all weathers, and encourages participation in the running of the Branch. The Fellowship provides stewards for Brigade competitions, also 'patients' for examinations and demonstrations; it is much in demand for catering at St John events in the Counties, and for background help at cadet enrolment ceremonies and at camp; above all, its Branches have contributed valuable funds to St John through sales of work, raffles and many original forms of fund-raising.

The third object is met too. Branches find many thoughtful ways to prove to their elderly or chronic sick members that they remain members of the St John family. One London Branch sends a birthday card to each member; for those who have outlived most relatives and friends, it may be the only one they receive. Most Branches hold a Christmas Party with gifts for members, and visit those who cannot attend meetings. Contact between Branches allows visits to those in hospital away from their home area, and members who move are welcomed by their 'receiving' Branch.

The St John Fellowship is open to anyone who has served St John in any capacity. Under its constitution, Branches are self-governing and self-financing, and can admit to membership anyone acceptable to the Committee. There is no age limit, and there are a number of young members who had to resign from the Brigade owing to their work or for health or domestic reasons. All aspects of the work of the Order are represented; a former Matron of the St John Ophthalmic Hospital in Jerusalem is an honoured member.

The Fellowship is proud that its members include the former Lord Prior, Sir Maurice Dorman. It is grateful for the support it has received from the Order, from the Chief Commander, St John Ambulance, and from Headquarters, County and Area staff. Above all, it rejoices in the joy it gives to those who have devoted their lives to the service of mankind. The Fellowship now enjoys success among serving and former St John Ambulance members, and this is due in no small part to the initiative and dedication of Sheila Puckle, its founder secretary.

The Fellowship supports those who have completed their service and allows them to maintain contact with the Order and its Foundations. Within the Brigade, at the younger end of the scale, some action was needed to encourage members to continue their service and recruit others. Children were not forgotten, for a new pilot scheme is currently under way, designed to attract the very young and provide an identity within the St John family. This will be based on the black and white colours shared by the Order and the badger. Currently five Counties are taking part in a pilot scheme and the 1st of January 1987 will see the birth of the Badgers nationwide. This black and white animal has been given a variety of personalities with which children can identify, whilst others can find humour and an important sense of belonging to their own special Badger Set. Eventually a wide range of Badger materials – for example tee-shirts, lunch-boxes and greetings cards – will be available to enhance this identification process.

Badgers will be able to join a Set at the age of six and remain there until ten years of age, when they become Cadets. The Set (the members of the Badger Burrow) will have its own identity and leaders. These may be parents, ex-Cadets, or auxiliary members, and will not have to take promotion examinations. Badgers will wear an adaptable and inexpensive uniform, and will have a flexible programme of activities designed to stimulate interest and develop the concept of the Brigade and its aims. The award is to be fun as well as achievement-orientated and small mementoes of different Badgers will be given at each completed stage.

Youth also requires incentive and in 1985 Her Majesty the Queen approved a new award for young SJA members between the ages of 16 and 25. To gain 'The Sovereign's Award' candidates should have completed five years of Brigade service and hold current statutory certificates for 'First Aid' and 'Caring for the Sick'. A cadet will be required to hold the Grand Prior's Badge and an adult member must hold a certificate for 1,000 hours of voluntary duty. In addition each candidate must have shown initiative in a St John Ambulance community project and a research project. These conditions must be completed over a period of three years. The aim of this new award is to encourage a greater sense of community spirit and personal achievement, developing initiative and providing experience, particularly during the transition stage from Cadet to Adult membership. Those who gain the award will receive a certificate, and a badge will mark the holding of the award. The badge will be as that of the Sovereign Head of the Order of St John, with a scroll inscribed 'Sovereign's Award'. This scheme took effect from 1 July 1986, the Brigade thus embarking on its second century with this royal challenge to youth which is at once an incentive to service and a statement of faith in the future.

*

This story cannot end without considering the overall contribution of the Brigade during its century of service and assessing its impact on society and its current position as a voluntary organization. The Brigade has always been acknowledged as the pioneer practical first-aid organization, but it has also evolved as society itself has changed, providing new forms of service both at home and overseas. It is important to recognize that the help provided by the Association and the Brigade was given where there was a genuine need. There was nothing contrived or artificial about the direction of the Brigade's effort and nothing half-hearted about the dedication of those who put it into effect; nor is there now.

The years during which the Brigade made its greatest impact on society in Britain were of course those immediately following its creation, the decade from 1926 to 1936 and the period from 1950 to 1965. The first was natural and inevitable, the second covered a period of depression and subsequent revival, while the third followed the creation of the National Health Service and coincided with changes in social behaviour. Its lean years were those immediately following the two World Wars, when the people of Britain had no wish to continue the wearing of uniform or to be 'organized'; all they wanted was the opportunity to enjoy the peace for which they had fought. Even in its worst years, however, the Brigade proved able to meet all the many and varied requirements placed upon it. Only in the late 1960s was there need for real concern over manning levels, when it was becoming clear that younger men were not replacing those who were ending their active service, and the average age of the Ambulance members rose sharply. These were also years of improved technology as well as greater social liberation, when patterns of behaviour were more relaxed. The pace of these changes, as well as their nature, was sufficient to outrun the normal evolution of the Brigade. If the interest and motivation of younger members were to be maintained there would be a need for new techniques of leadership and greater physical and mental stimulation. The years between 1965 and 1985 saw the Brigade rise to the challenge of change.

Changes in structure and uniform were necessary if the Brigade was to present a new image to the public, and changes in the approach to training were required not only to comply with the new statutory regulations, but also to provide a focus for greater motivation and increased recruitment. Now the results of those changes are awaited and it will be several years before their impact on the Brigade and the public can be assessed. The campaign to bring St John Ambulance more to the forefront of public awareness has only recently begun, and already its eye-catching and controversial message has caused much discussion within St John. The response of the public will be measured by the number of Brigade recruits, the number of auxiliaries and the degree of financial support. Meanwhile, in whatever direction society evolves it will continue to require the services of voluntary organizations such as the British Red Cross Society, St Andrew's Ambulance Association and St John Ambulance. Although the British government has opened the way for other organizations to teach and practise first aid, there are none with the commitment, competence and experience of these three which have served the community for so long. Coordination and cooperation between these great charitable organizations will be of increasing importance in the years ahead and St John has an important role to play in this.

St John Ambulance will still, therefore, be needed in the future, though not in precisely the same way as in the past nor in the same form. If the last years of its first century of service have called for change, the years which will take it into the twenty-first century will be no less critical, for these will see an assessment of St John's relevance to a future Britain. Any failure of conviction or commitment, any lowering of standards and any missed opportunity to respond to new requirements could lead to the belief that St John Ambulance has outlived its usefulness. The individuals who have guided and trained the Brigade over the years have made their mark and passed on, but the cornerstones of the organization remain of vital importance for the future. Now, more than ever before, St John Ambulance needs the guidance of the medical and nursing professions to chart a course for new responses to changing first-aid requirements; to provide a focus for better informed welfare work and to train the cadets and their leaders at all levels in those specialist aspects of first aid and nursing without which St John would become simply a series of separate groups of well motivated do-gooders. The selection of younger, more active leaders has been given a high and urgent priority, and the attempt to provide greater challenge and more responsibility for younger people deserves to succeed.

Public recognition of the Brigade's work in the form of recruits and money will be of great importance for those organizations which call on St John for help. Some of the donations to St John Ambulance following public duty are ludicrously small, when compared with the effort and self-denial of the volunteers. Even if a scale of contributions to St John could be accepted for voluntary duty, the cost to organizers would be considerably less than that of hiring a profit-making organization. However, this is only one side of the equation; the other is that a hired group would probably not have the commitment and back-up of the modern Brigade. Further, the costs which would be incurred if a municipal ambulance service were to undertake the Brigade's public duty and welfare work would be an additional burden on the taxpayer.

By its past services the Brigade has earned the privilege of serving the public and it must now renew that warrant as a branch of St John Ambulance. It has much to be proud of: pioneer of first aid and Comforts Depots; public duty over a wide variety of functions; Aeromedical and Air Wing; military and naval reserves in war; youth training through the Cadets and the Sovereign's Award; welfare and social care, as well as a high standard of behaviour and skill during emergencies. All this service throughout Britain and the Commonwealth is entirely voluntary and has been so from the beginning. The Brigade has therefore been a force for good and has justified the comment of King Edward VII so long ago. It has been a good uniform and, even though materials and designs have changed, it is still a good uniform; much good has come from it and its work has not yet ended.

Above all, the Brigade has been a practical expression of the aims of the Order of St John of Jerusalem, which holds a unique place in Britain as a working Order of Chivalry whose voluntary activity today maintains to the full its ancient Hospitaller motto:

> *Pro Utilitate Hominum*:
> For the Service of Mankind.

APPENDICES

APPENDIX 1

THE ORDER OF ST JOHN

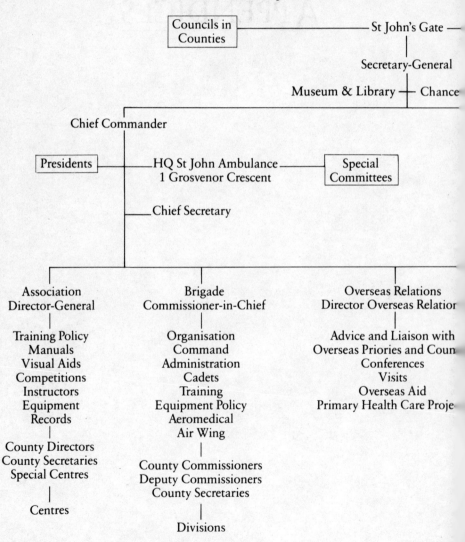

Councils in Counties —— St John's Gate ——

Secretary-General

Museum & Library ┼ Chance

Chief Commander

Presidents

HQ St John Ambulance
1 Grosvenor Crescent —— Special Committees

Chief Secretary

Association Director-General	Brigade Commissioner-in-Chief	Overseas Relations Director Overseas Relation
Training Policy Manuals Visual Aids Competitions Instructors Equipment Records	Organisation Command Administration Cadets Training Equipment Policy Aeromedical Air Wing	Advice and Liaison with Overseas Priories and Coun Conferences Visits Overseas Aid Primary Health Care Proje
County Directors County Secretaries Special Centres	County Commissioners Deputy Commissioners County Secretaries	
Centres	Divisions	

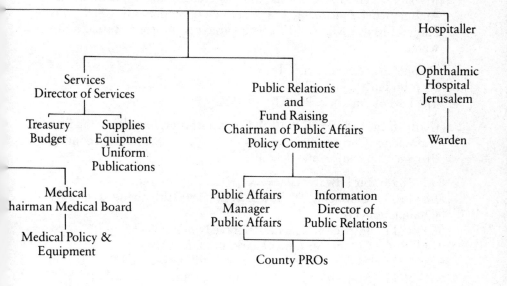

Priories and
Overseas Establishments

Hospitaller

Services
Director of Services

Public Relations
and
Fund Raising
Chairman of Public Affairs
Policy Committee

Ophthalmic
Hospital
Jerusalem

Treasury
Budget

Supplies
Equipment
Uniform
Publications

Warden

Medical
hairman Medical Board

Public Affairs
Manager
Public Affairs

Information
Director of
Public Relations

Medical Policy &
Equipment

County PROs

APPENDIX 2

OFFICERS IN COMMAND OF THE BRIGADE

1887–1893 The Brigade was administered by the Director of the Ambulance Department, the first Superintendent of which was Surgeon-Major Manley, VC. The Directors in order of succession were:

Colonel Francis Duncan, CB
Sir John Furley, CH, CB
The Earl of Limerick, PC, CB

(*Note*: from 1887 to 1905 W. J. Church Brasier, founder of the first Ambulance Corps in Britain, was the principal assistant, becoming Brigade Chief Superintendent in 1895)

1893–1898 Sir Edward Thackeray, VC, CB (Commissioner)
1898–1903 Colonel C. W. Bowdler, CB (1900 title changed to Chief Commissioner)
1903–1911 Inspector-General Belgrave Ninnis, CVO
1911–1924 Colonel Sir James Clark, Bt., CB, CMG
1924–1931 Major-General Sir Percival Wilkinson, KCMG, CB
1931–1943 Major-General Sir John Duncan, KCB, CMG, CVO, DSO
1943–1947 General Sir Clive Liddell, KCB, CMG, CBE, DSO
1947–1949 Lieutenant-General Sir Henry Pownall, KCB, KBE, DSO, MC
1949–1956 Lieutenant-General Sir Otto Lund, KCB, DSO
1956 Brigadier T. Daly, CBE, MC (3 months' office only)
1956–1962 Major-General J. M. Kirkman, CB, CBE
1962–1967 Rear-Admiral Royer Dick, CB, CBE, DSC
1967–1973 Lieutenant-General Sir William Pike, KCB, CBE, DSO

Appendix 2

1973–1978   Major-General D. S. Gordon, CB, CBE, DSO
1978–1980   Major-General P. R. Leuchars, CBE
1980–1984   Major-General Sir John Younger, Bt., CBE
1984–1986   Major-General P. R. Leuchars, CBE (until June 1986)
1986–   Mr A. J. Sunderland (from June 1986)

APPENDIX 3

CHIEF COMMANDERS AND DIRECTORS GENERAL

The merger of the Association and Brigade in 1968 resulted in a change of policy to create one overall coordinator of both functions. The Counties were each to have a Commissioner for the Brigade and a Director of the Association and these titles were reflected at National Headquarters. In the Counties the title of Commander St John Ambulance was created to show that both branches were coordinated. Today the Chief Commander has a coordinating role, while the Commissioner-in-Chief and Director General continue to control the normal work of their respective branches.

CHIEF COMMANDERS

1970 Sir William Pike, KCB, CBE, DSO
1976 Sir Maurice Dorman, GCMG, GCVO
1980 Major-General P. R. Leuchars, CBE

DIRECTORS GENERAL

1970 Sir Hugh Stephenson
1972 Neville Marsh, CBE
1977 Professor H. C. Stewart, CBE
1978 P. A. Lingard, CBE, TD
1982 D. Seymour
1985 R. G. A. Balchin

APPENDIX 4

THE BRIGADE'S CHIEF SURGEONS

The first title for the Brigade's principal medical officer was Medical Officer-in-Chief. This later changed to Chief Surgeon and subsequently to Surgeon-in-Chief.

1896–1901	Sir William MacCormac
1901–1905	Surgeon-General Sir John Reed, KCB
1905–1915	Edmund Owen
1915–1931	Sir William Bennett, KCVO
1931–1936	Colonel C. I. Ellis, CMG
1936–1950	Nigel Corbet-Fletcher, OBE
1950–1951	F. H. Edwards
1951–1960	Major A. C. White-Knox, OBE, MC
1960–1966	H. S. Taylor-Young
1969–1972	Marcus M. Scott
1972–1975	Colonel R. Ollerenshaw, ERD, TD, QHS, DL, BM
1975–	J. C. Graham, OBE

APPENDIX 5

SUPERINTENDENTS-IN-CHIEF
(The original title was Lady Superintendent-in-Chief)

1911–1939	Lady Perrott
1939–1942	Mrs St John Atkinson
1942–1960	Lady Louis Mountbatten, GCIE, GBE, DCVO
1960–1970	Marjorie, Countess of Brecknock, DBE
1970–1983	Lady Moyra Browne, DBE
1983–	The Lady Westbury

CHIEF NURSING OFFICERS

1952–1960	Miss Noreen Hamilton
1960–1965	Miss Lucy Duff-Grant
1965–1972	Dame Barbara Cozens, DBE, RRC, QHNS
1972–	Miss Rosemary Bailey, SRN, SCM, MTD, RNT, DN (Lond.)

APPENDIX 6

COMMISSIONERS FOR THE BRIGADE OVERSEAS

1903–1911   Colonel C. W. Bowdler, CB
             (Commissioner for Special Services
             and The Brigade Beyond The Seas)
1911–1920   Major-General J. C. Dalton
             (1912 title changed to Chief Commissioner)
1920–1930   Major-General Sir R. Havelock Charles, GCVO,
             KCSI, Bt.
1930–1950   Colonel Sir James Sleeman, CB, CMG, CBE, MVO
             (In 1950 the appointment was merged with that of the
             Chief Commissioner, Home, then Sir Otto Lund)

DIRECTORS OVERSEAS

1968–1975   Sir Hilton Poynton, GCMG
1975–1981   Sir Leslie Monson, KCMG, CB
1981–   Sir John Paul, GCMG, OBE, MC

APPENDIX 7

THE SERVICE MEDAL OF THE ORDER OF ST JOHN

First authorized in 1895, the Service Medal was officially approved by the Prince of Wales, Grand Prior of the Order, in June 1898. The first list of awards included John Furley, Sir Herbert Perrott, William Church Brasier, Dr Sam Osborn and C. J. Trimble, all of whom made a prominent mark on the Brigade's history.

The medal is circular, 1½ inches in diameter. It was originally struck in silver, but is now made from cupro-nickel, rhodium plated. The design of the piece has remained the same from its inception:

Obverse: A bust of Queen Victoria, with tiara and veil within a circle on which is embossed 'VICTORIA. D.G. BRITT. REG. F.D. IND. IMP'.

Reverse: A complex design containing, in the centre, the Royal Arms within the Garter. Between the Garter and an outer border, between sprigs of St John's wort, are four circles, containing respectively a Crown, the Arms of the Prince of Wales as Grand Prior, the Badge of the Prince of Wales and the Arms of the Order. The wording on the outer border is 'MAGNUS. PRIORATUS. HOSPITALIS. SANCTI. JOHANNIS. JERUSALEM. IN. ANGLIA.'

Ribbon: 1½ inches wide, black with two white stripes, resulting in five equal divisions.

Suspension: Originally by a ring but now from a straight bar.

The medal is normally awarded to members of St John who have completed fifteen years of efficient service, but it should not be referred to as a long-service medal, for at one time it was awarded to people who had made a specific, conspicuous contribution to the Brigade or the

Order. It is unique among modern medals in that it retains the bust of Queen Victoria, sculpted by her daughter Princess Louise.

In 1911 Chapter-General authorized the award of a bar for a further five years' service. The first design showed the words '5 years' service' but in 1924 this was changed to an eight-pointed cross between two sprigs of St John's wort. When the ribbon is worn alone, the award of a bar or bars is represented by the wearing of a small silver or gold cross affixed to the ribbon.

When worn with other medals and decorations, the medal follows campaign medals and other service medals and will normally be seen as the last medal in a group of British medals. It will be followed by any foreign decorations awarded.

APPENDIX 8

THE LIFE SAVING MEDAL OF THE ORDER OF ST JOHN

Sir Edmund Lechmere was the first to suggest that the Order of St John should sponsor a medal for saving life on land where the rescuer's own life was in danger. He was particularly concerned that bravery in the mines should be rewarded and between 1870 and 1874 he put forward his ideas. At a Chapter Meeting in 1874 his view was endorsed and medals struck in silver and bronze were authorized, Lechmere himself providing the dies. In 1907 gold medals were authorized.

The medal is circular, 1.4 inches in diameter and there have been two designs:

First Design 1874–1888: The obverse showed the eight-pointed cross, without embellishments, within a circular border containing the words 'Awarded by the Order of St John of Jerusalem in England'. The reverse showed sprigs of St John's wort with scrolls surrounded by the words 'For Service in the Cause of Humanity'. This was suspended from a black ribbon, having a white cross embroidered directly on the ribbon.

Second Design: In 1888, the year of the Royal Charter, a new design was instituted. The wording 'For Service in the Cause of Humanity' was transferred from the reverse to the obverse, where the eight-pointed cross was now embellished with the lion and unicorn. The reverse was redesigned, with a longer title for the Order. Suspension is still by means of a ring and the original plain black ribbon has been given narrow scarlet and white stripes at each edge.

The medal is worn on the right breast, although for a period from 1905 to 1949 it was worn with other medals on the left breast.

The award of bars for subsequent acts of bravery was authorized in 1892. The bar consists of a narrow rectangle having the badge of the Order within a circle between two sprigs of St John's wort; when the

214

ribbon is worn alone the possession of a bar is indicated by an emblem consisting of a metal cross of the Order mounted on a white enamel circle.

Those who wish to learn more of the medals and insignia of the Order of St John are referred to Charles W. Tozer's excellent book *The Insignia and Medals of the Order of St John*, published by J. B. Hayward (Simprints) in 1975.

APPENDIX 9

TROPHIES

AMBULANCE

Award for the team gaining highest aggregate marks in all sections
1 The 'Dewar' Shield
2 The 'Symons Eccles' Cup
3 The 'Hong Kong' Shield

Award for the winning team in the Individual section
The 'Trimble' Shield

Award for the winning team in the Team Test section
The 'Hingston' Rose Bowl

Award for the team leader gaining highest marks in the Individual section
The 'Ellis' Cup

NURSING

Award for the team gaining highest aggregate marks in all sections
1 The 'Perrott' Shield
2 The 'Corbet Fletcher' Cup
3 The 'Stewart' Cup

Award for the winning team in the Individual section
The 'Chalmers' Cup

Award for the winning team in the Team Test section
The 'Mountbatten' Cup

Award for the team leader gaining highest marks in the Individual section
The 'Ellis' Cup

Award for the team gaining highest marks in the Individual sections Nos. 2 and 4 combined
The 'Marguerette Golding' Trophy

Award for the team gaining highest marks in the Individual sections Nos. 1 and 3 combined
The 'Mountgarret' Cup

AMBULANCE CADET

Award for the team gaining highest aggregate marks in all sections
1 The 'White-Knox' Cup
2 The 'Schooling' Cup
3 The 'Pownall' Cup

Award for the winning team in the Individual section
The 'Jarvis' Cup

Award for the winning team in the Team Test section
The 'Barne' Cup

Award for the team leader gaining highest marks in the Individual section
The 'New Zealand' Cup

NURSING CADET

Award for the team gaining highest aggregate marks in all sections
1 The 'Dunbar-Nasmith' Cup
2 The 'Mountbatten' Cup
3 The 'Pownall' Cup

Award for the winning team in the Individual section
The 'White-Knox Individual' Cup

Award for the winning team in the Team Test section
The 'Emdon' Cup

Award for the team leader gaining highest marks in the Individual section
The 'Phyllis Birch' Trophy

Award for the winning team in the Home Nursing Individual sections (excluding bedmaking)
The 'Tweedale' Cup

Award for the winning team in the bedmaking section
The 'Bedmaking' Cup

SELECTED BIBLIOGRAPHY

St John Ambulance Publications

The Annual Reports and Accounts of the Chapter General of the Order of St John.

The Annual Reports of the Chief Commissioner St John Ambulance Brigade.

The Report of the Chief Commissioner into the Mobilisation of the Brigade, Col. C. W. Bowdler, 1900.

'The Black and White Budget'. Selected articles.

Chivalry
The St John Ambulance Gazette   } These were the titles of the
The St John Review   } periodical journal issued for
                                       St John personnel.

The St John Ambulance Association, Its history and its part in the Ambulance Movement, N. Corbet-Fletcher, London 1929.

Champions of the Cross, H. A. R. Edgell, Norfolk 1983.

The Knights of St John in the British Realm, Sir Edwin King, London 1967, revised Sir Harry Luke.

A Short History of the Order of St John, E. D. Renwick, London 1969, revised I. M. Williams.

Centenary Book, St John Ambulance Kent, 1877–1977, Robert Percival, Kent 1977.

The St John Ambulance Brigade, Leicestershire Centenary, 1882–1982, L. Lee, Leicester 1983.

General

The Imperial Yeomanry Hospitals in South Africa, London 1902.

Report on the Medical Arrangements in the South African War, Surgeon-General Sir W. D. Wilson, KCMG, London 1904.

The South African Field Force Casualty Lists, 11 October 1899–31 May 1902, Ilford 1972.

The Work of the Portland Hospital in South Africa, Portland Hospital Committee, London 1901.

Selected Bibliography

Separate Reports of the Joint Work of the British Red Cross Society and Order of St John for the Boer War, 1914–18 War and 1939–45 War, London 1921 and 1949.

The Public Record Office Medal Rolls 68/AMC/301 and WO/100 series.

The London Gazette

First Aid. A valuable source for the late years of the nineteenth and the first part of the twentieth century.

On Active Service with the St John Ambulance Brigade, South African War 1899–1902, W. S. Inder, Kendal 1903.

Brigade in Action, D. G. F. Acutt, Weymouth 1947.

Malta, Sir Harry Luke, London 1949.

The Insignia and Medals of the Order of St John, C. W. Tozer, London 1975.

The British Red Cross in Action, Dame Beryl Oliver, London 1966.

A Good Uniform, Joan Clifford, London 1967.

In the Service of Mankind, Joan Clifford, London 1971.

The Red Cross and the White, H. St George Saunders, London 1949.

The George Medal, W. H. Fevyer, London 1980.

MORI Report: 'The Public's Image of St John Ambulance', London 1982.

INDEX

221